New
Directions
in
Mediation

We dedicate this volume to
Kenneth Boulding and James Laue
—peacemakers who were both insightful scholars
and devoted practitioners.

New
Directions
in
Mediation

Communication Research and Perspectives

Joseph P. Folger
Tricia S. Jones
editors

SAGE Publications
International Educational and Professional Publisher
Thousand Oaks   London   New Delhi

For information address:

 SAGE Publications, Inc.
2455 Teller Road
Thousand Oaks, California 91320

SAGE Publications Ltd.
6 Bonhill Street
London EC2A 4PU
United Kingdom

SAGE Publications India Pvt. Ltd.
M-32 Market
Greater Kailash I
New Delhi 110 048 India

Printed in the United States of America

Library of Congress Cataloging-in-Publication Data

Main entry under title:

New directions in mediation : communication research and perspectives
     / edited by Joseph P. Folger, Tricia S. Jones.
          p.   cm.
     Includes bibliographical references and index.
     ISBN 0-8039-5550-2.   —   ISBN 0-8039-5551-0 (pbk.)
          1. Communication.   2. Mediation.   I. Folger, Joseph P., 1951-
     II. Jones, Tricia S.
P91.N378   1994
302.2–dc20   93-32784

94   95   96   97   98   10   9   8   7   6   5   4   3   2

Sage Production Editor: Astrid Virding

Contents

Introduction

NOT LONG AGO, mediation and other forms of alternative dispute resolution were clearly the exception rather than the rule in discussion and practice of conflict management for interpersonal, organizational, and community disputes. It was rare to find a general understanding of mediation, much less acceptance of the idea of applying mediation to anything other than labor-management or international conflicts. But considerable change has taken place.

Mediation currently serves as the most common dispute resolution mechanism in alternative dispute resolution programs (Kressel & Pruitt, 1989b). The rise of alternative dispute resolution (ADR) in the past 15 years has highlighted the role that third parties enact in a wide range of conflict arenas. Sparked by ideological and practical concerns, this movement has created diverse options for third-party intervention.

Disputes that were once addressed solely through adjudication are, in many cases, now addressed by alternative forms of third-party intervention such as mediation. For example, in 1975 there were only 12 community dispute resolution centers in the United States. By 1986 there were more than 400 court-annexed or community-based mediation programs in which family, neighborhood, landlord-tenant, small claims, and business-related disputes are mediated (Johnson, 1993).

Mediation and ADR are becoming institutionalized. For family and marital disputes several states now require mediation for all custody issues in divorce cases. In the private sector a market has developed for dispute resolution services that can provide out-of-court settlements for large- and small-scale business disputes. Organizations have developed internal procedures to address conflicts, with increasing attention given to ombudspersons, patient representatives, open-door grievance programs, hearing officers, and so forth. Middle managers have increasingly been viewed as dispute-resolvers—a reconceptualization of managerial role that has sparked considerable interest in the skills and problems associated with organizational mediation and informal thirdpartyship (Karambayya & Brett, 1989; Kolb & Sheppard, 1985).

There are several reasons for the maturation of mediation and ADR. The growth of the alternative dispute resolution movement and the visibility of supporting professional organizations such as the American Bar Association's Standing Committee on Dispute Resolution, the Society for Professionals in Dispute Resolution, and others have dramatically increased public awareness of third-party work. Basic social changes over the last decade in employer-employee relationships and the erosion of traditional adversarial models of intervention in labor-management and provider-client disputes have focused attention on the changing roles for third parties. Attempts at intervention in international conflicts have also given third-party work a high profile, focusing attention on mediators' ability to effectively manage disputes ranging from hostage-taking situations to the negotiation of extremely complex international treaties (Pruitt, 1981; Touval & Zartman, 1989; Zartman & Touval, 1985).

With these expanding applications of mediation came a corresponding pressure from scholars and practitioners to achieve a more accurate understanding and a more perfect application of the mediation process. Across the social sciences researchers have compared forms of third-party intervention (Pruitt et al., 1989), examined influences of third-party moves (Jones, 1988), assessed intervention skills (Moore, 1986; Sheppard, 1984), and evaluated outcomes (Carnevale, Lim, & McLaughlin, 1989). When considering mediation as a body of knowledge, however, most of us involved in and committed to its study and practice feel the need for continuing discussion and examination.

This volume is offered as a part of the ongoing consideration of theory and research on mediation. Unlike other works on the topic, this book attempts to inform both scholars and practitioners of new directions in mediation theory and research from a communication perspective. The following section provides a broad conceptual background for understanding a communication perspective on mediation. The assumptions, strengths, and limitations of adopting a communication approach for understanding mediation will be discussed, followed by a preview of the individual chapters in the book.

A Communication Perspective on Mediation

Conflict scholars have long acknowledged the absolutely central role that communication plays in dispute management, often arguing that communication is the sine qua non of conflict. Without question, communicative behavior, both verbal and nonverbal, creates, reflects, and remediates conflicts (Folger, Poole, & Stutman, 1993; Hocker & Wilmot, 1992). And, central to a communication perspective is the realization that conflict is a socially created and communicatively managed reality occurring within a socio-historical context that both affects meaning and behavior and is affected by it.

The basic assumptions of a communication perspective in the study of conflict and negotiation have been suggested by Putnam and Folger (1988) and Putnam and Roloff (1992). Drawing heavily from pragmatic and interpretive metatheory, three principles guide this perspective. The first principle is the attention to micro-analysis of specific verbal and nonverbal cues, including the patterning and development of process over time. These behaviors are the foundation for understanding the evolution of conflict. Without appreciation for these structures and functions, scholars cannot attend to the developmental aspects of the process and their impact on outcomes. Furthermore, the structure and functions of messages change the nature of the interaction and are changed by them. Thus examining communication at a micro-level necessitates a process orientation in which simple message sequences are understood within larger dynamic sequences.

Some communication research has focused on structural/functional analysis of mediation, examining the pragmatic features and sequencing of messages. For example, Donohue, Allen, and Burrell (1988) have looked at verbal immediacy and language intensity cues to determine mediator competence. Jones (1988, 1989a) has conducted phase analyses of mediation and has isolated mediator-disputant and disputant-disputant patterns of interaction that distinguish agreement and no-agreement mediation. And, Jacobs (1990; Jacobs, Jackson, Stearns, & Hall, 1991) has explained the structure of argument in mediation interaction. As a whole, this research and other contributions in this area have helped us understand the nature and impact of communication components within the larger dynamic. And, without question, most of the research in mediation from a communication perspective focuses on structural/functional analyses.

As important as structural/functional analyses of mediation may be, exclusive attention to these factors is not sufficient to explain the illusory influence of communication in mediation. Ultimately, behaviors have influence because they have meaning to the participants in the mediation process. And, meaning is not inherent in the behavior, it is continually created and recreated throughout the process of social interaction. Thus the second principle of a communication perspective is the appreciation for the social construction of meaning and the interpretive structures used to uncover meaning in communication. Research from an interpretive orientation addressing the question of constructed meaning in mediation examines how disputants and third-party perspectives are revealed and negotiated as the interaction unfolds. In this work, the disputants' and third-parties' values, their views of justice and their orientations to conflict (Littlejohn & Shailor, 1986), and their interpretations of each other's behaviors (Dingwall, 1988; Greatbatch & Dingwall, 1989) provide insight into the bases of productive and unproductive conflict.

The attention to social construction of meaning in mediation has resulted in an almost exclusive reliance on discourse-analytic examinations of mediation, where contextual and/or ideological influences affect the way conflict discourse unfolds in intervention settings. Grimshaw (1990) suggests that discourse analysis enables an understanding of how participants make sense of discourse that is produced within known and specified contexts of text and situation.

As Folger et al. (1993) indicate in their discussion of an interactional perspective, context is key to identifying the rules and structures people use to make sense of discourse, to construct social meanings, and to use messages to accomplish multiple goals. Mediation, like communication, does not take place in a vacuum. All social action is embedded in layers of context that act and interact to influence both the form, essence, and function of actions and the individuals who produce them. The interrelation between text and context necessitates the assessment of context as the third general principle of a communication perspective. Just as text affects context, context affects the use of and meaning of textual elements, that is, communication. Assessing context is made more complex by the multiplicity of loosely boundaried forces, such as relational, social, cultural, and institutional contexts. Existing communication research addressing contextual influences on mediation has examined how mediators' backgrounds and training shape their interventions (Folger & Bernard, 1985, 1986), the influence of organizational constraints on adjudicative and mediative options (Karambayya & Brett, 1989), cultural influences on conflict management (Nadler, Nadler, & Broome, 1985; Ting-Toomey, 1985), the impact of institutional constraints on educationally based mediation programs (Burrell & Vogl, 1990), and communities as settings for mediating neighbor disputes (Folger, 1991).

The communication perspective (and its preceding theory and research from more purely systemic/pragmatic and interpretive perspectives) is well suited to the interests and questions generated by the expanding arena of mediation practice. There are many fundamental questions about what mediation *is* and what it becomes as it is employed in new social contexts and is practiced by a range of people with various backgrounds and diverse training experience. The communication perspective is well equipped to clarify how third-party interventions are constituted in new settings. Its microfocus has suggested ways to see the process in less global terms. Its emphasis on process allows us to conceive of and study intervention in a less static, snapshot-like way. It encourages us to see how any given move in an intervention is influenced by what has come before and will influence later moves. Its emphasis on the construction of meanings encourages us to think of disputes and intervention moves as being at play on several interpretive fields simultaneously. It reveals how disputants and third parties rely on specific interpretive premises and assumptions and it points to potential disruptions if disputants' premises are incongruous.

Overview of the Chapters

The chapters in this volume present ideas about mediation process from a communication perspective, often opening truly innovative areas for contemplation and translation into practice. The contributors have drawn from the premises discussed previously to examine and enrich our understanding of mediation by: (1) providing theoretical perspectives that help us conceive of mediation and understand third-party work as it unfolds in ongoing interaction—how taking a communication perspective can reveal new ways of understanding the structure of intervention processes; (2) illustrating through micro-analysis of mediation discourse how specific communicative acts shape the realities of mediators and disputants, thus influencing the process and outcomes of mediation; (3) detailing contextual influences on intervention processes and suggesting critical contextual factors that should be gauged in order to guide mediation more effectively; and (4) beginning a dialogue with practitioners about how these ideas can be translated into practice and soliciting suggestions for further practice implications of a communication perspective on mediation. This volume is organized in four sections that correspond to these four areas of enrichment.

In the first section, Communication Perspectives on the Nature of Discourse in Mediation, the three contributors present suggestions for different ways of seeing mediation through a communication lens. Although all three share the same basic assumptions underlying a general communication perspective, each rings a unique theoretical note. Folger and Bush, in their chapter on "Ideology, Orientations to Conflict, and Mediation Discourse," examine how the implicit orientations to conflict on which mediator intervention approaches are based actually reveal broader ideological assumptions about social relationships and human development. They offer a critique of problem solving as a basis for third-party intervention in nonadversarial conflict settings and discuss practice implications of their perspective, including a consideration of how training models may bias mediators ideologically to emphasize the problem-solving approach. Jones, in "A Dialectical Reframing of the Mediation Process," suggests that dialectical tensions in relationships between interactants serve as a critical context that affects issue identification and development and serve as the genesis for the evolution of conflict and the mediation process. Drawing from work in family therapy and interpersonal communication theory, she discusses primary relational tensions that may affect mediation and presents basic strategies mediators may use to resolve or manage these tensions. Cobb's chapter, "A Narrative Perspective on Mediation: Toward the Materialization of the 'Storytelling' Metaphor," reveals her framing of intervention discourse as narrative. She sees mediation process as shaped by narrative structures that influence the development and direction of the interaction as the process unfolds and argues that the mediator's role is clarified when the implicit narrative structure of the discourse is acknowledged. Her discussion raises important questions for mediation training and practice and reminds us that reliance on narrative structure is inherent in most mediation models.

In Shaping Reality Through Discourse, the second section of the volume, three chapters present exemplary discourse analyses that reveal the power of discourse to shape the realities of mediators and disputants. The first contribution, by Littlejohn, Shailor, and Pearce, "The Deep Structure of Reality in Mediation," presents an interpretive model of mediation and illustrates the power of this model through an analysis of a divorce mediation case. Their model assumes that there are three critical parts of social reality—moral reality, conflict reality, and justice reality—that must be considered to understand how mediators may privilege certain realities and impact disputants' orientations and outcomes. Greatbatch and Dingwall's chapter, "The Interactive Construction of Interventions by Divorce Mediators," presents a unique and sorely needed analysis concerning the influence of disputants' behaviors on mediator's realities and actions. Working with discourse analyses of divorce mediation cases, the authors demonstrate how specific disputant responses may constrain mediators' options for intervention. The final chapter in this section, " 'Talking Like a Mediator': Conversational Moves of Experienced Divorce Mediators," by Tracy and Spradlin, takes a close look at how expert mediators use language and conversational control to establish their realities in mediation.

Highlighting differences in language use, topic management, and interactional structuring, they challenge previous conceptions of mediator styles and end with suggestions for practitioners.

The third section of the volume concerns Contextual Influences on Intervention. These chapters focus on the impact of social, institutional, or cultural influences on mediation models, training, and practice. Donohue and Bresnahan discuss "Communication Issues in Mediating Cultural Conflict." They provide a general discussion of the importance of culture in intergroup conflict processes. Using a case example for illustrative purposes, they overview models of cultural difference and explain how certain models of mediation are more or less congruent with specific cultural assumptions. In "Teach Your Children Well: Recommendations for Peer Mediation Programs," Jones and Brinkman suggest that the developmental level of children, their cultural and social contexts, and the institutional context of public education are important considerations for the successful implementation of peer mediation programs. Within each of these areas they provide specific recommendations for people interested in creating or evaluating such programs. Turning their attention to organizational contexts, Karambayya and Brett's chapter, "Managerial Third Parties: Intervention Strategies, Process, and Consequences," presents a comprehensive model of the influences that shape third-party roles and intervention outcomes in organizational settings. They review existing literature on this new and powerful arena for mediation.

The fourth section of the volume, Practitioners' Perspectives, offers three practitioners' views on themes, theoretical frameworks, and research claims in this volume. Carl M. Moore suggests that research and theory on mediation needs to be grounded in an appreciation of why third parties are important in strengthening the social fabric. He sees mediation as an appropriate means to build and restore a sense of community in social groups throughout society. Janet Rifkin cautions that theoretical advancements in our understanding of mediation need to be translated into designs for practice. Without converting theoretical insights into useful training programs, practitioners are not able to enact new forms of intervention and may only be rewarded for maintaining current approaches. Finally, in an effort consistent with Rifkin's concerns about translating theory to practice, Christopher W. Moore demonstrates how two sets of ideas in this volume can be useful to third-party practitioners. Moore extends Tracy and Spradlin's framework by discussing additional ways that third parties establish credibility with disputants. He then offers a case study from his own experience that illustrates Littlejohn, Shailor, and Pearce's analysis of how disputants and third parties negotiate moral, conflict, and justice realities. Moore's analysis demonstrates the types of insights astute practitioners can take from perspectives offered in this volume.

Acknowledgments

This book stems from a deepening interest in mediation within the field of communication. Over the past several years, scholars and practitioners have turned to each other to understand the dynamics of third party intervention. As a result, there are many new ideas and insights about practice that stem from a communication perspective. These ideas have been talked about at conventions, training seminars and mediation programs and are already shaping third-party work in exciting ways. This book is an attempt to capture some of these ideas and make them available to a wider audience.

We would like to thank our colleagues in communication who have encouraged us to develop this volume, especially Linda Putnam, David Seibold, and Randall Stutman. We are also very grateful to practitioners at the Center for Conflict Resolution (Madison, Wisconsin), the Columbus Ohio Night Prosecutor's Program, the El Paso County Mediation Programs, the Ann Arbor Mediation Center, the Queens Mediation Center, the University of Denver Mediation/Arbitration Clinic, and the Hofstra University Law Clinic for contributing to our own backgrounds as mediators. And, we would like to thank our students at Temple University for their helpful discussions of many ideas in this book.

We are indebted to Sophy Craze at Sage Publications for her guidance on this project and to Astrid Virding for her editorial assistance. We would also like to thank Mary Beth Flynn for her careful work on the index for the volume.

–Joseph P. Folger
Tricia S. Jones

Part One

Communication Perspectives on the Nature of Discourse in Mediation

How do our underlying orientations to conflict shape expectations about third-party involvement? In what ways are orientations to conflict driven by broad ideologies about social relations and social interaction? What is an alternative to a problem-solving conception of conflict intervention?

1

Ideology, Orientations to Conflict, and Mediation Discourse

Joseph P. Folger
Robert A. Baruch Bush

Emergent Conflict and the Critique of Mediation

Recent assessments of dispute processing within the American justice system point to the emergent nature of conflict during intervention (Felstiner, Abel, & Sarat, 1980-1981; Mather & Yngvesson, 1980-1981; Sarat, 1988; Cobb, 1991, this volume). These assessments emphasize that disputes and third parties do not remain unchanged during the course of intervention. Rather, "Disputes, even after they emerge and are articulated, are indeterminate. They do not exist in fixed form prior to the application of particular dispute processing techniques; they are instead constituted and transformed as they are processed" (Sarat, 1988, p. 708). When fully elaborated, this statement includes two distinct but related claims: that disputes are influenced by third parties as they unfold in intervention; and that third parties themselves are influenced by the disputes they address —intervenors' moves are shaped by characteristics of the dispute, by disputants, and by the unfolding interaction during intervention. In short, both conflicts themselves and the processes used to handle them are malleable.

Studies of how discourse unfolds in intervention support the claim that conflict and intervention is emergent and malleable. Close analyses of third-party moves demonstrate, for example, that, in practice, the line blurs between adjudication and mediation. At times, mediators and arbitrators act similarly when they intervene in disputes. Third parties with adjudicative mandates (e.g., small claims or family court judges) intervene in ways that typify mediators (Philips, 1990; Wall & Rude, 1989). Judges often negotiate, encourage compromise, and involve parties in creating settlement options. Conversely, mediators in labor, divorce, and community disputes often act adjudicatively. They make implicit or explicit judgments about how issues should be framed, which settlement terms are preferable, or which interests need to be addressed (Folger & Bernard, 1985; Greatbatch & Dingwall, 1989; Jacobs, in press; Kolb, 1983, 1989; Lam, Rifkin, & Townley, 1989; Shapiro, Drieghe, & Brett, 1985). Moreover, several general models of third-party strategies suggest that intervenors act contingently; they are influenced by how much value the parties place on achieving their goals, how much common ground there is (Carnevale, Conlon, Hanisch, & Harris, 1989), whether absent parties need protection (Folger & Bernard, 1985), how many issues are on the table, how complex the issues are (Carnevale & Pegnetter, 1985), and how defensive or hostile disputants are (Donohue, 1991; Hiltrop, 1985, 1989; Kochan & Jick, 1978).

This evidence supports the view that conflict in intervention is emergent and malleable—third parties may be as responsive to characteristics of the dispute, disputants, and unfolding interaction as they are to the formal intervention mandates they bring to the process. The resultant "transformation" of disputes in intervention is itself a dynamic process. Characteristics of the emerging dispute, coupled with third-party dispositions about cases and issues, prompt third-party moves. These intervention moves in turn trigger disputants' actions and reactions, ultimately shaping how the conflict unfolds and what the intervention becomes.

The claim that conflict in intervention is emergent has raised some particular concerns about mediation, as a form of third-party intervention (Cobb, 1991, this volume). It is especially clear with mediation, given its informal character, that the process has no fixed form but rather is constituted by the series of moves that third parties and disputants enact. However, precisely because of the growing evidence that conflict is emergent, critics contend that mediation in particular—in contrast with more formal processes like adjudication—is an inherently and severely flawed instrument for handling conflicts. The general argument is that, if conflicts themselves are malleable—if third-party actions in response to contingencies of the case and vagaries of unfolding interaction can reshape and define the conflict itself—then outcomes are potentially vulnerable to intervenors' dispositions, preferences, and prejudices. The best safeguard against this is adherence to procedural formalities and structures that at least reduce process malleability and thus render conflicts less vulnerable to such third-party influence. In other words, given the malleability of conflicts to begin with, malleability of process, though inevitable to some degree, should be minimized to counteract the effect of third-party influence.

As applied to mediation, this argument leads to the conclusion among critics that mediation's extreme malleability makes it an inherently flawed and dangerous forum for handling conflict. The fundamental flaw is that, because of its lack of formality and structure, mediation cannot adequately regulate third-party interventions and even tends to encourage abuse. Without rules of law guiding mediators' response to parties' issues, mediators can alter the very terms of disputes that the parties themselves have framed. Without formal rules of evidence and procedure, less skillful or powerful parties are likely to be at a serious disadvantage during the process. Moreover, without public scrutiny of or accountability for what goes on in the privacy of mediation sessions, there is no way to monitor or limit the kind of abuses just mentioned. As a consequence, when conflicts are mediated, social justice issues can be suppressed, power imbalances can be ignored (or reinforced), and outcomes can in fact be determined by covertly imposed third-party values despite the rhetoric of "mutually acceptable settlement" (Abel, 1982, 1988; Fineman, 1988).

This critique of mediation based on the emergent nature of conflict has raised some important concerns about the way mediation is practiced at present. However, it suffers from a serious weakness. The critique does not fully acknowledge that it rests upon what is essentially an ideological position about what should and should not happen when conflicts occur, and why. That is, "emergent conflict" theory claims that "transformation" of conflict is inevitable, in mediation or elsewhere. If so, the critics cannot be saying that mediation is flawed because it transforms conflict—because the same is true for all other means of handling conflict. The real and unarticulated point of the critique must be that mediation is problematic not simply because it transforms conflict, but because it inevitably does so in ways that are bad or harmful. This kind of argument has to be based on a set of claims about what *should* happen in emergent conflict, and the concern that it will not happen in mediation. Such claims are embedded in an overall ideological consciousness that is left unarticulated and unquestioned in the critique.

Nevertheless, despite these flaws in the critical argument, we share many of the critics' concerns about the way mediation is widely practiced at present. We agree that conflict is emergent and third-party influence inevitable. We also agree that the forms of third-party influence found in mediation as presently practiced are problematic. Therefore, like the critics, we are dissatisfied with the character of mediation at present. However, we differ with the critics' view that mediation is *inherently* flawed. We suggest that the destructive forms of mediator influence currently found in mediation are by no means inevitable.

We ground our approach to both current mediation practice and its critics on an understanding of the ideological foundations of mediation and other forms of dispute processing—making explicit what the critics for the most part leave implicit. We start by assuming that views of mediation—supportive or critical—rest on claims about what interactions and outcomes *should* occur in conflict situations and *why*. These claims rest on ideological foundations that are often deeply rooted in a culture and therefore rarely unpacked and examined. From these foundations arise conceptions of conflict and approaches to intervention, which generate positive or negative views of particular processes such as mediation and specific forms of practice.

Our objective is to show how the discourse that occurs within and about mediation is linked to broad ideological orientations about the nature of the social world, its structures and processes. To reach this objective, we briefly examine the links between conflict, discourse, and ideology, in general. We then show how current mediation practice is shaped primarily by one orientation to conflict—problem solving—and clarify how problem solving is driven by a prevailing ideology of Individualism. We then describe an alternative conception of mediation, one that is built upon a less well articulated orientation to conflict—a transformative view—and show how it stems from an emerging Relational ideology.

Ultimately, as implied above, our analysis offers a critique both of current mediation practice *and* of those who reject mediation altogether because they see its virtues vitiated by the inevitability of unchecked and oppressive third-party influence. These forms of influence, which we also criticize, occur because mediation as currently conceived and practiced is built upon an orientation to conflict that makes such practices likely if not inevitable. Although this orientation has powerful roots in our individualistic culture, it is not absolute or unchangeable.

We believe, therefore, that it is possible to construct and support a form of mediation based on an alternative conception of conflict that we and others envision. If this is done, the emergent nature of conflict and the informal and open character of mediation become, not detrimental, but of enormous positive value. In short, by reaching to the level of ideology on which views of conflict and intervention are based, both current mediation practice and its critique can be transcended.

Conflict Discourse and Ideology

Our analysis of mediation—as a form of conflict discourse shaped by ideology—is grounded on two premises derived from recent studies of the construction and representation of ideology in everyday discourse. The first premise is that "ideologies" are organizing frameworks that people use to view, interpret, and judge their surrounding world. Although ideologies are often held as cognitive values or expectations, they are acquired and expressed through social phenomena; people learn (and recreate) ideologies through participation in groups and relationships (Billig et al., 1988). Because ideologies are lived, they are evidenced in discursive practice and "can be studied through members' interpretations and expressions in talk" (Van Dijk, 1987, p. 13).

The second premise is that people's discursive choices create important social consequences. The choices people make in constructing messages, responding to others' actions, or deciding when or whether to speak, influence expectations and behavior. These choices ultimately distribute power, establish the acceptability of social relationships, and constrain the ability to imagine or enact alternative social arrangements (Billig et al., 1988; Mumby, 1988; Mumby & Putnam, 1992; Potter & Witherell, 1987; Thompson, 1984).

Studies that specifically examine conflict discourse rely on these two premises to display how our ways of thinking about conflict are acquired and expressed in social interaction. Disputants and third parties adopt ideologies of conflict or "conflict realities" that are used in experiencing and interpreting conflict discourse (Littlejohn, Shailor, & Pearce, this volume). These "conflict ideologies" carry implicit notions of what conflict is, as well as expectations about what moves or responses are possible or required in specific contexts, what role third parties play, and what outcomes are desirable. Grimshaw (1990, p. 298) characterizes these expectations as "norms about how conflict talk should be conducted." Studies of conflict discourse reveal the implicit views of conflict people hold and demonstrate how these views are enacted in a wide array of contexts.[1]

These studies begin to offer a useful account of how conflict discourse is influenced by ideology, but we believe the account is not yet complete. Thus far these studies have focused on *conflict* ideologies—ways of thinking about conflict per se—without relating them to broader ideological frameworks affecting society as a whole. In fact, orientations to conflict are themselves reflective of and driven by broader ideologies in society that shape views of human nature, social relationships, and societal structures in general (Aubert, 1963; Coser, 1956; Mack & Simmel, 1955; Snyder, 1957). As Likert and Likert (1976, p. 14) note, "The strategies and principles used by a society and all its organizations for dealing with disagreement and conflict reflect the basic values and philosophy of that society." Societal values and philosophies establish prevailing orientations to conflict; they determine which views of conflict are sovereign and restrict the emergence of alternatives.

Therefore, a full account of the relationship between conflict discourse and ideology—in mediation or other forums—requires an understanding of how orientations to conflict are themselves rooted in larger ideological frameworks. In the next section, we examine the orientation to conflict that currently exerts a pervasive influence on mediation, and we suggest the broader ideological framework on which it rests. We show how this underlying ideology, and the orientation to conflict it supports, lead to the form of mediation practice that critics find problematic.

The Problem-Solving Orientation and Its Ideological Roots

In the dispute resolution field, collaborative problem solving is often cast as the ideal version of conflict resolution. It is, in many ways, the household view in theorists' and practitioners' discussions of the way successful conflict unfolds.[2] The problem-solving orientation is woven through conflict literature in the fields of law (Fisher & Ury, 1981; Menkel-Meadow, 1984), psychology (Likert & Likert, 1976; Maier, 1967; Maier & Solem, 1962; Pruitt, 1983; Pruitt & Rubin, 1986), business/management (Blake & Mouton, 1964; Filley, 1975; Kepner & Tregoe, 1965; McKersie, 1964; Pruitt & Lewis, 1977; Ruble & Thomas, 1976; Schmidt & Tannenbaum, 1960), and communication (Borisoff & Victor, 1989; Folger et al., 1993; Putnam & Poole, 1987).

Although characterizations of problem solving vary somewhat, all rest on the same fundamental orientation to conflict. Any orientation to conflict includes both a view of what conflict is, as a social phenomenon, and a corresponding view of what the ideal response to conflict should be. Conflict is seen as the manifestation of a problem in need of satisfaction. That is, a problem exists because of a real or apparent incompatibility of needs or interests that makes satisfaction of needs impossible for one or more of the parties. Although the resulting dissatisfaction may spark controversy and disputation, the conflict is at heart an unsolved problem—a problem of how to satisfy simultaneously what appear to be incompatible, unmet needs.

Following from this view of conflict, the corresponding view of the ideal response to conflict is integrative and collaborative problem solving. Resolving conflicts means finding solutions that meet the needs of all parties concerned and thus lead to universal satisfaction:

The capacity of a group to develop new, innovative solutions to difficult problems is especially important in resolving conflicts constructively. Where disagreements or conflicts exist, there typically is no readily available solution seen by all parties as acceptable. A new, innovative, integrative solution which will meet the needs and desires of *all* interested parties must be found. (Likert & Likert, 1976, p. 133)[3]

Problem solving is widely espoused in discussions of third-party intervention in general (Ury, Brett, & Goldberg, 1988) and mediation in particular (Folberg & Taylor, 1984; Haynes & Haynes, 1989). It is now well documented that, in mediation as currently practiced, disputants and third parties usually act in ways that are consistent with this orientation to conflict. Three types of evidence, from a range of studies in diverse mediation settings, point to specific ways in which the problem-solving orientation is enacted in mediation.

Global Assessments of Parties' Circumstances

As disputants offer their opening stories (i.e., chronologies of events that led to the present circumstances), mediators tend to search for and define problems that need to be solved or addressed. Mediators fold historical background, chronologies of events, and expressions of frustration or anger into more global assessments of problems that can be addressed through the process. Shapiro et al. (1985) find, for example, that early in labor grievance mediations, third parties ask themselves what kind of case or problem is in front of them, so that they can begin formulating possible solutions. Mediators tend to consult a "repertoire of case patterns they know" that allows them to make a "quick cognitive evaluation of the potential outcome of a case" (Shapiro et al., 1985, p. 112). Similarly, Carnevale, Conlon et al.'s (1989) contingency model of mediation posits that, early in the process, mediators assess whether there is sufficient common ground between parties to reach a mutually acceptable solution.

These findings suggest that problem solving forms a template through which mediators view parties' contributions from the outset of the process. The problem-solving orientation necessitates that intervenors not focus on individual comments or move-by-move interaction. Instead, it encourages them to unearth underlying interests and needs, thereby identifying the problem that these needs create. Like an artist who steps back to peruse a large canvas after every few brush strokes, a mediator working within a problem-solving orientation repeatedly steps back from the comments parties make to see the problem that disputants' statements reveal.

Settlement Orientation

We noted above that mediators have considerable leeway to influence substantive issues and process during intervention. Substantial evidence suggests that mediators orient their intervention strategies primarily toward the creation and acceptance of settlement terms that solve disputants' problems. At times, these strategies challenge the disputants' own preferences or willingness to reach agreement. Intervention moves such as selective facilitation (Greatbatch & Dingwall, 1989); reframing (Lam et al., 1989), reformulations, and directive questioning (Jacobs, in press) enable mediators to shape arguments, frame proposals, and influence process.

This evidence suggests that mediators gear interaction toward settlement, sometimes being influential in ways that raise questions about their role as neutral intervenors (Bernard, Folger, Weingarten, & Zumeta, 1984; Folger & Bernard, 1985; Greatbatch & Dingwall, 1989). This tendency is consistent with a problem-solving orientation. If the goal of intervention is to solve problems for disputants, mediators are likely to rely on intervention strategies that expedite movement toward agreement. Agreements provide tangible evidence that solutions have been created.

Dropping Concerns That Cannot Be Treated as Problems

Donohue's (1991) research on divorce mediation suggests that mediators selectively address issues. Donohue compared agreement and no-agreement divorce mediation sessions and found that in agreement sessions, mediators focused on substantive issues that could readily be examined within a problem-solving framework. In the agreement sessions, mediators talked about interests because the couples were ready to hear one another's interests. In the no-agreement sessions, couples frequently raised relational issues of trust, self-worth, and so on. These concerns tended to stymie mediators' efforts, prompting responses that seemed almost inappropriate for the issues the parties raised: "The no-agreement disputants talked about relational problems while their mediators pursued factual issues" (Donohue, 1991, p. 164). Donohue reports that the no-agreement sessions lasted half as long, on average, as the agreement sessions because relational issues arose in these sessions and mediators swerved from these obstacles in the road, avoiding background events and relationship history that might thwart the creation and acceptance of solutions.

Mediators' willingness to drop relational issues is consistent with the characterization of mediation as "future oriented." Parties' discussion of past events often focus on questions of interpretation—how one party's perspective of an event could be different from the other's. These contradictory views frequently reveal how trust is lost. Sidestepping consideration and discussion of these past events is a way to keep the process "future-oriented"—moving away from relational issues and toward the identification of tangible problems and their solutions.

The tendency to drop issues that cannot be treated as problems is obviously consistent with a problem-solving orientation to conflict. Some issues disputants raise are readily addressable as problems; they lend themselves to definable parameters and concrete arrangements or exchanges that can be formulated as solutions and articulated in settlements. Relational or "personal identity" (Grimshaw, 1990) issues, however, are more difficult to address in problem-solution formats (Sillars & Weisberg, 1987).

Mediators may try to reframe these more elusive issues into problems that have tangible solutions. However, if disputants resist the reframing or reframing appears impossible, mediators may see no alternative other than dropping the issue or case.[4]

The foregoing discussion suggests that much of the practice of mediation at present stems from an overall problem-solving orientation to conflict. However, as we noted above, demonstrating how any view of conflict shapes discourse offers only a partial explanation of people's behavior in fractious situations. The question remains, *why* is the problem-solving orientation so influential, what explains its appeal and its power for those in the dispute resolution and mediation fields? To explain this, we must identify the broader ideological premises on which it rests. These premises explain why problem solving is so entrenched as an orientation to conflict and why alternatives are often unseen, untried, or overtly resisted.

The strength of the problem-solving orientation derives from the fact that it stems from and is closely aligned with an Individualist ideology that is central to the mainstream culture of the United States. This framework, which applies not only to conflict but to every arena of social life, views the human world as made up of radically separate individual beings, of equal worth but with different desires (i.e., perceived needs), whose nature is to seek satisfaction of those individual needs and desires. Society is important because it can serve as a neutral facilitator (or referee) of the process of individual satisfaction. Given this view of the nature of the human world, the highest value is the satisfaction of individual needs and desires, and the greatest evil is the existence of unmet needs and dissatisfaction. Moreover, since all individuals are equal in worth, this value is most completely served—and evil avoided—when equality is preserved, when different individuals' needs and desires are simultaneously satisfied.

This Individualist view of the human world has dominated Western culture in some form for roughly the last 250 years. It can be traced from the writings of Hobbes and Locke to present-day philosophers like Dworkin (1977), Nozick (1974), Rawls (1971), and others. It underlies and informs modern political economy, from Adam Smith to Karl Marx. It has driven, in recent history, the civil rights, women's rights, and human rights movements—and their antecedents in the previous century. It underlies Western democratic theory and institutions. In all of these areas, the Individualist vision has been seen as heralding the liberation of all individuals, each to achieve full satisfaction in his or her own terms.

Problem solving is essentially aligned with Individualistic assumptions about human nature and social interaction. As an orientation to conflict it embodies the view that conflicts represent problems faced by autonomous individuals in achieving mutual needs satisfaction. Further, it reflects the view that conflict resolution can and should involve finding solutions that maximize the satisfaction of every individual involved. In short, the larger ideological context explains why the problem-solving orientation to conflict is so appealing and powerful within the dispute resolution field: It is a view of conflict that expresses the deeply rooted Individualist ideological premises of the society as a whole. Indeed, alternative dispute resolution processes such as mediation are seen as valuable precisely because they offer the opportunity to provide joint satisfaction to disputing individuals, an opportunity that does not seem to exist in formal adversary processes. As a consequence, when processes such as mediation are actually practiced, they naturally enact the problem-solving orientation that makes them seem valuable in the first place, in Individualist terms. Even though problem solving represents a shift away from an even more harshly individualistic orientation—it replaces a worldview of strict self-interest with a worldview of enlightened self-interest—nevertheless, its premises are basically individualistic.

Thus, underlying the specific practices of most mediators is a general problem-solving orientation to conflict, and driving both specific behaviors and the general orientation is a deeply rooted Individualist ideological framework. This, in our view, is the fully traced relationship between ideology, orientation to conflict, and actual conflict discourse in mediation.

Tracing this relationship reveals important insights regarding both current mediation practice and its critics. As noted above, the greatest concern is the likelihood of unchecked and oppressive mediator influence in the conflict process. Our analysis shows that the main cause of the behaviors condemned by the critics is the overall problem-solving orientation itself, with its Individualist ideological base. That is, mediators engage in influencing and controlling behaviors because they see conflicts as problems—obstacles to satisfying incompatible sets of needs—and see their primary mandate as finding the best solutions to those problems. Mediator influence is justified implicitly by the Individualist value of providing maximum satisfaction. However, according to the same Individualist perspective, mediation ultimately is a flawed and dangerous *form* of problem-solving, because it ignores the value of justice/equality, which is just as important in Individualism as satisfaction. Solving problems of unmet or incompatible needs means solving them justly and this requires the kind of formality and rules found only in judicial forums. Unconstrained third-party influence gives rein to third-party biases that inevitably produce disparate treatment, unjust results, and unequal satisfaction. Put differently, Individualist mediators inevitably act as problem solvers, but in doing so their interventions often are unjust, thus compromising Individualism itself.

Our analysis of the links between ideology, conflict orientation, and practice support this critical view of mediation up to a point; but our analysis also shows where the limits of this view lie. As long as the world—and the phenomenon of conflict—are seen in Individualist terms, one cannot but agree with mediation's critics. However, it is not inevitable that the Individualist framework itself be accepted. If it is not, if an altogether different ideology is instead taken as the starting point, then the picture is very different—not because the same mediation practices would no longer seem problematic when followed, but because those practices would no longer be followed to begin with. In short, given that ideology drives orientations to conflict and actual discursive practice, a different, *non-*Individualist ideology might engender an orientation to conflict *and* a form of mediation practice that not only avoids the evils of oppressive third-party influence, but realizes goods that an Individualist ideology barely imagines.

We believe that such an ideology is emerging that views human nature and social interaction in *Relational* rather than Individualist terms, and that gives rise to an orientation to conflict quite different from the problem-solving view. In the next section, we summarize this different view of conflict, show how it can be enacted in mediation practice, and characterize the emerging Relational ideology on which it is based.

The Transformative Orientation and Its Ideological Roots

Few attempts have been made to articulate what a true alternative to a problem-solving orientation might look like, including alternative views of both what conflict is and what the ideal response to conflict should be. Envisioning an alternative to the problem-solving orientation starts by rejecting its basic premise that conflicts need to be viewed as problems. Instead, disputes that emerge from people's substantive concerns, dissatisfactions, and interpersonal or relational tensions can be seen, not as problems, but as opportunities for human growth and transformation.

Specifically, a conflict is seen, in this *transformative orientation,* as a potential occasion for growth in two critical dimensions of human development: *empowerment* and *recognition.* Growth in *empowerment* involves realizing and strengthening one's capacity as an individual for encountering and grappling with adverse circumstances and problems of all kinds. Growth in *recognition* involves realizing and strengthening one's capacity as an individual for experiencing and expressing concern and consideration for others, especially others whose situation is "different" from one's own. Growth in both of these dimensions *together* is the hallmark of mature human development, as we discuss below. And in the transformational orientation, conflict is viewed as a rich field for human growth along both of these dimensions. Conflict creates numerous opportunities for empowerment. For example, it allows people to clarify, for themselves, what causes them dissatisfaction and what contributes to their satisfaction. It also makes it possible for them to realize and strengthen their own capacity and their own resources for addressing both substantive concerns and relational issues. In short, conflict gives people the occasion to develop and exercise self-determination, in deciding for themselves how to define and address difficulties, and self-reliance, in actually putting their decisions into effect. Moreover, conflict creates opportunities for recognition—for acknowledging, although not necessarily accepting or agreeing with, the situations and perspectives of others. The emergence of conflict automatically confronts each party with a differently situated other, holding a very different viewpoint. This in itself gives rise to the possibility for the individual to feel and express some degree of understanding and concern for another, despite diversity and disagreement. Conflict thus gives people the occasion to develop and exercise the capacity for tolerance and empathy. In sum, the transformational orientation views conflict not as a problem to be gotten rid of or solved, but as a rich opportunity for growth, to be exploited to full advantage.

Following from this view of conflict as opportunity for human growth, the corresponding view of the ideal response to conflict is not problem-solving, but *transformation* of the individuals involved, in both dimensions of human growth. Using conflicts productively means exploiting the opportunities they present for empowerment and recognition to change and transform the parties as human beings. It means encouraging and helping the parties to realize, draw from, and strengthen their inherent capacities for both self-reliance and empathy. If these capacities are realized, the response to conflict itself transforms individuals from fearful, defensive, and self-centered beings into confident, open, and caring ones, ultimately transforming society from a shaky truce between suspicious enemies into a strong network of trusting friends.

With few exceptions (Bush, 1989; Northrup, 1989; Riskin, 1982, 1984) the transformative view of conflict has not been widely discussed in published accounts of mediation, nor has it been systematically examined in the mediation practice or training literature. Despite its emerging and largely undocumented state, we can suggest several key elements that characterize mediation practice when it is based on the transformative orientation to conflict.

Micro Assessments of Parties' Moves

The focus of mediators' assessments in this orientation remains largely at a micro-level. In contrast to problem solving's initial global assessment of how individual comments contribute to the definition of some overall problem, mediators examine each interactive turn—disputants' statements, challenges, questions, narratives—for the possibilities each affords for transformational opportunities. The mediator focuses on the brush strokes, rather than the larger, emerging image on the canvas. Parties' individual statements and exchanges are seen as significant in themselves because they are the places where mediators locate choices that the parties can be empowered to make, and where mediators find openings that allow parties to acknowledge the other's perspective. Opportunities for parties to be empowered or to recognize the other can arise in discussion of substantive issues, relational and identity concerns, or the process of intervention itself. Building on these opportunities requires a sustained focus throughout the intervention on individual contributions as they are offered.

Encouraging Parties' Deliberation and Choice-Making

In keeping empowerment central in the process, mediators actively clarify parties' available choices at all key junctures and they encourage parties to deliberate among options. Throughout the process, mediators identify and display opportunities for parties to make choices and they ask parties to acknowledge that their choices are the basis for agreement-making (or for impasse). The parties' choices are treated as central at all levels of decision making, including decisions about process, substantive issues, and relational or identity concerns.

Thus, in sharp contrast to a problem-solving practice, mediators enacting a transformative orientation consciously try to avoid shaping issues, proposals, or terms for settlement, or even pushing for the achievement of settlement at all. Rarely, if ever, would they challenge the parties' own expressed preferences. Indeed, though they may offer suggestions, they usually avoid voicing opinions of their own about issues or proposals, limiting themselves, instead, to raising questions for the parties to consider and decide. Instead, mediators are often insistent about urging, and helping, the parties to make their decisions deliberately—to consider information and options fully before deciding what to do on any issue.[5]

Encouraging Parties to Consider Each Other's Perspectives

In keeping recognition central, mediators actively explore the potential that one party's statements hold for the other's insight. Mediators consider each turn at talk as a potential opening for the listening party to consider the other's circumstances, life situation, or sense of self. The third party takes an active role in turning the interaction toward a consideration of these opportunities for recognition. Starting with parties' statement-by-statement descriptions of past events in their opening narratives, mediators look for places where each party can consider the other's perspective. Parties' different interpretations of the past are often important in allowing them to consider alternative perspectives of shared events. With this transformative emphasis, mediation is less "future oriented" than that conducted within a problem-solving framework. Without the press for defining problems and finding solutions, the moment-to-moment interaction during the process takes on greater significance—it becomes the ground on which a new basis for interaction among the parties is built.

Within a transformative approach mediators not only reinterpret, translate, or reframe parties' statements and viewpoints but, in doing so, they ask parties to acknowledge the value of such reformulations—they encourage parties to consider how recognition of the other's perspective is central to the mediation process and to a productive response to conflict in general. Parties are allowed the possibility of exploring issues that cannot be readily addressed as problems. Issues of identity and relationship can be as important as more tangible substantive outcomes. As a result, "settlement terms" in this orientation encompass a broader range of accomplishments than are typically itemized in problem-solving agreements. These accomplishments might include explicit statements of misunderstandings that were alleviated by the process, alternative views of the other that were developed, or "news" about the other that was not known before the process began.[6]

The above discussion suggests that mediation practice can, and for some mediators does, rest upon an overall transformative orientation to conflict. And when this is the case, practice takes on a very different character than when the problem-solving orientation holds sway. The question remains, *why* do some mediators adopt a transformative orientation, despite the pervasiveness of the problem-solving view? Here too, the answer lies in the broader ideological framework on which the transformative orientation rests.

The appeal of the transformative orientation is due to its connection to a Relational ideology that is emerging to challenge the dominant Individualist framework. This emerging Relational ideology has not yet been fully articulated; however, there are statements in different fields, using different language and constructs, that, taken together, suggest the outlines of a single unifying framework. The Relational framework is a response to perceptions in these different fields that the Individualist worldview gives an impoverished account of the human world and its potential. Most important, Individualism's categorical description of persons as radically separate beings fails to account for many important aspects of human life in which connection to others is the primary quality of experience; and its focus on self-satisfaction as a value is demonstrably inadequate as the basis for moral theory, in a world where its pursuit increasingly appears to be responsible for more evil than good.

The Relational framework, like the Individualist, views the world as made up of persons with individuated consciousness and with diverse needs and desires; but it also sees these diverse beings as possessing an inherent form of consciousness that *connects* them to each other. Specifically, every person has two inherent human capabilities. The first is the capacity for consciousness of the full range of human experience—pain and pleasure, joy and sorrow, clarity and confusion, and so forth. The second is the capacity for realizing that every other person has the same kinds of experiential capacities as oneself. It is this inherent and uniquely human capacity for *relating to* the experience of others that constitutes the structure—a structure of human consciousness—that connects every individual human being to every other, at least potentially. Of course, this connective structure itself rests upon a capacity for reflection and awareness that, even though inherent, is only realized through the actions of individuals encountering one another, reflecting upon one another's predicaments, and gaining awareness of each other's common humanity.

The Relational view therefore sees the world as containing *both* the plurality of individual selves and the (potential) unity made up of the network of their relationships. Society is important, in this view, because it is the medium for the process of human relations, through which potential connections between individuals are realized. Implicit in this whole framework is the view that the development of potential relations into actual ones involves an elevation from a lower to a higher state of being or nature. That is, in developing conscious awareness of others' common humanity, instead of regarding others as things to be used for one's own ends, the individual moves from a lower to a higher state of being. When individuals experience awareness and concern for both self *and* other, they rise to a higher, fully human existence. And as individuals develop a fully human consciousness, the world as a whole develops from hostile jungle to friendly civil community.

The highest value that emerges from this vision of the human world is not the satisfaction of individual desires, but the development of the higher potential of both the individual and the world itself through activating the human capacity for awareness of and concern for both self *and* other. In moral terms, the value translates into a consciously and freely chosen extension of consideration to others. When the self-aware individual freely chooses to put concern for others on a par with concern for self alone, this is a kind of self-transcendence that expresses the uniquely human capacity for relating to others, and thus concretely realizes the potential for human interconnection and elevates both the individual and the world to a higher state of being. The primary function of society, as medium for human interconnection, is both to provide opportunities for individuals to grow in strength through self-awareness, and then to encourage them to use that strength to give consideration to others.[7]

It should be clear that the transformative orientation to conflict is driven by the Relational view of human nature and society. This orientation embodies the view that conflicts represent opportunities, for individuals who have inherent but latent capacities for self-awareness and self-transcendence, to achieve fuller development of those capacities. It further reflects the view that the ideal response to conflict can and should involve helping individuals to take advantage of these opportunities by making choices that call forth these highest human qualities. Thus, as with Individualist ideology and problem solving, underlying the practices of certain mediators is a transformative view of conflict, and driving both practice and orientation for these mediators is a larger Relational ideological framework.

Tracing this relationship fully, as we have tried to do above, clarifies why we see the critique of mediation practice as limited and unduly pessimistic, even though we agree that much of current practice is problematic. The key point is that we start from a different ideological basis—the Relational framework. We therefore agree that the patterns of mediation practice involving excessive mediator influence are problematic—but not for the same reasons as the critics. Our objection to such influence is not primarily that it works injustice and distributes satisfaction unequally. Rather, our objection is that it disempowers *all* parties and squanders opportunities for empowerment and recognition throughout the process. It may thwart equal satisfaction, but we are even more concerned that it thwarts the human development for which mediation is so potentially valuable.

At the same time, our framework demonstrates that this is not an *inherent* problem of mediation. It is rather an inherent problem of the problem-solving approach to conflict as played out in mediation. When practice is driven by a transformative orientation instead, the controlling and influencing mediator behaviors that the critics find objectionable are largely *avoided*. That is, the care taken by transformative mediators to empower the parties results in minimizing the risk of mediator influence. Thus what the critics seek to avoid by rejecting mediation altogether can be avoided instead by rejecting the *approach* to mediation that stems from the problem-solving orientation.

However, there is an even better reason, in our view, to consider shifting the basis of mediation practice from a problem-solving to a transformative orientation to conflict. Not only would such a shift avoid the evils of oppressive mediator influence; more importantly, it would open up the possibility of using the full potential of mediation as an instrument for human development, a potential that is being largely ignored at present.

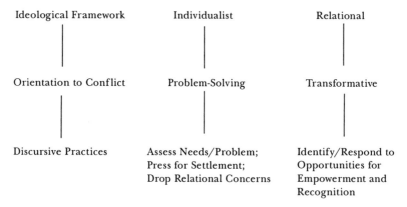

Ideological Framework	Individualist	Relational
Orientation to Conflict	Problem-Solving	Transformative
Discursive Practices	Assess Needs/Problem; Press for Settlement; Drop Relational Concerns	Identify/Respond to Opportunities for Empowerment and Recognition

Figure 1.1. Summary: Ideologies, Views of Conflict, and Discourse

Conclusion: Ideology, Views of Conflict, and Discourse

In this analysis, we have attempted to define what mediation is, and what it might become, by examining how it embodies orientations to conflict and ideological visions of human interaction. Figure 1.1 summarizes the framework guiding our discussion; it displays the relationship between discourse, orientations to conflict, and ideological frameworks.

Our analysis suggests that it may be critics' limited expectations about human interaction and conflict that yield a damaging, though in some ways warranted, assessment of mediation. Those who reject mediation because it is vulnerable to mediators' influence stand firmly within the Individualist framework, taking for granted the value (and perhaps inevitability) of problem solving as an ideal process. If this framework remains unquestioned, or if one believes that it is the only approach to conflict that people are capable of, then these critiques may well be the death knell for mediation. We may have to accept, for instance, that in practice mediation and adjudication easily become indistinguishable because both are variations on a recognizable theme—they epitomize the same Individualistic expectations about human relationships and social interaction. They start with similar expectations about treating concerns as needs-satisfaction problems, they remain limited to self-referential views of parties' interests, and they are aimed primarily toward the creation and adoption of satisfying solutions—solutions that can be either imposed by a third party, with greater or lesser guarantees of fairness, or constructed by the disputants.

As long as Individualistic assumptions go unacknowledged or unquestioned, alternative views of conflict—and thus of mediation—remain opaque. Questioning these assumptions necessitates that we imagine and develop processes that realize rival objectives by demanding different discursive practices. We believe that practitioners can construct a reality that follows a transformative view of conflict by placing empowerment and recognition at the heart of mediation practice. Indeed, we see instances where this orientation is already enacted, although it is not often recognized or documented.

The transformative orientation needs an accessible language that can give voice to those who know it intuitively and aspire to enact it. Where do opportunities for empowerment and recognition arise during the process? What are appropriate third-party interventions, given the goals of empowerment and recognition and the educative objectives of the transformative view? How do the typical ground rules and process guidelines of mediation, as we have come to define them within a problem-solving orientation, undermine transformative possibilities? What does a mediation process look like that fosters transformative discourse? How do institutions that house and administer mediation respond to transformative approaches to mediation? Are our courts, community centers, and private practice offices so steeped in Individualist ideology that these institutions prevent a transformative approach from being enacted? What institutional assumptions and practices would have to change in order to facilitate mediation that is based on Relational assumptions?

Once these questions are addressed, we believe that the transformative view of conflict will lose the utopian image some have assigned to it. It was only a few decades ago that many theorists and practitioners thought problem solving and "win-win" approaches to negotiation and conflict were quixotic, especially in the face of truly divisive conflicts. As this approach was articulated and exemplified, however, daunting impracticalities soon seemed like minor technical difficulties. Practitioners came to think problem solving was possible because theorists indicated it was. Third-party practice then confirmed its perceived utility. We see the transformative view of conflict walking a similar path as theorists and practitioners articulate the inadequacies of prevailing Individualistic views of conflict and imagine the possibilities of a Relational alternative. In an important sense, current debates about the viability of mediation can spark a much more significant reexamination of our assumptions and expectations about conflict in general.

Notes

1. See Brenneis (1988), Grimshaw (1990), Silbey and Merry (1986), Penman (1987), and Littlejohn, Shailor, and Pearce (this volume) for summaries and illustrations of this research.

2. Stewart (1987) and others recognize, however, that problem solving is a Western view of conflict.

3. Strict or purist conceptions of problem solving contend that the only process that warrants the problem-solving label is the one in which a truly creative solution is found that fully meets all parties' needs. Other "bargaining" forms of problem solving, where parties give up or ignore some needs to reach agreement, are frequently labeled "compromising"—a different and less desirable conflict orientation. That is, for some who identify conflict styles, problem solving is reserved for the ultimate creative process that appears to transform confrontation into artistic creation and disputants into collaborators. We view bargaining and compromising as integrally tied to the problem-solving process. The essence of all problem-solving behavior is that interests are viewed self-referentially. When parties interact within a problem-solving orientation, they address the needs of others primarily because it enables them to satisfy their own needs.

4. We are not suggesting that substantive and relational issues are mutually exclusive. We agree with Grimshaw (1990, p. 284) that "Whatever the putative stakes . . . , it appears that all conflict talk involves some negotiation of identities and of the appropriate nature of interpersonal (i.e., structural, organizational) arrangements." Nonetheless, disputants do give emphasis to substantive or relational issues and third parties must respond to issues that are brought to the fore.

5. The transformative orientation to conflict does not foreclose the possibility of parties addressing a specific issue or dispute as a problem. Problem solving is one option that parties might choose. The difference is that this orientation does not privilege problem solving; it asks parties to decide whether the concerns they face should be treated as problems or as something else (e.g., open-ended discussions of historical circumstances, a basis for gaining insight into each other's actions, etc.). Disputants are thus empowered to decide this question as well as others. As a result, specific "problems" may be solved once the parties have chosen to view them as such, but this orientation looks beyond the provision of solutions to the transformation of the individual disputants through the experience of empowerment itself.

6. Some might argue that problem solving itself is a means to transformative ends—that although the process itself does not claim transformative objectives, transformative outcomes can occur after the problem-solving process transpires.

Once parties reach a solution by creatively addressing joint needs, they can recognize each other's situation and learn that the problem-solving approach is, itself, a way to handle conflict in the future. There are several reasons why this view of problem solving does not constitute a transformative orientation as we have described it.

First, transformative possibilities for both empowerment and recognition that are possible within a problem-solving orientation are left to parties' retrospective and, in some ways, serendipitous insight. In contrast, the transformative orientation is self-consciously educative; it attempts to enhance parties' awareness of empowerment and recognition as goals of the process. Second, the sense of empowerment problem solving entails is limited to the disputants' belief that defining issues as problems is the ideal approach to conflict. This provides a narrow sense of the options people have for addressing life's concerns. Third, the self-referential approach to interests that lies at the heart of the problem-solving orientation is inconsistent with the other-directed nature of recognition.

7. The Relational view has not yet been embodied in a complete or definitive statement; it is a framework that is still being formulated. Nevertheless, it is possible to identify works from many fields that not only reflect aspects of this ideology but are coming together to constitute it. Among the most important of these are the works of Carol Gilligan (1982, 1988) in moral theory and psychology, and Michael Sandel (1982) in political philosophy. Many others express and contribute to the vision in some degree. These include: in law, feminist scholars like Sherry (1986), West (1988), Henderson (1987), and Minow (1987); in sociology, Bellah and his colleagues (Bellah, Madsen, Sullivan, Swidler, & Tipton, 1985, 1991), and Evans and Boyte (1988); in history and political science, Epstein (1984), Pocock (1975), and other "new republican" writers; in organizational theory Morgan (1986), Mumby (1988), Mumby and Putnam (1992), and, cutting across philosophy, sociology, and law, MacIntyre (1981), Bernstein (1983), Ferguson (1984), MacNeil (1984), and other "communitarian" or "dialogist" theorists.

What are the conflicting tensions that influence how third-party interventions unfold? How does a dialectical view of discourse capture these tensions and the patterns of interaction they produce? What strategies do the third parties and disputants use to deal with these tensions?

2

A Dialectical Reframing of the Mediation Process

Tricia S. Jones

BY NOW, most conflict scholars are aware that mediation has come of age in the practical sense, but concerns linger about our ability to generate theories of mediation process and consequence. As the blush fades from the initial experience of mediation as alternative dispute resolution, conflict scholars and practitioners are stepping back to take a sober and realistic look at the extent of our knowledge. They are finding more consensual focus, but less theoretical advancement.

In their recent volume summarizing contemporary mediation research, Pruitt and Kressel (1989) summarize the "key themes" in this work:

> The efficacy of mediator behavior as a function of the nature and stage of the dispute and the characteristics of the disputants; the importance of studying not only formal mediation but the informal

mediation of everyday relationships, and the effect of the wider social context in which conflict is embedded. (p. 4)

Apparently, mediation scholarship is moving toward acknowledging the relevance of mediation contexts: the interplay of context and text, situation and behavior.

But, to what extent are we developing theories that explain the functional and constructive contribution of context? We may be concentrating too heavily on amassing detailed and insightful descriptions of action within context. In fact, Kressel and Pruitt concluded in their summary and critique that we seem to be able to describe behavioral sets and even identify exigencies related to their occurrence, but we have little explanatory capability when pushed to discuss the "whys" of mediation interaction and process.

The absence of theory is not only an academic concern. The lack of theoretical explanation negatively affects mediation practice. Mediators are not provided with explanatory models that enable them to be more strategic as interveners, as Kressel and Pruitt (1989a) note:

> Mediators appear influenced by immediate stimulus (such as rising hostility) and perhaps by a generalized preference for a particular style of mediation, but not by any integrated perspective about the proper response to various underlying dysfunctional dynamics. The situation seems much more primitive in this regard than what prevails in psychotherapy—another type of "conflict" intervention—in which therapist behavior is typically rooted in theories of personality development or family dynamics. (p. 426)

Rather than attempting to develop a specific theory of mediation process, this chapter presents an argument for the heuristic value of a new perspective on mediation process, a metatheoretical suggestion. That perspective, derived from dialectical approaches to understanding interpersonal relationships and their development, assumes that relationship is the primary context of interest in mediation and that a communication perspective is essential to understanding the generative synergy of communication and relationship.

This perspective is not presented as the answer to all theoretical inadequacies in the study of mediation. In fact, the goal here is to ask mediation scholars to try a different way of looking at mediation process, to test the fabric and alter the cut if necessary, but to challenge the traditional. Following the lead of family therapy and relationship development theorists, the perspective may actually generate a variety of middle range or particularistic theories tailored to specific mediation situations.

In order to accomplish this aim, the initial section of this chapter suggests why relationship should be privileged as a primary context. Then, the interrelation of relationship and communication is used to support the adoption of a communication perspective in mediation theory and research. A review of some of the previous ways communication scholars have conceptualized relational factors in mediation serves as contrast for what may be accomplished from the new perspective. Finally, an overview of the dialectical perspective enables discussion of the potential contributions for thinking about and doing mediation.

Relationship as Context: Conflict's Underpinning

Relationship is the keystone of conflict. To some degree, all conflicting parties are in "relation" by virtue of their direct or indirect impact on the conditions and behaviors of the others. However, *relationship* is being used here to indicate a more permanent, substantive, and/or intimate experience with the other. The extent of this experiencing can be labeled relational salience, or the degree to which the relationship impacts life experience.

Relationship is interdependence, the genesis for conflict. By definition, relationship involves interdependence between parties in order to coordinate action, negotiate understandings, and distribute resources. Yet, it is the very nature of interdependence that guarantees conflict. Without some degree of relationship the motivation for conflict is almost nonexistent, limited to situations in which individuals experience conflict as a transitory, animalistic response to immediate attempts at interference or dominance. The degree of operative interdependence is the probable degree of experienced conflict.

The relationship between conflicting parties serves as a context that gives meaning to their text or behaviors. It is not the only information necessary to understand the complex unfolding of the conflict or its resolution. Yet, the more idiosyncratic the relationship, the more the knowledge of the relational context is necessary to interpret action.

Obviously, the degree to which the relationship between parties actually triggers conflict or determines its nature and intensity varies considerably. An episode of "random" violence or an impersonal one-shot negotiation by proxy differs in degree and kind from the nature of conflict occurring between divorcing spouses. And, the salience of the relationship as context may fluctuate within a given situation where alternate contexts interact.

Yet, for most mediators, relational context is significant given the types of disputes requiring their attention. The impetus for mediation and its recent popularity lay in the realization that traditional methods of dispute resolution were insensitive to relational parameters and influences. Especially in disputes between members of long-term, intimate relationships, reliance on dispute processes that privileged a nonresponsive, legalistic authority were attacked as inappropriate and ineffective (Nonet & Selznick, 1978; O'Connor, 1981; Riskin, 1982). Although relational factors to a dispute may have been used as information considered during processing, the relational bases of the dispute were not allowed to alter the processing method itself. This fueled criticism that these dispute resolution methods merely increased tensions and hostilities, increased recidivist conflict, and thus were economically inefficient (Cahn & Cahn, 1970; Felstiner et al., 1980-1981; Fraser & Froelich, 1979).

Alternative dispute resolution processes, modeled after European and Asian experiences (Doo, 1973; Felstiner, 1974; Gulliver, 1979), were developed and specifically targeted to handle "relational conflicts," that is, interpersonal, family, and neighborhood disputes. Mediation became the preferred method because flexibility of process enabled consideration of relationship factors, preserved the decision-making power of disputants, and decreased the adversarial (and thus defensive) nature of the interactions (Moore, 1986).

In fact, current developments in mediation suggest a tendency to more informal processes, and thus, a growing need for mediation theories that recognize the importance of relational context. American mediators have traditionally been relationally detached from the disputants in order to protect the appearance of a "neutral" or "nonvested" status, unlike mediation models in nonindustrial societies (Merry, 1989). Yet, mediation in organizational contexts (Kolb & Sheppard, 1985) and other manifestations of "informal thirdpartyship" (Sheppard, Blumenfeld-Jones, & Roth, 1989) involve a mediator who is ensconced in a relationship with the parties and who has considerably more knowledge of the relational dynamics between disputants than the "traditional" mediator. In some cases, the third party may be a part of the dispute proper, or at least a factor in its development.

The benefits and drawbacks of more informal applications of mediation have been addressed by others (see Karambayya & Brett in this volume as well as Kolb & Sheppard, 1985). Regardless of the outcome of that debate, the use of mediation in increasingly informal contexts is likely to continue.

De-Emphasizing Relationship: An Overview of Mediation Theory and Research

A review of theoretical approaches to conflict and, more specifically, to mediation reveals that relational context has received little attention, as is true for other contexts—social, cultural, or institutional. Strides in understanding the "figure" of mediation have come at the expense of even elementary considerations of the "ground."

Contemporary conflict theories have built upon the foundation of assumed hedonism, rationality, and intentionality; usually constricting relationship conceptualization to economic exchanges (Northrup, 1989). Thomas (1989) labels this the legacy of game theoretic approaches to conflict and questions our continuing reliance on these assumptions as we appear to move beyond strict game theoretic models.

Over-reliance on game theory

Although mediation theories may include reference to or discussion of relational context, they rarely highlight its potential for influence. And, to date, they have failed to seriously unpack how that influence may be exerted.

What is called for may best be understood in contrast. It is the difference between acknowledging that relational tensions may alter the general level of emotionality or defensiveness present, or between classifying parties' relationships to determine their effect on or association with other variables of interest, *and* examining how relationship defines the nature of the conflict interaction as well as its unfolding. The former is more tangential, the latter is more essential.

Suggest move from relationship as influence to relationship as context

Earlier theories of mediation did not intend to highlight relationship as context to the extent described above. Their interests were guided by other questions of importance. For example, Wall (1981) presented a social exchange model of mediation in which three key relationships are posited: mediator-disputant, mediator-other disputant, and disputant-disputant. His interest, however, lay in suggesting and explaining mediator strategies and tactics based on social exchange premises rather than in-depth assessment of relational factors. Carnevale and colleagues have developed a theory of contingent mediator behavior that assumes effective mediators are adaptive to situational factors (Carnevale, Lim, & McLaughlin, 1989). Their focus has been to develop taxonomies of mediator behaviors, dispute features, and outcomes; and to suggest when and how combinations of these factors result in maximum effectiveness. Interestingly, relational attributes are not key in their treatment of dispute features. They have yet to explore fully the influence of a thorough knowledge of the relationship between disputants and/or between the mediator and disputants. These mediation theories, generated for alternate purpose but illustrative for the point, are not the exception to the rule. In general, other mediation theories are less cognizant of relational factors or treat relationship similarly (Moore, 1986).

Descriptive analyses of mediation, with particular emphasis on mediator strategy and tactics, comprise the majority of mediation research in the past two decades. These studies rarely investigate relational parameters as serious influences on mediation process or outcome. This omission does not negate the value of the research, but it is noteworthy, especially when the descriptive studies examine mediation of disputes between members of long-term, intimate relationships.

For example, Pruitt and colleagues have reported in-depth analyses of community mediation hearings and factors related to the long- and short-term success of mediation outcomes, but do not include relationship type or relational issues in their analysis (Pruitt et al., 1989). Several research programs in divorce mediation have contributed significantly to our knowledge of the association of demographic characteristics of divorcing couples and their decision to mediate, reactions to mediation, conflict behaviors, and dispute outcomes (Kelly & Gigy, 1989; Pearson & Thoennes, 1989; Roehl &

Cook, 1989). None of these comprehensive analyses has explored relational influences on mediation process.

Even interpretive, ethnographic studies of mediation grounded in the fundamental connection between context and practice tend to emphasize organizational settings, the mediator's positional status, and the mediator's ideology rather than the history and present degree of relational tensions between the disputants (Kolb, 1989). However, the basic presupposition of the importance of context in interpretive research highlights the potential for this type of investigation to explore relational influence.

Constituting Relationship: The Need for a Communication Perspective on Mediation

A search for relationship in conflict theory logically presumes a search for communication, given the mutually constitutive nature of communication and relationship. As Roloff (1987) suggests, "interpersonal communication constitutes the production, transmission, and interaction of symbols by *relational partners*" (p. 489, emphasis his). For communication to be comprehensible there must be context, and relationships are the preeminent social context, setting the "boundaries within which interpersonal experiences are evaluated" (Bochner, 1984, p. 611).

Consonant with the traditional theories of conflict, communication has generally been controlled or eliminated in conflict research, seen more as a confounding or insignificant factor than as an integral component of the construction of a conflict (Putnam & Jones, 1982). Mechanistic views of communication in conflict necessitate the de-emphasis of relational bases and deny the evolutionary nature of conflict as a discursive process structuring context and communication interchangeably.

What is needed as a precursor for serious conceptualizations of relational context is an appreciation for a communication perspective in studies of mediation. Such a perspective extends beyond the identification and examination of communication variables in conflict, although that is undeniably a part. Discussing negotiation theory, Putnam and Roloff (1992) identify three features of a communication approach applicable to the study of mediation: (1) examination of microelements of behavior with an emphasis on patterning, (2) a focus on dynamic, developmental features of negotiation, and (3) an effort to uncover how meaning is dependent upon relational, social, and cultural contexts. As Northrup (1989) suggests, we must actively support conceptualizations that prize the evolutionary and developmental realities of conflict process, that acknowledge the multiplicity of contextual levels operating to produce meaning, and that prove commensurate with the complexity of the phenomenon under investigation.

Through communicative acts relationships are accomplished, transformed, and evaluated. This is particularly evident in conflict interaction because problematic relationships tend to be cause, consequence, or both in conflictual situations. Indeed, sociolinguistic analyses of dispute discourse reveal an increased reliance on relational accounts rather than rule-based accounts in the justificatory recitation of conflict situations. People often feel the need to recount relational factors that impact their understanding of the conflict and find relatively little latitude for such relational accounts in legalistic procedures (Conley & O'Barr, 1990b). When given opportunity, such as that provided by the informality of mediation, relational accounts may eclipse other interactional devices for establishing and communicating the dispute framework.

"Conflict talk" usually involves negotiation of relational parameters and resultant identities. Grimshaw (1990) asserts that "*all* conflict talk involves *some* negotiation of identities and of the appropriate nature of interpersonal arrangements" (p. 284, emphasis his).

These same principles of communication resound through relational communication theory (for a good summary of interpersonal communication theory and relational theory, see Bochner, 1984). Originally identified with the pragmatic approach of the Palo Alto group (Watzlawick, Beavin, & Jackson, 1967) this work introduced the notion of report and command dimensions of communication, digital and analogic language, symmetrical and complementary interaction patterns, metacommunicative behavior, punctuation of communication episodes, confirming and disconfirming responses, and the power and form of paradoxical injunctions. Later, relational theory concentrated on explorations of basic dimensions of relational communication: trust, intimacy, and control (Millar & Rogers, 1987). And most recently, it has focused on the role of communication in creating and transforming relationships through the life span of the relationship. In many ways the principles of a "communication perspective" to conflict as discussed by Putnam and Roloff (1992) mirror the basic tenets of pragmatic perspectives on relational communication.

A Select Review of Communication Research in Mediation

Most of the mediation research contributed by communication scholars in the past decade reflects a communication approach, or pragmatic perspective in terms of microanalysis of behavior, to identify patterns and appreciation for dynamic, development characteristics of conflict. However, it has been less successful at reflecting the commitment to recognize and consciously address the impact of relational, social, and cultural contexts.

Two research programs in divorce mediation, studies by Jones and by Donohue and colleagues, exemplify communication research that incorporates certain aspects of a communication approach without fully embracing an exploration of relational contexts. Interestingly, both scholars were analyzing data from the same data pool of divorce mediation audiotapes originally collected and made available by Dr. Jessica Pearson.

Through interactional analysis, both programs of research were interested in microanalysis of communication behavior in mediation. Coded interaction was examined using lag sequential analyses to discover patterns of mediator-disputant behavior. However, different theoretical assumptions underlay the content analytic systems used in the respective research.

Initially, Jones (1989a) intended to revise traditional taxonomies of mediator behavior to incorporate more relational sensitivity. These taxonomies separated behavior into content and process functions, where content strategies focused on involvement in substantive decision making and process addressed establishing communication flow between the parties (Bartunek, Benton, & Keys, 1975). Four major taxonomies were reviewed (Kochan & Jick, 1978; Kressel, 1977; Sheppard, 1984; Simkin, 1971). None included explicit delineation of strategies or tactics that were relationally oriented; an understandable omission considering these taxonomies were developed for use with traditional mediation applications. Needing a taxonomy better suited to the nuances of relational concern in divorce mediation, Jones's taxonomy added supportive communication tactics involving confirmation, empathic expression, and face concerns and instructive tactics that involved relational negotiation as well as substantive instruction by the mediator. She then revised a recently developed content analysis system for mediation to correspond to the strategies and tactics in her taxonomy (Jones, 1985).

Distinctive patterns of mediator-spouse and disputant-disputant interaction in successful and unsuccessful mediation sessions were identified through lag sequential analysis (Jones, 1989a). Key differences in mediator-spouse patterns of interaction revealed that mediators in successful sessions controlled the provision of information by guiding disputants to talk for themselves rather than the other disputant. Protecting the disputant's own voice and his or her ownership of personal information was critical to reducing tension and distributive inclinations. Mediators in unsuccessful sessions were pulled into reciprocating disagreement with disputants, positioning themselves as a clear and present adversary; while mediators in successful sessions engaged in and stimulated reciprocal exchanges of problem-solving behaviors. Predictably, disputant-disputant patterns suggested strong symmetricality in distributive behaviors, resistance to information acquisition strategies by other disputants, and failure to generate problem-solving cycles independently. Other investigations examined interaction patterns of mediator responses to disputant behaviors and gender differences in the ways mediators responded to husbands versus wives during joint and caucus mediation sessions (Jones, 1987).

Donohue's research was prompted by the need to determine "which mediator communication strategies and tactics, in response to which disputant negotiation strategies and tactics, would create a collaborative dispute resolution context" (1989, p. 323). Diez's (1984, 1986) theoretical contributions to understanding communicative competence in conflict served as the underpinning of subsequent interaction analyses.

Diez (1984) originally based her work on Hyme's ideas of communicative competence as a native speaker's ability, within his or her speech community, to interpret and produce language appropriate to situations—situations that were understood in terms of relational features including social distance, status, and power elements that shift with activity and setting. Her interpretive, ethnographic investigations of educational bargaining teams led her to develop her model of negotiation competence (Diez, 1986) in which she identified three types of discourse work involved in negotiation: coherence work (linking concepts together, making sense of the "story"), distance work (controlling relational immediacy and informality to communicate psychological distance, role distance, and social distance), and structuring work (organizing the interaction through the sequencing of information and turns at talk).

Diez's ideas served as the basis for a model of mediator competence operationalized as the use of "three primary content strategies; structuring the process of mediation, reframing the disputant's positions, and expanding the information resource" (Donohue et al., 1988, pp. 108-109). Patterns of mediator-disputant interaction in agreement and no-agreement divorce mediation were examined using lag sequential analysis to address the central research question stated earlier. Disputant strategies were coded as attacking, bolstering, or integrative (for full explanation of those strategies, see Donohue, 1989). Structuring interventions had more relative merit than others in terms of creating cooperative interaction among disputants. Examinations of timing differences in the use of specific strategies revealed that agreement mediators were more likely to intervene after integrative disputant behaviors while no-agreement mediators were more likely to intervene after attacks.

Developmental processes have received attention through phase analyses of divorce mediation interaction, typifying the second emphasis in a communication approach to mediation. There are two key issues in phase modeling: how to constitute a phase and how to determine the dynamics that generate changes in interactions from phase to phase. Previous research has contributed to our understanding of basic phase structures and patterns of interaction characteristic of the phases. However, because "change over time is at the heart of phase modeling," it is unfortunate that "most descriptive phase models gloss the question of what causal mechanisms generate movement from phase to phase" (Holmes, 1992, p. 95).

Phase models of negotiation (Douglas, 1957, 1962; Gulliver, 1979; and for a thorough review, see Holmes, 1992) differ in the number and specificity of hypothesized phases; yet all agree that movement in "successful" conflict interaction shifts from differentiation to integration, antagonism to coordination. Similarly, several models of phase structures in mediation are basic elaborations of negotiation phase theories (Haynes, 1982; Irving, 1981; Moore, 1986; Wiseman & Fiske, 1980).

Jones (1988) examined phase structures in agreement and no-agreement divorce mediation. Developmental structures in agreement mediations supported suggested phase models: an initial agenda-building phase in which issues are identified and structured, followed by an information-exchange phase where disputants tell their "stories," leading to a negotiation phase where alternatives are presented and evaluated, and finally culminating in a resolution phase where agreements are achieved and finalized. However, no agreement mediation evidenced a tendency to de-emphasize or omit the agenda-building phase, to linger overlong on the information exchange that often degenerated into escalating differentiation and increasing polarization and belated attempts to instill problem-solving that quickly aborted. How or why these phase structures occurred is not addressed; the causal mechanisms remained unknown.

Understanding a Dialectical Perspective: Applying the Basics to Mediation

The preceding review of communication research in mediation suggests that, despite some progress, we have yet adequately to address relational context as a generative force in mediation. We can classify behaviors as indicative of some relational coloring, such as identifying more or less confirming comments or assessing levels of relational distance. We can identify phases of interaction and behaviors characteristic of those phases. But these accomplishments do not seem commensurate with the complexity of relational context, or of mediation.

What is needed is a way of thinking about mediation (and conflict in general) that is more dimensional; a theoretical perspective in which behavior is understood as "both-and" rather than "either-or." For example, where an agenda suggestion is recognized as both opening a topic for discussion and closing off others instead of either one or the other. Dimensionality also involves "de-linearizing" current conceptions of mediator-disputant relationships. Mediators are not third parties who act on others without being acted upon, yet most of our theory implicitly or explicitly confirms this view. And, dimensionality argues for an appreciation of a less instrumental understanding of mediation—where mediation is appreciated for its ability to change the way people relate to each other and to society as well as its ability to accomplish resolution of a specific dispute. A dialectical perspective on mediation offers the opportunity to "dimensionalize" our thinking; to "cube" our "square" conceptions. The following sections present an overview of the dialectical perspective and relate these basic ideas to mediation. Although it is not possible to explore this perspective fully, the last segment of this section suggests avenues for further exploration.

A "dialectical" perspective is commonly assumed to refer to Hegelian conceptions of thesis, antithesis, and synthesis, or to a Marxist discussion of oppressive systems. In addition to these meanings, *dialectic* has also been discussed as a rhetorical invention, a decision-making structure, and as a property of social interaction (Weeks, 1977). It is the latter sense of the term that concerns us.

Basseches (1981) defines *dialectic* as "developmental transformation (i.e., development through forms) which occurs via constitutive and interactive relationships" (p. 46). The notion of a dialectic of social interaction is the idea that concepts of transformation and contradiction underlie all social activity and its meaning. Moreover, meaning and relational context are mutually generative.

Dialectic is not limited to a given domain or application. Rather, dialectic conceptions operate as a perspective, or metatheory. Dialectical perspective is emerging throughout the social sciences, replacing the more reductionist, demonstrative analytic metaphors (Gergen, 1980; Rychlak, 1968), like the rationalist and mechanistic conceptions of conflict discussed earlier.

Communication researchers have used dialectical perspectives to examine a variety of relationships including first-time parenthood couples (Stamp & Banski, 1992), adolescent and adult friendships (Legge & Rawlins, 1992; Rawlins, 1983a, 1983b, 1989, 1992), blended relationships involving friends as co-workers (Bridge & Baxter, 1992), and stepfamilies (Cissna, Cox, & Bochner, 1990). Yet, critics are already calling for dialectical communication studies to give equal emphasis to process and contradictions (Goldsmith, 1990) rather than repeating mistakes of earlier approaches that de-emphasized how interactions unfold longitudinally (Alberts & Driscoll, 1992; VanLear, 1991).

Dialectical perspective in family therapy is becoming popular (Backman, 1988; Buss, 1976; Cronen, Pearce, & Tomm, 1985; Dolliver,

1972; Hoffman, 1985) as a means of accomplishing second-order change in family systems (Watzlawick, Weakland, & Fisch, 1974). Even some conflict theorists are beginning to entertain the utility of dialectical approaches to conflict (Kolb & Putnam, 1991). Although a coherent set of theoretical premises is still evolving, certain tenets of the perspective are identifiable: that (1) oppositional forces form the basis of all social phenomena, (2) that change is constant, (3) that social phenomena are defined by the relations among their characteristics, not by the characteristics themselves, and (4) that dialectical tensions are never eliminated, but rather managed (Montgomery, 1992).

Conforth (1968) identifies two root concepts that qualify a theory as dialectical: process and contradiction. The centrality of the process element is that all things undergo constant change resulting from the conflict or tension between opposing or contradictory elements. Although tensions shift they are never eliminated and the motivation for change remains (Goldsmith, 1990). Thus to understand process we must first appreciate contradiction, or the motivating force.

The Notion of Contradiction

A contradiction is present whenever two forces are interdependent (the dialectical principle of unity) yet mutually negate one another (the dialectical principle of negation) (Baxter, 1990). Rawlins (1992) discusses two broad, analytical classes of contradictions, interactional and contextual. The former concerns interactional dynamics that create and manage contradictions and the latter consists of socio-cultural conceptions that frame the interaction, such as the tension between the public and private sanctioning of a relationship, for example, marriage. Interactional contradictions, the focus of this discussion, were eloquently summarized by Bochner (1984) in one of the earliest discussions of dialectical principles in communication:

> The dialectical qualities of interpersonal communication make it obvious that things are not always what they seem . . . talk may inhibit what it exhibits—expressiveness mandating protectiveness, revealing necessitating concealing, openness petitioning discretion, weakness used to dominate, freedom as a constraint. (p. 610)

One example of an interactional contradiction is supplied by Kelvin's (1977) discussion of the tensions underlying self-disclosure or openness, which he calls the tolerance of vulnerability. To disclose information is to put oneself into a vulnerable position, yet, such disclosures are necessary for the relationship to grow and enrich. Thus, to disclose may be hurtful by making us vulnerable, but not disclosing is also potentially hurtful by limiting our abilities to benefit from social interaction. A similar reading of this tension is given in Rawlin's (1983a) study of openness/closedness or expressiveness/protectiveness in friendship.

These contradictions are inherently relational, as Rawlins (1983a) concludes, "the potential oppositions produced by the functioning of communication place the experience of contradiction at the center of relational life" (p. 255). Moreover, dialectical perspectives must be understood within a relational context rather than as individualistic creations or cognitions. As Baxter argues (1988), "although the dialectical contradictions . . . are experienced and acted upon by the individual parties, they are situated in the relationship between the parties" (p. 258).

Thus, to understand the contradictions operating in any given situation, we must attend to all operative relationships. Dialectical theorists in family therapy argue that all relationships between interactants (therapist-client as well as client-client) constitute context that influences interaction (Bopp & Weeks, 1984). Extending the argument to mediation indicates the need to understand relational tensions between mediators (in a co-mediation model), between mediators and disputants, and between disputants.

Several contradictions or dialectical tensions have been identified throughout the interpersonal and family literature: autonomy/connection, predictability/novelty, affection/instrumentality, judgment/acceptance, expressiveness/protectiveness, ideal/real, public/private, openness/closedness, continuity/discontinuity, affirmation/nonaffirmation, instrumentality/affection, power/solidarity (Askham, 1976; Baxter, 1989; Montgomery, 1992; O'Donnell, 1990; Rawlins, 1992; Stamp, 1992; Yerby, 1992). Other dimensions are possible, as well.

It is difficult, if not impossible, to generate a definitive list of dialectical contradictions. Not all situations or relationships involve the same tensions. For example, blended relationships (Bridge & Baxter, 1992) involve tensions of impartiality and favoritism but marriages traditionally do not. And, if similar tensions are occurring, relationships may differ in terms of the salience of those tensions to the relational partners, for example, judgment/acceptance dimensions are critical to some friends and almost irrelevant to others (Rawlins, 1989). No list of tensions can be considered universal and applicable to any and all relationships.

[*mediation is about facilitating change*]

Because more than one contradiction may be operating at any given time, a further difficulty is to identify the contradictions most responsible for motivating change (Bochner, 1984). A critical task in applying dialectical perspective is to understand the operant tensions and to determine their primacy.

Given the number of potential tensions, dialectical theorists identify a basic or primary contradiction and examine how secondary contradictions operate in relation to it. An analogy exists in Goffman's argument that multiple levels of meaning or frames are possible; thus necessitating the establishment of a primary framework (Putnam & Holmer, 1992).

Although primacy is a function of the situation, many theorists argue that two dialectics are likely to be primary in most relationships: autonomy/connection and predictability/novelty (Bochner & Eisenberg, 1987). The autonomy/connection dialectic, also labeled the independence/involvement dilemma (Tannen, 1986), involves the tension between establishing intimacy and interdependence in a relationship and maintaining an individual identity and autonomy of action. The predictability/novelty dialectic concerns the need to be able to predict what will happen in the relationship in order to be secure, but the need to maintain levels of novelty or ambiguity to motivate interest and growth. Baxter (1989) argues that we should consider openness/closedness, described earlier, as a third primary dialectic, especially considering the role of disclosure in building involvement or intimacy.

Even without investigation, one could posit the existence of basic contradictions in mediation. Clearly, the tensions between openness and closedness exist with the same, if not exacerbated, threat of vulnerability due to heightened awareness of information as commodity. Tensions of autonomy and connection encompass the very essence of the relationship requiring these disputants to work together in order to disengage (to some extent) from their problematized interdependence. And, the need for predictability in behavior so that interactants may trust in the capacity of the other to seek and implement resolution in consistent ways is buttressed by the equivalent need for all parties to be open to novelty or change in order to create innovative processes and outcomes. In addition, some suggest that tensions between cooperation and competition serve a dialectical function unique to conflict interaction (Kolb & Putnam, 1991). Impartiality/favoritism dilemmas noted in blended role relationships (Bridge & Baxter, 1992) are also clearly indicated in a process so recently consumed with questions concerning the nature, even the possibility, of impartiality/neutrality.

Yet, beyond suggesting that these basic contradictions will probably operate in any mediation, it is not possible to confidently elaborate on other potential contradictions and their primacy. It is important to recommend that alternative tensions be considered in terms of the relationship between the interactants. Such consideration will be more critical for informal mediation processes, as suggested earlier, because those situations involve ongoing relationships between all parties, where management of dialectical contradictions and extent of relational development may be triggering events to the mediated dispute itself.

Complicating the identification of tensions is the notion that contradictory forces shift over time. Dimensional primacy is a function of interactional progress or relational development. The very force that compels the change may become obsolete as others ascend. So, identifying primary tensions requires sensitivity to process.

The Notion of Process

Change through process is the second root concept of a dialectical perspective. The link between contradiction and process is summarized by Baxter (1988): "These basic dialectical oppositions or tensions form the exigence for communicative action between the parties and constitute the basis of change and development in the relationship" (p. 258).

There are two implications of the dialectical sense of process or motion. First, this conceptualization of process challenges the idea of discrete particles, events, or components that can be understood alone. It argues that change is basic and that all social activity must be studied as activity rather than action (Hoffman, 1985). Second, process is communicatively constituted, as Boszormenyi-Nagy's dialectical theory of family therapy suggests. The key to identifying and analyzing motion is to comprehend activity patterns as cyclic, nonlinear, feedback mechanisms where functioning is the product of complex reciprocal interactions (Boszormenyi-Nagy & Spark, 1973; Boszormenyi-Nagy & Ulrich, 1981). And, care should be taken to avoid assuming that relational change follows a unidirectional path, for example, ever-increasing openness, predictability, or connection (Altman, Vinsel, & Brown, 1981).

In order to appreciate change, one must see how that change is constituted communicatively through developmental patterns or cycles of behavior. This entails an examination of how the dialectical contradictions are discursively altered so that the tension shifts, as does the motivational force that affects the nature of the relationship.

Appreciating change and managing change are quite different. It is easier to recognize a dialectical contradiction than to work it out. In his discussion of goals in discourse, Craig (1986) suggests that communicative competence may be seen as one's ability to discursively manage dialectical contradictions, and he calls for theoretical developments addressing these concerns. To date, very few have answered this call.

Those who have tend to discuss strategies abstractly, rather than detailing the various ways they can be accomplished discursively. As Montgomery (1992) suggests, there are countless forms for any function, like "being open." We have little understanding of how form affects function. More work needs to be done identifying specific discursive patterns and tactics that instantiate these general strategies (Cupach, 1992). This is a truly rich area for mediation and conflict scholars.

One of the premier theorists in this area, Baxter (1988, 1990), has identified four generic strategies to manage contradictions: selection, separation, neutralization, and reframing. Although these strategies clearly involve communication, they exemplify more abstract discussions of strategy.

Selection occurs when a social actor realizes the coexistence of both aspects of the contradiction, but chooses to emphasize one pole as dominant to the exclusion of the other. For example, a mediator often strategically selects autonomy or closedness in interactions with disputants, intentionally hiding personal information and assessment in order to reinforce the relational perception of detachment and neutrality. Disputants, especially those who are "terminating" their relationship (or at least some externally sanctioned definition of that relationship) may select aspects of autonomy while attempting to deny retentions of connection, even in the case of parenthood. Rather than legitimating one pole over the other(separation) involves the coexistence of poles, but not their simultaneous application. Instead, topics or issues are segregated and strategically handled. There are two forms of separation: cyclic alternation and topical segmentation. In the former, one pole of the contradiction is privileged at one point in time, and the other at a different time. Caucuses provide a perfect example of this strategy in mediation. In joint session, the disputant may be completely nondisclosive about details of the dispute and relationship. However, in caucus, where privacy protects disclosures, he or she is extremely open and informative. In topical segmentation, topics or issues are divided in terms of which will be treated in one extreme manner and which will be treated in the other extreme. For example, disputants may be very open about their financial situations but very closed about their romantic involvements. In divorce mediation, topical segmentation is often built into the process by procedurally restricting property and support issues from entering into discussion of custody and visitation arrangements.

Neutralization involves strategies in which the extremes of the contradiction are realized, but the intensity of the contrast is intentionally dampened or neutralized. These strategies are more subtle than those already mentioned. Two forms are noted by Baxter (1988, 1990). The first, moderation, occurs when one uses messages that do not privilege either dimension, such as small talk or chit chat. Often, mediators begin sessions or buffer discussions with digressions into social pleasantries. These behaviors perpetuate the sense of connection and attention while avoiding confrontation of tensions that are substantively and/or relationally based.

The second form of neutralization, disqualification, occurs when the contrasting elements are handled indirectly or ambiguously. Strategic disqualification has received considerable attention from communication researchers (Bavelas, Black, Chovil, & Mullett, 1990) and sociolinguistic scholars investigating "indirect" behavior (Tannen, 1986). There are a variety of ways to be equivocal or indirect, including denying the context of the message, denying the content of the message, denying being the sender of the message, and denying sending the message to a specific receiver. Mediators and disputants may use indirect acts to avoid seeming rude or insensitive when they cannot refuse to answer or respond to another within the mediation session. In general, these strategies are more understood in terms of discursive accomplishment than any others mentioned here. Considerable opportunity exists for the investigation of strategic equivocation in mediation interaction.

The fourth strategy, reframing, is the most sophisticated. It requires a perceptual transformation in which the original poles of the contradiction are no longer seen as oppositional. Reframing differs substantively from the other three general strategies in that it is the only one that does not present the poles of the contradiction as zero-sum opposites. This is more Bateson's sense of reframing as contextualizing a relationship, learning new understandings of the social context (Putnam & Holmer, 1992). For example, mediators may accomplish reframing by helping divorcing parents understand that their separate existences are not truly autonomous, but are a different form of connection than previously experienced; that through the custody and visitation arrangements for their children they are actually sharing more interdependence and thus, more connection. Or, mediators may help disputants realize that their reluctance to share information actually divulges important information about their feelings and vulnerabilities in the dispute. Finally, disputants may help a mediator see that their desire to compete is actually a cooperative understanding between the parties; an agreement to disagree and act out positionally.

These strategies, as well as others to be detailed by further analysis and investigation, are key to process in an immediate and longitudinal sense. Their use manages immediately experienced tensions but also propels the larger interactional or relational development.

Perhaps the most important contribution of a dialectical perspective to our understanding of mediation process is its ability to help identify strategies that trigger phase development in mediation, that accomplish the critical shift from antagonism to coordination. Gulliver (1979) foresaw this possibility in his characterization of propulsion through phases:

> The whole process is given persistence and movement by the basic contradiction between the parties' conflict and their need for joint action. This contradiction generates opposing dispositions . . . that give the possibility of continuous impetus toward some final agreement and outcome. (p. 186)

Parallel processes in relational development stages have been hypothesized in Baxter's (1988) four-phase model where autonomy/connection is primary and tension-management strategies function to move from phase to phase. Her hypothetical processes bear resemblance to actual patterns discussed in Masheter and Harris's (1976) study of a divorcing couple's process involving redefinition of their relationship in terms of autonomy and connection at three points in time.

Not only can we hope to identify forms of strategies that trigger developmental progress, we can examine alternative phase structures for varying outcomes. Not all disputes will require the same progression, and attempts to boilerplate phase models may be disadvantageous (Charny, 1986).

Concluding Suggestions

The core argument in this chapter is that relational context should be studied as a key generative force in mediation and that a dialectical perspective affords a promising orientation for theoretic development in this vein. Central to this argument is the expressed need for a relationally sensitive theory to include the basic principles of a communication approach (Putnam & Roloff, 1992), but to move beyond the relational orientations evident in previous communication research in mediation.

A dialectical perspective adheres to the notions of contradiction and process. Contradictions, or relational tensions, act as pressures that motivate strategic management. This management alters the operative tensions and moves the relationship or interaction to a different state. Thus, change is a function of contradiction and vice versa. Examples of contradictions and strategies for their management have been presented in terms of an initial application to mediation. Within this discussion some suggestions for fruitful future activity have already been presented. Other suggestions, or questions, are presented now in the parting hope that others will pursue the application of a dialectical perspective in the study of mediation and conflict.

Contradictions result from the nature of the relationship. Basic exploratory research could assess the types of contradictions experienced by interactants or, from a more critical perspective, the types of contradictions uncovered by careful analysis of mediation discourse. Are there general tensions that are at play in all mediation? How do mediation contexts (distinguished by level of formality or type of dispute, etc.) differ in the types of contradictions operating and the primacy of certain contradictions? How can we tap our knowledge of the relationship between disputants (or between mediator and disputants in the case of organizational mediation or informal thirdpartyship) to diagnose relational context?

The management of contradictions produces change. Given the traditional interest in instrumentality in mediation, investigation of strategies for tension management may be of keen interest for theoretical and pragmatic reasons. There are two general lines of investigation that need serious attention. The first involves a fuller understanding of the varieties of strategies and their discursive formations, as mentioned earlier. The second concerns the efficacy of those strategies. What is the relationship between forms of strategies and their effectiveness in resolving the tension? Are there situations in which certain forms are better than others? At a broader level, how do strategies differ in terms of general effectiveness, and what exigencies mediate those relationships? And, once we understand efficacy conditions, how can we teach mediators to recognize situational factors and employ the appropriate strategy with the appropriate form?

Returning to Gulliver's (1979) call for a better understanding of forces that trigger movement between phases, examinations of specific strategies (and forms) that seem to demarcate phases are immediately pursuable. Yet, the phase ideas raise a variety of other questions about timing that prove intriguing. When is strategy use most effective and how can we determine timing cues within the unfolding of interaction? Are there different developmental cycles detectable for certain disputes or relationship types? Can we develop contingency phase theories of mediation and assess their relationship to mediation outcome in the nonrelational sense?

These questions demonstrate the length and complexity of our intellectual journey, should we seriously embrace a dialectical approach to mediation. Even so, they also, hopefully, hint at its rewards.

What does an understanding of the narrative structure of discourse reveal about disputant and third-party interaction? How does a narrative perspective help to define a third-party role that avoids a false distinction between content and process?

3

A Narrative Perspective on Mediation

Toward the Materialization of the "Storytelling" Metaphor

Sara Cobb

IT IS WIDELY ACCEPTED that mediation is a storytelling process—training manuals, research articles, and trade books discuss the story that disputants tell in relation to its legal, psychological, and interpersonal benefits. In fact, it is widely held that the telling of one's story in mediation serves simultaneously the ethical mandate, "participation" (Harrington, 1985), as well as the pragmatic mandate to move "from story to settlement" (A. Davis, 1986).

But what does it mean "to tell a story"? What are the discursive conditions that enable and/or constrain that process? What are the ethics and the pragmatics of storytelling? What role does storytelling play in agreement construction or mediation efficacy?

To date there is little research in mediation that can address these questions.[1] This is because within the field of mediation "storytelling" is still a *metaphor* that does little more than suggest that disputants tell stories, much less provide a coherent theoretical frame for understanding and evaluating the storytelling process *within mediation practice.*

Although there are preliminary studies of narrative process in mediation, this research has yet to coalesce into a developed, narrative framework. For example, Shailor (in press) has examined the hierarchical organization of stories in mediation, using the Coordinated Management of Meaning theory.[2] Through case studies he notes that stories of relationships can contextualize stories of lifescripts or episodes (or vice versa). In earlier work, Shailor and Pearce (1986) have examined the reflexive relationship between context and process in mediation; using a rule-based approach, they examined the relationship between the stories disputants told, the interaction system, and the mediation process; Littlejohn and Shailor (1986) described the "deep structure" of mediation as a function of rules of meaning and action. Although these studies examined the disputants' "stories," they did not draw from narrative theory for their analysis.

Rifkin, Millen, and Cobb (1991) used a "storytelling" perspective to highlight paradoxical features of mediation process. Cobb and Rifkin (1991b) have examined the construction and transformation of discourse "positions" in mediation and found that the first narrative that is told colonizes subsequent narratives. Although both of these studies detail findings pertaining to mediation process from a narrative perspective, neither has "unpacked" the assumptions about narrative that are operant. What is needed is a theoretical base for describing narratives from which intervention technologies and research methodologies can be developed.

This chapter is an attempt to move us beyond metaphor, to materialize "storytelling" as a set of micro-level discourse practices central to the pragmatic and ethical goals of mediation. To this end, I (1) review approaches to narrative theory and identify three features of narrative that are pertinent to the analysis of mediation—coherence, closure, and interdependence, and (2) discuss these features in relation to the content/process distinction that is core to the concept of intervention in mediation. Ultimately, I suggest that the "materialization" of the storytelling metaphor, although it challenges core assumptions in mediation theory, affords both practitioners and researchers new ways to understand and intervene in conflict.

A Theoretical Base for "Storytelling"

In the past 10 years and across multiple disciplines, narrative theory has been adopted as a frame for the analysis of social action.[3] At the philosophical level, as Fisher (1987) has pointed out, narrative is not only a theory for analysis but a fundamental condition for communication and social being. Although there is considerable argument about the scope of the narrative approach,[4] there is considerable agreement that experience is organized via narrative.

In addition to the philosophical literature on narrative, there is considerable research in communication using narrative as a unit of analysis. This literature on narrative can be (albeit roughly) divided into two camps: the structuralist approaches and the poststructuralist approaches.

The structuralist approaches have largely been used to examine and address narrative structures and features *as variables* of communication processes.[5] Chatman's (1978), Genette's (1980), Prop's (1968), and Frye's (1963) examinations of plot types, temporal order, and character roles within the *fictive* narrative have been used in communication studies to address narrative competence and narrative coherence. For example, "story grammars," as topologies, have been used as variables in the analysis of narrative comprehension (Mandler, 1982; Omanson, 1982; Ohtsuka & Brewer, 1988) and cultural competence (Brady, 1981; Cronin, 1980; Nicholas, 1982; Polanyi, 1985). Story structures have also been used to make claims about *intra*-narrative coherence, as exemplified by Agar and Hobbs's (1982) account of global, local, and themal coherence, as well as Ohtsuka and Brewer's (1992) discussion of temporal ordering in narrative. Structuralist approaches to narrative often operate as ethnographies, using sociolinguistic methods to account for the relation between culture and narrative (Carter, 1988; Hofer, 1991; Katriel & Shenhar, 1990; Maynard, 1988; Sherzer, 1980).

Explicitly or implicitly, these structuralist approaches share Chatman's (1978) distinction between story (the actual set of events) and the discourse (the telling of those events).[6] The interest in these approaches is in *representation* of real events as a whole, as a unit, as a structure. This emphasis is equivalent to Saussure's focus on *"langue"* and demonstrative of the exclusion of *"parole";* narrative, in this respect, has been studied as a structure autonomous from

the social, political, and fundamentally *interactive* contexts in which
it is unfolded. It is this attentive focus on the unfolding of narrative
in interaction that characterizes the poststructural approaches to
narrative.

Poststructural approaches to narrative have been used to examine
storytelling as a practice (Bennett & Feldman, 1981; Goodwin, 1990;
Labov & Fanshel, 1977; Sarbin, 1986; Sluzki, 1992). By dissolving
the distinction between *story* and *discourse,* the study of narrative
ceases to function as an analysis of *representation* and begins to operate
as a description of the evolving and reflexive relationship between
story *content* and story *telling* (Feldman, 1991; Gergen, 1986; Mishler,
1986; White & Epston, 1990).[7]

For example, O'Barr and Conley (1985), in their studies of small
claims court narratives, noted that persons construct stories that
inevitably contain negative outcomes that persons then use to build
a "theory of responsibility"; these "theories" function (inductively
or deductively) to construct blame and responsibility (p. 689). O'Barr
and Conley show that narrative "adequacy" is a function of the
structural relations within the story between agents, actions, and
recipients of those actions; these structural relations are, in turn, a
function of the situational rules for storybuilding as well as the
interpretative (cultural) frames of litigants (Conley & O'Barr, 1990a).
It is the reflexive relation between structure and the situational/
cultural rules for enactment that constitutes a poststructural narrative theory.

And it is these more poststructural approaches to narrative that
I suggest would be useful for "filling in" the storytelling metaphor
in mediation for two reasons: first, the ideology of mediation is
"antithetical to the structural approaches to narrative—the distinction between *story* and *discourse,* between events and their representation, if adopted, would lead mediators to look for the "real"
story, the one that purports to have the best fit between the telling
and the events themselves. However, the focus in mediation is *not*
on accurate representations of real events, for indeed, mediation
presumes that there is no *one* true story; rather, the focus in mediation
is on the differences/similarities in the representational forms
themselves, a focus that essentially evaporates the representational
function of storytelling. Second, poststructural approaches to narrative in mediation enable the examination of the *practice* of storytelling as it functions reflexively to construct the context in which

stories are told. This blurs the distinction between the story and its telling, between the content and the process in mediation. A post-structural narrative perspective not only begins to focus attention on the role of discourse in mediation (and after all, it is a "talking" practice), but it permanently *includes* the mediator as a co-partici-pant in both the construction and the transformation of conflict narratives. Once included, rather than neutral and detached, the mediator becomes responsible for the process, which requires, in turn, the management of content: The pragmatics of mediation are thus interconnected to the politics of the process.

In keeping with a poststructural perspective, to understand nar-rative construction *requires* a focus on narrative transformation—the nature of the stories that unfold is dependent on the process of the telling; to explain the pragmatics of narrative process, in turn, *requires* attention to narrative politics; as they unfold, some stories become dominant, others can be marginalized. This chapter discus-ses three features of narrative that can contribute to our under-standing of the pragmatics and the politics of mediation: narrative coherence, narrative closure, and narrative interdependence. Col-lectively, these features facilitate the description of *how* conflict stories are constructed and transformed as well as forecast the collapse of the content/process distinction in mediation.

Coherence and the Structure
of Conflict Narratives in Mediation

Conflict stories, like "theories of responsibility," construct the logical, causal linkages between actors, their actions, and outcomes defined as problematic; the coherence of a conflict narrative is a function of the degree of fit between these portions of the story. *Coherence* refers to unity exhibited in (and constructed by) the part/whole relationships of narrative components *within* a given narrative (Agar & Hobbs, 1982) and *between* narratives (White & Epston, 1990). By *narrative components* I refer to plots (sequences of events ordered via a causal logic), character roles, and themes (values). *Within* the narrative, each of these parts functions to construct the meaning of the other parts: for example, the sequenced intentional actions or unintentional events that lead to property damage (plot) reflexively function to constitute the role of the characters as villains and victims (character roles), as well as the value system (themes) that is used to interpret the action (MacIntyre, 1981). But the coherence of any one narrative is dependent upon its relation to other narratives.

Inter-narrative coherence is a function of the resonance of part/ whole relationships across multiple narratives; these part/whole relationships exist (1) *within* a speaker's narrative system and (2) *between* speakers' narrative systems. Each speaker's narrative system is a "web" of narratives that is both reflected in and constructed by any given narrative (Packman, 1992, personal communication); these webs are particularly pertinent to the analysis of any mediation narrative. For example, persons come to mediation with a story about a particular set of events, character roles, and themes; these stories themselves are fit into a web of stories from the individuals' personal histories, from the stories told in their families and significant social networks, and from the cultural stories that function as archetypes (Pearce & Cronen, 1980) or "filters," shaping our presentation of everyday stories (Dollerup, 1984).

From this perspective, any story that is told is "nested" in a hierarchical structure of meaning that provides context for shaping the construction of a story.[8] The conflict story (or the "theory of responsibility") that is advanced in mediation constructs and consolidates the part/whole relations within the story line under construction *in relation to* the lived narratives that comprise and enact relationships (Shotter, 1984). For example, a father may tell a story about his daughter's disobedience that resonates to other stories in the family about sexuality, motherhood, and patriotism; altering the story about the daughter's "disobedience" impacts the meaning of other stories within the narrative web. The meaning of a conflict narrative is thus connected to and constitutive of a meaning *system*. Even though only portions of the system are constructed in the mediation session, the narrative web is both reflected in and constructed by the "told" story.[9] The construction of a portion of the narrative web functions to materialize and consolidate the meaning of the entire web, whether it is "visible" or not (Cobb, 1992b).[10]

Inter-narrative coherence is also a function of the interaction *between* speakers' narrative systems. Between speakers, in the interaction, narratives are interactively developed, modified, and contested as disputants elaborate portions of their own and each other's conflict stories. The coherence between narratives is constructed conjointly as disputants create junctures where their stories can be compared/contrasted: The character roles in a disputant's story are contested and reformulated in the other's story, or the values celebrated in one story become values denigrated in another. From this perspective, conflicts are the *product* of inter-narrative coherence, as Haynes and Haynes (1989) have indirectly noted in their description of divorce mediation: Couples come into mediation with the parameters of the conflict coalesced and solidified. Haynes and Haynes describe their work as "opening" couples' stories to new interpretations.

Narrative coherence both within and across narratives is never total. Even though it is always present to some degree (given that narratives are never told outside the interpretative frameworks that construct the part/whole relations), the consolidation of the narrative's meaning is never complete. The degree of coherence is, in turn, a function of a second feature of narrative that materializes the "storytelling" metaphor: *narrative closure.*

Closure and Conflict Narratives in Mediation

Conflict stories are notoriously rigid, readily reenacted, and recalcitrant to change, not because persons are unwilling to resolve conflicts but, rather, because the conflict stories themselves are self-perpetuating—they exhibit "closure." Narrative closure refers to the autopoetic process through which narratives seal off alternative interpretations to themselves (Varela, 1979). Although interpretative theories often lead toward a rampant relativism, the determinacy of narrative meaning is quite obvious in everyday life; in *theory,* narratives are open to infinite interpretations, but in *practice,* their interpretations are limited, if not almost entirely closed. This is because interpretation is a "living tradition" (MacIntyre, 1981) embedded in specific role relationships and local practices. Although these traditions delimit possible meanings, so does the narrative itself in order to meet the discursive requirements of the local interpretations, relationships, and practices.

Although closure is never complete, narratives generate closure by *stabilizing* sites in the narrative that threaten to alter the part/whole relations that comprise narrative coherence. These sites are locations in the narrative from where the plot-character-theme relationships could be destabilized(ing) (Sluzki, 1992) through the alteration of plots, character roles, and themes: changes in plots destabilize narrative causality,[11] changes in character roles destabilize the victim/victimizer positions assigned, and changes in themes can potentially reorganize the moral frameworks used to evaluate action. For example, if Person A comes to mediation to request that Person B pay for the repair of a car, Person A will have to show how Person B is responsible for the damages. Clearly, the adequacy of the "theory of responsibility" will be a function of the role relationship of A and B: if A is a parent that has authorized B to use the car, it will be problematic to suggest that B should pay the damages, given cultural understandings about parent/child relationships. However, if B is a coworker that asked to borrow the car, the request for damages becomes more plausible. Narrative adequacy is also a function of the plot sequences constructed—if Person B caused the damage through carelessness and then lied to protect herself, Person A's request becomes extremely legitimate. But if Person B damaged the car when a streetlight malfunctioned, the request for damages can be undermined. We can predict where the sites for contestation will appear: causality, role relations, and values.

The discursive "work" to close off alternative interpretations requires the contextualization of sites in the narrative that are more unstable, where the meaning can be multiplied (Derrida, 1978). This is done by "enframing": disputants contextualize unstable sites by elaborating a subplot that accounts for or explains the event, the character roles, or the theme that is at issue. Disputants often stabilize narratives in this way *before* other disputants contest these sites and, in fact, I would predict that much of this stabilization takes place before the mediation session itself, as persons rehearse telling the story in their own network.

As is the case with narrative coherence, there are variations across narratives with respect to closure; some narratives are more stable than others. There are two factors that differentiate narratives with respect to stability (closure): narrative completeness and cultural resonance. The more "complete" the narrative, the less vulnerable it is to alternative interpretation and transformation; the more complete the narrative, the "deeper" the hierarchical structure.[12]

Narrative structure can be modeled on both horizontal and vertical dimensions. The horizontal structure unfolds the sequence of events in a main plot; the vertical structure refers to the contextualizing narratives that enframe portions of the main plot line, stabilizing meaning at key sites in the narrative. Vertical structure is variably constructed in interaction; portions of the horizontal structure may be told *after* telling narratives that contextualize the characters' roles or vice versa—the sequence of telling cannot be predicted on the basis of structure.[13] In addition, the vertical complexity of the structure cannot be predicted—portions of a narrative can be enframed by any person in the session, during any turn. Because narratives are variably constructed, there are differences across disputants' narratives with respect to narrative closure—some narratives will exhibit more stability than others. For example, children's stories are likely to be less stable than adults' stories (Cobb & Rifkin, 1991a). From this perspective, variations in closure can be seen as a function of narrative completeness or complexity.

Variation in narrative closure can also be a function of the cultural resonance—some stories are more resonant to dominant cultural myths than others. For example, stories that exhibit a rule-based logic are more effective in legal settings than stories exhibiting a relational logic (Conley & O'Barr, 1990a). Because women are more likely to tell "relational" stories, their stories are more likely to be transformed by others, perhaps contributing to the construction of mediation agreements where their "interests" are not present (Germane, Johnson, & Lemon, 1985). Narratives that resemble dominant cultural stories have more stability because the broader culture has already done the "work" to seal off discursive sites where these meanings can be contested. As I have noted, however, closure is never complete and contestation is inevitable in mediation, as disputants refute, deny, and elaborate the discursive context in which they are located by self and other. It is in this process of contestation and re-formulation that the *interdependence* of conflict narratives is visible, a third feature of narrative that contributes to the materialization of the storytelling metaphor.

The Interdependence of Conflict Narratives in Mediation

Conflict narratives function, as I have mentioned, as "theories of responsibility." As such, they connect a negative outcome to an agent's actions, provide a rationale for those actions, and discuss the effect of those actions on others (self). With great regularity, disputants construct the "other(s)" as responsible for the negative outcome, which has two discursive consequences: (1) the construction of the self as victim, and (2) the construction of the other as victimizer.[14]

Within and between conflict narratives, victim/villain roles are interdependent: Within one narrative, the validity of the victim's position rests on the construction of the villain's; between narratives, victim/villain roles are constitutive of *patterns* in account sequences—accusations lead to justifications and usually, renewed accusations.

In mediation, disputants construct "other" via negative discourse positions, while they construct self via positive discourse positions. A negative discourse position is a delegitimate social location (Fairclough, 1989), constructed via the attribution of bad intent or the assignment of negative character traits/labels (Cobb & Rifkin, 1991b).[15] In mediation they are synonymous with the victimizer roles. Positive discourse positions are social locations in discourse that are constructed via the attribution of good intent and positive character traits/labels; they are synonymous with victim roles. For example, Betty tells a story about her eviction that was caused by Susan's "meddling" that, in turn, was caused by Susan's jealousy. Relatedly, Betty describes herself as a woman who "minds her own business" and is able to "let go of the past" (as opposed to a jealous person who "hangs onto the past"). The victimizer role is *dependent* on the victim role—the very morality that is used to delegitimize other is often reversed in the legitimization of self.

Between conflict narratives, interdependence is visible in the account sequences that structure interaction. Accusations (in which victimizer positions are constructed) are followed by justifications, denials, and excuses (Cobb, 1992b; Garcia, 1991). Although Garcia has noted that not all accusations are paired with justifications, denials, or excuses (for disputants do not necessarily attend to each and every accusation—they presumably attend to those that are the most problematic for their own narrative), her findings prove that the accusation/justification/denial/excuse pattern continues despite the regulation of turns: persons defend themselves and blame others.

The interdependence of positions in conflict narratives entrenches blaming in mediation and instantiates adversarial relations; as each party legitimizes self, they delegitimize the other. As each is delegitimized, they inevitably work to alter the narrative in which they are negatively positioned; but narrative analysis shows that justifications, denials, and excuses function to reproduce (more often than evolve) the narrative in which disputants are delegitimized (Cobb & Rifkin, 1991b; Rifkin et al., 1991). This accounts for the cycles of escalations in which conflicts are enacted. Here narrative theory provides a rationale for third-party intervention in conflicts: Disputants *inside* of narrative structures reproduce conflict stories as they try to transform them. The resolution of conflict requires the intervention of a third party precisely because the third party can alter persons' discursive positions and, in the process, generate a new pattern of interaction, a new interdependence.

Taken collectively, these three narrative features—coherence, closure, and interdependence—suggest that the stages of the mediation process alone cannot regulate either the construction or the transformation of the conflict narratives: (1) conflict stories are constructed with varying degrees of coherence; (2) they exhibit varying degrees of closure; and (3) the redundancy in interactional sequences, the evidence of narrative interdependence, suggests that the telling of conflict stories, contrary to mediation ideology, may, in fact, reproduce rather than resolve the conflict.

"To be able to tell your story" is no insurance against marginalization or domination. Pallai (1991) has noted that domination and marginalization are a function of the degree to which persons can be self-defining in discourse and, I would add, the degree to which those self-definitions are elaborated by others (Cobb, 1992a). If we tell stories about self and they are not elaborated by others, we are effectively silenced, even though we "tell our story" (Belenky, Clinchy, Goldberger, & Tarule, 1986). To take a narrative perspective on mediation requires that we examine the implications of narrative coherence, closure, and interdependence as features of conflict narratives for a new understanding of the relationship between narrative process and narrative politics.

Mediation as Narrative Intervention

Current mediation theory equates mediation intervention with the regulation of the mediation process (Marlow & Sauber, 1990; Polenski & Launer, 1986; Rogers & McEwen, 1989). This regulation includes, generally, providing a context for "telling your story," venting and listening, regulating speaking turns, scheduling public and private sessions, exploring alternatives, creating options, and building an agreement. The regulation of the mediation process is presumed to function independently of the regulation of the content, but the narrative perspective challenges this distinction.

Narrative Coherence and the Process/Content Distinction

If, as I have suggested, there is variance in narrative coherence across stories, it follows that some disputants' stories are more coherent (more complete and more culturally resonant) than others. This variance occurs despite the regulation of the mediation process (Cobb & Rifkin, 1991b).[16] The political consequences of this variance are twofold: (1) less coherent stories may be dominated or marginalized by the more coherent narrative; and (2) less coherent stories may not provide a satisfactory base for the construction of agreements.

Theoretically, less coherent narratives, those whose part/whole relations are problematic, incomplete or not culturally resonant, are less likely to be elaborated by others (Cobb & Rifkin, 1991b) and therefore more likely to be marginalized, subsumed within a more coherent narrative (Lubiano, 1992). Consensus is not forged from equal parts of multiple stories—consensus evolves via the subduction (inclusion) of narratives that threaten the coherence of the dominant story (Gramsci, 1971).

Variation in narrative coherence also has implications for how we understand the construction of mediation agreements. If there is disparity between narratives in terms of coherence and if the less coherent narrative is not adopted or elaborated by others (being instead colonized by the dominant, more coherent narrative), then the agreement will not be reflective of both disputants' stories. Even if the less coherent narrative is not colonized, it does not, by definition, contain the same amount of information that a more coherent narrative contains: Plot structures may be incomplete, themes may only be implicit, character roles may lack rationales, cultural myths may contradict the meaning of the story. The result is that less coherent narratives may contribute less to the structure and content of the mediation agreement.

Disparity in the coherence of narratives in mediation can lead to the marginalization of disputants and the construction of unfair agreements. The only remedy is the regulation of story *construction;* this would involve the formulation of a set of questions that can be asked of both disputants to facilitate the development of complete narratives as well as culturally resonant narratives. The narrative perspective in mediation implies that mediators need to regulate the construction of stories with respect to narrative coherence; this mandate defies the traditional distinction between the process of mediation and the content of the dispute: To regulate the process, mediators must manage the construction of content.

Narrative Closure and the Process/Content Distinction

The concept of narrative closure also poses a threat to the process/content distinction core to mediation: If we accept the notion that narratives seal off alternative interpretations via the contextualization of sites where meaning is unstable, mediation becomes a process requiring the destabilization of narratives via the disruption of the vertical and horizontal organization of narrative structure.

If we assume that conflicts endure due to the stability of the conflict narrative (and that conflictual interactional patterns are inevitably the result of this stability), the mediation of conflict mandates the "opening" of narratives to alternative interpretations. This not only necessitates the examination of the vertical narrative structure for sites where meaning is potentially unstable, but it requires mediators to contest the meaning at these sites, essentially undoing some of the "work" done by the disputants to seal off alternative interpretations to their stories. *Destabilization* can be accomplished via the use of circular questions (Fleuridas, Nelson, & Rosenthal, 1986; Tomm, 1987),[17] reframing (Putnam & Holmer, 1992; Watzlawick, Weakland, & Fisch, 1974), positive connotation (Selvini-Palazzoli, Boscolo, Ceechin, & Prata, 1980; Solomon & Rosenthal, 1984), and externalization (White & Epston, 1990). This process of destabilizing narratives effectively dissolves the distinction between mediation process and narrative content. Again, the regulation of the process involves the regulation (control) of the content.

Narrative Interdependence and the Process/Content Distinction

Narrative interdependence also challenges the taboo in mediation requiring the process/content distinction: Positive and negative discourse positions are mutually constitutive, within each narrative and across two or more narratives. Within each narrative, one person's positive position is contingent on the other's negative position; across narratives, accusations lead to justifications that lead to more accusations. This pattern entrenches the conflict and rigidifies the moral frames used to understand and evaluate characters' roles. As the moral order solidifies, delegitimized disputants remain imprisoned in the other's narrative, unable to participate in the construction of their own legitimacy.

Changes in interactional patterns require alterations in the discourse positions constructed by disputants for self and other, a shift from negative to positive positions for "other" within each speaker's narrative. This *transformation* can be accomplished via positive connotation and lead toward the development of what Sluzki (1993) has referred to as a "better-formed" story.

All three of the features of a poststructural perspective on narrative—that is, narrative coherence, narrative closure, and narrative interdependence—function collectively to challenge current assumptions about the nature of mediation as a process for conflict intervention. Once adopted, however, the narrative perspective does more than simply challenge mediation theory—it also enables us to describe conflict intervention as narrative construction, narrative destabilization, and narrative transformation. In this way, a narrative perspective offers a theoretical framework that not only challenges existing assumptions about mediation practice, but also provides a basis for reconceptualizing conflict intervention.

Conclusion

"Storytelling" is more than a metaphor—the practice of storytelling, as well as the content of specific stories, has import for the development of new technologies for intervention as well as new analytic frames for understanding those interventions. This, in turn, shakes the foundation of the ethical mandates related to neutrality and empowerment: if the regulation of the mediation process requires the regulation of narrative content, how can mediators remain "detached," "unbiased," or "equidistant"? If mediators must control the transformation of stories, who is responsible for the construction of the agreement?

The materialization of the storytelling metaphor opens a Pandora's box of questions about the politics and the pragmatics of mediation practice. However, it also makes material the stories that are told in mediation—they have structural and processual features that affect the resolution of conflict and the social construction of disputants' (as well as mediators') worlds.

Notes

1. There is a growing body of research on negotiation that describes narrative process. For example, Linda Putnam (1992) has used "storytelling" as a metaphor to describe the role of story construction in the negotiation process; she argues that negotiation efficacy is dependent on the co-construction of stories.

2. Developed by Pearce and Cronen (1980), this theory is a heuristic device for understanding and explaining both regularity and transformation in an individual's meaning system, as well as the interaction system as a whole. Shailor used the "hierarchy of meaning" to model the hierarchical structure of stories in mediation.

3. See Polkinghorne (1988) for a description of the use of narrative across multiple disciplines, particularly chapters 3-5.

4. See Rowland's (1988) critique of Fisher as well as Fisher's (1988) reply to Rowland.

5. Many of these studies are rooted in linguistics and sociolinguistics. The research on narrative structures examines coherence and cohesion between narrative components while the research on narrative features includes, for example, analysis of asides, hesitations, and ellipses. See Stubbs's (1983) account of narrative analysis, specifically chapter 2: "On Speaking Terms: Inspecting Conversational Data," pp. 15-39.

6. This distinction was previously known as the "fabula/syuzhet" distinction in the structural analysis of fiction. See Ohtsuka and Brewer's (1992) discussion of this distinction. More generally, see Culler's (1975) *Structuralist Poetics: Structuralism, Linguistics and the Study of Literature.*

7. For this reason, narrative analysis has often been equated with poststructural approaches to discourse—*parole* enables the examination of the social construction of meaning (the "how" of meaning); this project, in turn, necessitates the inclusion of the observer/time/culture/interaction toward the description of social processes; see Derrida (1980). See Mishler (1986) for a discussion of the epistemological implications of the narrative perspective, specifically the section "The Impact on Our Views of Scientific Knowledge," p. 132.

8. This is an appropriation of Pearce and Cronen's (1980) hierarchy of meaning to describe the reflexive relation between narratives. Shailor (in press) has made this point, mapping the structure of the stories disputants use to contextualize the story under construction.

9. Pearce and Cronen's (1980) notions of implicative and contextual force are useful for understanding the relationship between a narrative system and a story under construction.

10. This was a finding from a narrative analysis of a mediation session in which a conflictual interactional pattern was reinstantiated when one disputant made a

reference to a *portion* of their justification narrative. Even though the agreement had been signed, the fight was renewed as this narrative was referenced. The accusation/justification pattern continued.

11. In mediation, much of the work to stabilize narrative interpretation takes place with respect to the intentions attributed to disputants: Each side describes the other as "intending to harm," and consequently, disputants contest various portions of the other's narrative as they "work" to open the narrative to alternative interpretations (Cobb, 1992b).

12. This notion of "vertical narrative structure" is an adaptation of Pearce and Cronen's (1980) hierarchy of meaning; they presumed that meaning is always a function of the contexts that are themselves contextualized by other levels of meaning. See Shailor's (in press) use of this hierarchy to distinguish the contextual functions that stories in mediation perform; some stories about relationships enframe stories about episodes, or vice versa. This hierarchy is reflexive in nature and therefore both stable and evolving. See Cronen, Pearce, and Tomm's (1986) "Radical Change in the Social Construction of the Person."

13. Once again I refer to Garcia's (1991) research as well as mine (Cobb, 1992b), because both studies indicate patterning in account sequencing *despite the regulation of turns.*

14. In practice, disputants do not attribute the negative outcome to their own intentions or to fate, chance, or luck. Instead, they systematically attribute bad intentions to the "other." For this reason, the attribution of negative intent in narrative seems to be a discursive requirement for the construction of a conflict narrative (Cobb, 1992b).

15. This formulation is a discourse-based equivalent to Watzlawick, Beavin, and Jackson's (1967) observation that identified patients are described by others as either crazy or bad.

16. For example, even though there is an "information-gathering" stage, the questions that mediators ask are not systematized—and there are no guidelines for asking questions. See Cobb (1992a) for a format for systematizing questions.

17. See Gadlin and Oulette (1987) for a discussion of the application of circular questions to mediation. See also Sluzki's (1992) description of the microphysics of narrative transformation.

Part Two

Shaping Reality
Through Discourse

How do disputants' and third parties' views of morality, conflict, and justice influence developments during intervention? How can third parties and disputants deal with deep differences?

4

The Deep Structure of Reality in Mediation

Stephen W. Littlejohn
Jonathan Shailor
W. Barnett Pearce

CONFLICT MANAGEMENT involves handling differences in the goals, interests, and opinions of various individuals or groups. The key concerns of conflict managers are how to resolve such differences, how to facilitate a win-win solution, or how to create an atmosphere in which such differences can be tolerated without disrupting the lives and work of those involved. The statements made in any conflict reflect an underlying social reality, and the differing goals, interests, and opinions expressed may or may not be based on a shared reality. When they are not, managing the conflict can become very difficult. As Lovins (1977) puts it, "Our society has mechanisms only for resolving conflicting interests, not conflicting views of reality" (p. 12).

In our research we have been especially interested in situations in which conflict arises from differing social realities (e.g., Freeman, Littlejohn, & Pearce, 1992; Littlejohn, Higgins, & Williams, 1987;

Littlejohn & Stone, 1991; Pearce, Littlejohn, & Alexander, 1989). We employ the term *social reality* as a general label for the meanings used by a communicator to interpret and act in a social situation. Social realities are ways of understanding one's experience worked out through interaction (Berger & Luckmann, 1966; Gergen, 1985; Littlejohn, 1992).

When the issues in a dispute are on the surface and reflect very little difference in underlying social reality, they are more easily resolved than when the issues lie at a deeper level. When differences involve incommensurate conceptions of morality, conflict, and justice, they may be very difficult indeed (Kressel & Pruitt, 1989a, p. 404). This kind of conflict is like one person trying to play chess and another person checkers on the same board.

Mediators themselves operate in a social reality that may or may not match that of the disputants. Mediation, then, involves a triad of realities among the disputants and the mediator, and the success or failure of the intervention may depend upon the extent to which the three realities match or coordinate and the degree to which the mediators and disputants take their potentially deep differences into account. Mediators bear a special responsibility here to acknowledge that they too operate from a constructed social reality, to understand what that reality consists of, to interpret the reality of the client, and to work toward some sort of coordination between these positions. As we shall see later in this chapter, this responsibility is not always assumed.

The Research

The research reported in this chapter is part of a series of interpretive case studies on mediation conducted at the University of Massachusetts (Littlejohn, Pearce, Hines, & Bean, 1986; Littlejohn & Shailor, 1986; Shailor, 1992; Shailor & Pearce, 1986). Interpretive research addresses different kinds of questions than most of the studies that have been done on mediation. Instead of centering on the generalizable effects of mediation and the common techniques of mediators, we focused on particular patterns of communication in specific episodes of mediation, including the ways participants themselves experienced those episodes. This kind of research requires examination of the actual discourse produced in particular cases of mediation and careful consideration of the circumstances of each case. When the discourse of mediators and disputants in actual cases are examined carefully, the various strengths and weaknesses of their practices can be revealed, and our research was therefore critical in orientation.

The investigation involved case studies conducted in conjunction with the Massachusetts Mediation Project in Amherst. It involved an examination of the methods and training used in the center, participation in simulated mediation sessions, live observations and examination of videotapes of a number of mediation cases, careful analysis of certain segments of discourse produced in these and other cases, interviews with mediators immediately following the observed sessions, and debriefings with the mediators and members of the mediation staff several days after each case.

We explored dimensions of social reality operating in mediated disputes, differences between social realities, and the possible difficulties of citizen dispute mediation in dealing with this state of affairs. We focused also on problems of coherence and coordination in mediation (Cronen, Pearce, & Harris, 1982; Pearce, 1989; Pearce & Cronen, 1980). Coherence is sense-making, the achievement of clarity in communication, and coordination involves meshing or organizing actions in such a way that the patterns of interaction seem logical to the various participants involved. We were interested in how disputants responded to one another and how those responses changed in the course of a mediation session. We were also interested in the ways in which mediator behavior brought about change in client responses.

The cases used in this phase of our research were eight in number and included: (1) a family dispute, in which a mother, her son, and the boy's stepfather tried to work out certain issues between them; (2) a consumer case, in which a customer and a tailor were contesting monetary compensation for what the customer perceived to be a poor alteration job on a jacket; (3) a case in which five roommates were objecting to certain behaviors of another member of their household; (4) a dispute between two roommate renters and an individual to whom they sublet the apartment during the summer; (5) a case involving an assault between two women in a love triangle; (6) the dispute of a couple in a deteriorating relationship; (7) a property division settlement between the partners in a relationship; and (8) a divorce case, in which a couple attempted to work out home ownership and child custody issues. The divorce mediation is discussed in more detail later in the chapter as an extended case study.

The Interpretive Model

Without presuming to be comprehensive, we came to define relevant social realities in terms of three parts—the moral reality, the conflict reality, and the justice reality. The moral reality includes one's assumptions about what constitutes a proper human life. Conflict reality includes a person's meanings for conflict itself. Justice reality is one's assumptions about the criteria by which conflicts should be settled. Similarities and differences in the realities of mediators and disputants can be analyzed in terms of this model.

The Moral Reality

Moral realities consist of assumptions about proper conduct. They are deep philosophical principles that define what it means to be a person and to live a life (MacIntyre, 1981; Shotter, 1984) and include one's most basic moral assumptions.

Drawing on the work of Bellah and his colleagues (1985), we identified four somewhat overlapping moral stances prevalent in American society—the biblical or authoritarian, which is based on scriptural direction or divine authority; the republican, which involves the idea of civic duty and public service; the utilitarian, which seeks the fulfillment of individual interests by negotiating agreements with others; and the expressivist, which calls for the pursuit of individual rights and free expression.

These realities are not necessarily incommensurate, though elements of them may be. The traditional and republican realities share a common vision of the importance of community. Utilitarian and expressivist realities place the self above the community. Republican and utilitarian realities both involve working together with others, although their notions of what that work should include differ substantially. Although Bellah and his colleagues think that individuals usually assume a predominant style based on one of these worldviews, members of a pluralistic society may adopt elements from a variety of worldviews and may from time to time move from one to another.

Conflict Reality

The second part of our model is conflict reality. This consists of participants' meanings for conflict itself. It is composed of two elements: a definition of conflict and an idea of how conflict should be handled. Numerous conflict realities are possible. The work of Zartman (1978) and Kilmann and Thomas (1975) was useful for identifying elements of the conflict reality. We used nine categories in our analyses. For purposes of discussion, these models can be grouped into three types.

Reliance on Outside Parties. Two models fit the category of reliance on outside parties. The *adjudicative model* sees conflict as different claims about a state of affairs to be resolved by an official on the basis of the weight of argument. Court trials and arbitration are examples. The *authority model* defines conflict as a difference of opinion or action to be settled by an authority in accordance with cultural or religious precepts. Such conflicts are often seen in primitive and traditional societies and in conservative religions in which a shaman, priest, or elder makes a decision based on special knowledge of laws and rules.

Conflict Management. Conflict management includes five models. The *conflict maintenance model* sees conflict as healthy, functional, or unavoidable and as something to be promoted, maintained, managed, or endured. The *economic bargaining model* is an exchange approach in which conflict is treated as opposing objectives to be resolved through negotiation and compromise. Collective bargaining is an example, and most mediation is designed to follow this ideal. The *power model* sees conflict as a struggle for resources in which the strongest side will prevail, as in fighting and war. The *coalition model* is a difference of opinion or interest that is settled by weight of alignment, as in an election. The *consensus model* is a difference of opinion on alternative solutions, which is settled by discussion and creative problem solving.

Avoidance and Prevention. The two *avoidance and prevention* models are libertarian and conflict avoidance. The *libertarian model* sees conflict as a difference arising from freedom of individual thought or action, to be settled by creating a condition under which interaction and intervention are minimized, thereby avoiding clashes. The *conflict avoidance model* defines conflict as personally disruptive and harmful or painful and to be avoided. The primary difference between these models is that the former is motivated by a desire to maximize personal freedom, while the latter is a result of fear or discomfort with conflict itself.

These nine images of conflict are not incommensurate and are often used in conjunction with one another. For example, power and bargaining often go hand in hand. Furthermore, different models may come into play at different stages of a conflict. For example, what begins as power conflict may become a bargaining situation, then be settled finally through adjudication. Yet each of the nine types emphasizes a unique quality or makes a particular aspect of conflict more salient than others, and not all are compatible. Conflict maintenance is hardly consistent with conflict avoidance, for example.

Although an exact fit between the moral and conflict realities has not been found, we think that certain correspondences are more likely than others. For example, people holding a traditional reality are more likely to adopt an authoritarian or libertarian conflict model. Republicans probably are more comfortable with adjudicative, consensus, and coalition models of conflict, and utilitarians almost by definition prefer economic bargaining.

Justice Reality

The justice reality consists of principles used to establish the proper outcome or consequences of conflict resolution. Three types of justice reality based in part on the work of Tedeschi and Rosenfeld (1980) were found in the various cases we examined. These include retribution, in which punishment is the criterion of justice; competition, in which winning is what determines justice; and distribution, in which justice involves the fair distribution of goods.

Retributive justice aims to punish wrongdoers. Although most theories of justice define *retribution* as antithetical to justice, many people in actual conflicts adopt it readily (Dikaioi, 1980). *Competitive justice* means maximizing gains and minimizing losses. Brute competition, although defined by most theories as unjust, is also readily adopted in the heat of dispute. Such a stance may be defended capitalistically by reference to larger social benefits. If everyone has an equal opportunity to compete, attempts to maximize gains and minimize losses may lead to an averaging effect that is socially just in the long run (Dikaioi, 1980). The third type of justice is *distributive*. Most theories of justice are distributive, because justice is most often defined as a fair distribution of resources. The catch, of course, is to establish the principles of fairness used in distribution (Perelman, 1963). Four general distributive principles are common.

Entitlement justice distributes resources according to prior qualifications such as ownership, rank, role, or class. For example, a spouse in a divorce mediation might argue that he or she should keep the house because of prior ownership. Although this type of justice may be prevalent in many traditional societies, modern societies have their own brands of this notion. Affirmative action and welfare entitlement programs are examples.

Equality justice divides resources equally without any consideration of other factors. Outside factors are not made part of the division formula because everything is split evenly. In a divorce mediation, for example, one might argue that the proceeds from the house be divided equally between husband and wife regardless of income or prior ownership.

The third principle of distribution is equity (e.g., Folger, 1984; Perelman, 1963). Because equity generally means "fairness," there is little agreement on exactly what equity is. For our purposes, we are adopting the definition of social psychological equity theories (Adams, 1965; Folger, 1984; Tedeschi & Rosenfeld, 1980; Walster, Berschied, & Walster, 1973), in which division is based on original contribution or productivity according to the principle, "to each according to work." Those who contribute more, get more. For example, a spouse may claim that he or she should get a larger portion of the house proceeds because of contributing more to the payments.

The final principle of distribution is social welfare justice. This norm would distribute resources according to some larger system benefit. The best known contemporary theory of justice (Rawls, 1974) is a social welfare theory. It imagines a society in which each person gets as much liberty as possible without constraining the liberty of others and that goods are distributed so as to benefit the least advantaged. This principle is stated otherwise as, "to each according to need," although other standards of social welfare could be adopted. An example of welfare justice would be a spouse desiring to get the entire house because he or she will have custody of the children, who need a home.

A Case Study

To explore the problems of divergent social realities in mediation and illustrate the interpretive model, let us turn now to one of our most interesting cases. The divorce case involved a dispute between a couple to whom we gave the pseudonyms Roy and Jane. According to the divorce decree, Roy was to keep the children and the house, and Jane was to pay child support. Jane appealed this judgment, and the case was brought to mediation, which took 7 hours in three sessions over a month's time. At the time of the mediation, Jane was living outside the home, and Roy was living with a new girlfriend and the children in the family home. In the end no agreement was reached, and the case presumably went to court.

One of the coauthors was present, behind a one-way mirror, during the entire mediation. He took copious field notes and videotaped the entire mediation. In addition, both disputants and the mediators were interviewed within days after the mediation was complete. We then viewed the entire mediation on videotape, listened to the audiotape recordings of the interviews, and together analyzed the case globally much as we had done in the earlier cases. Several segments of the mediation were later transcribed for more careful analysis.

The social realities of the husband and wife were quite different, and this difference explains in large part their inability to reach agreement. Although Roy's social reality is somewhat complex and difficult to characterize, it seems to emphasize three sets of assumptions about morality, conflict, and justice. His moral stance is traditional in the sense of valuing home and family above individual needs and wants. His view of conflict is libertarian in that he wants to be left alone with his new partner and to have his former wife Jane "get off his back." Roy's version of justice can be characterized as "social welfare justice," in that he seems to be arguing for a settlement that is best for the children and the whole family rather than the disputants as individuals.

Roy's discourse expressed a number of beliefs. He referred to the terms of the divorce decree as "vindication." He prided himself on

fixing up the house from a "wreck" to "an energy-efficient home,"
and he held an elaborate vision of a new family consisting of his
current partner and his children. He stated his desire to stay "separate" from Jane and not be "manipulated" by her. In his view, Jane's
actions since the divorce, including petitions to the family probation officer, her involvement in decisions about schooling for the
children, and her appeal of the divorce decree, were improper
attempts to maintain a relationship with him that directly assaulted
his attempt to build a new life.

During their marriage, Roy perceived Jane as "pulling his strings"
and "running him around" in ways that made him feel incompetent.
As Roy saw it, Jane always did the planning and directing of the
family. He related the following incident as a telling one. After they
were separated, Jane and Roy were having trouble finding depend-
able baby-sitters. One day Jane walked into "his" house without so
much as a hello, picked up the phone, and began to make arrangements for a new baby-sitter. Roy objected because he felt sure that
Jane would then "go out and tell the world" that she had to do all
the work in taking care of the children, despite the fact that he was
paying for it. Roy saw Jane as hedonistic, manipulative, and selfish—
traits that she "gets away with" because she is energetic and so-
ciable. As he stated:

> She sort of does it in spite of herself, and she has sort of a charismatic
> kind of personality. She's really bubbly, and she's really gregarious,
> and she's fun, you know, so she gets away with it, and she can run
> her little game on people for a while until they sort of figure out
> what's going on, you know.

Through the mediators, Jane proposed that Roy give her half of
the equity in the house immediately rather than wait for the children
to grow up. In a written plan, she suggested that he take a second
mortgage on the house to obtain sufficient funds. Roy was outraged
at this proposal, perceiving Jane as unreasonable and selfish. He
thought that the only way he could participate would be to sell the
house, in which so much of his self-concept is invested. In short, he
saw the proposal as yet another attempt to run his life:

> I feel indignant about putting so much work into the house and so
> much time and effort into providing a place to live for the family

and all of a sudden having Jane say, "Well, I'm sorry Roy, it's over, and I don't want to live with you any more, and therefore everything that you've done is null and void because I'm going to destroy it by taking half of it."

Roy characterized Jane as naive, having not considered the consequences of leaving him and now trying to avoid them. With little sympathy for her, he felt that she should stop looking for "a free ride" from him; specifically, he thought that she should get a job rather than go to school full time while demanding half of the equity in the house.

Roy agreed to participate in mediation in the hope that Jane would drop the appeal of the divorce decree. However, the actual experience of mediation held few surprises for him. He perceived Jane trying to "run her game" on the mediators. He noted that she cried in order to gain the sympathy of the mediators and pretended to be physically and psychologically threatened by him. At the same time, she tried to "run her program" on him by bringing in a type-written fact sheet that detailed how he could manage his finances in order to pay her half of the equity. On the other hand, he used mediation as the only available forum in which he could express his feelings to Jane because she refused to meet him or even talk on the phone. He wanted to explain that he was not being vindictive by refusing to renegotiate the judge's verdict; rather, he had good reasons for being adamant. These included his precarious financial position, his hopes for his new family, and his feeling that Jane's own predicament was self-inflicted and that she would have to deal with it by herself. To him (but not to Jane or the mediators), his purpose was clear: to "get Jane off my back," either by discouraging her by his intransigence or by responding to some "creative" proposal she might bring that would allow him to "pay her off" without "busting my budget."

In short, then, Roy had a somewhat complex social reality based on a traditional moral vision, a libertarian view of conflict, and a social welfare principle of justice. In sharp contrast to Roy, Jane's social reality was simple and clear. For Jane, the individual's wants and needs are preeminent, and relationships should be based on optimizing the "growth and development" of each person. Her view of conflict was one of economic bargaining, where the disputants negotiate and compromise. Justice, for Jane, was equality, and no settlement short of equal division of resources and responsibilities would suffice for her.

Jane perceived herself as competent and rational, and both of them acknowledged that Jane thinks and acts more quickly than Roy and that they are often "out of sync" with each other. Further, she felt that Roy did not appreciate her abilities, and that his insistence on living in a country home (rather than moving to a nearby college town) stifled her opportunities for growth. She characterized the last years of their marriage as a time in which she became much more self-aware and independent, in part because her work got her involved with some of the people at a nearby college:

> And I decided to sort of get into the ——— department, 'cause that's where it was . . . that's where I felt it was all related. It was really working for me, career-wise . . . I think Roy was a little resentful of that. I did meet new people. I was getting stimulated.

Her increasing ability to articulate her needs and act on them, she believed, made Roy fearful and suspicious. She said, "He always felt that my successes came at his expense."

Her competence enabled her to "juggle a lot of things," and she felt responsible both for her own needs and those of the people she was related to, including Roy and their children. For her, responsibility plus capability obligated her to take the initiative in all matters of family life. When the relationship with Roy was deteriorating, she initiated late-night conversations about their problems, scheduled counseling appointments for them, and in Roy's mind belabored the problem. Being a competent mother was very important to Jane, and she felt obligated to involve herself with and make plans for the welfare of their children. She was threatened by the presence of another woman in Roy's house and was horrified when she was told by Roy's new girlfriend that "I'll be doing the mothering now."

Jane's perception of Roy was more complicated and less explicit than his perception of her. She portrayed him as uncommunicative, irrational, threatening, and irresponsible as contrasted with her own qualities of being articulate, rational, and responsible. She did not seem to realize how important it was for Roy to establish his independence from her.

Jane sought mediation as a means of negotiating a more equitable settlement than the court had decreed, and she wanted a third party present because she feared Roy. She described a recurring pattern in which their attempts to discuss these issues had turned into shouting matches, and recalled one time in which he struck her and one of the children. As a result, she said, she was too threatened by Roy's "physical presence" to try to work things out without a third party present.

Both Jane and the mediators thought that Roy gave "mixed messages" during the mediation. On the one hand, he portrayed himself as unwilling to compromise and resentful of her "intrusion"; on the other, he depended on her to initiate a "creative" solution to which he could agree. Jane thought the mediators worked best by conducting a kind of "shuttle diplomacy," and blamed Roy for the failure to achieve an agreement. According to Jane, "he just did not want to deal with his part of it. He's still angry and vindictive."

Jane's reality, then, was individualistic, economic, and egalitarian. The mediators' social reality was typical and consistent with their training. Their moral stance was utilitarian. They aimed to accomplish an agreement by practical, responsible action. Their view of conflict was therefore one of economic bargaining, and their notion of justice was distributive. On the whole the reality of the mediators was akin to that of Jane, and their interventions adapted much more readily to Jane's reality than to Roy's.

The deep structures of these realities are like logics for action; they guide the ways in which the participants understand and respond to others. The pattern of interaction in the mediation is produced by a blend of these logics, and in this case the mediator's logic of action meshed more smoothly with that of Jane than with that of Roy.

For this reason the mediators become co-opted into the apparently unresolvable pattern of interaction of the couple. Jane wants to bargain, and Roy sees this as an attempt to manipulate. As the following excerpt between the mediators and Roy illustrates, the mediators do not seem to understand Roy's perspective here:

> **Mediator:** So, the question is: Is there, do you have anything to give to us that we could give to her?
>
> **Roy:** Well, you could tell her that yeah, I'm sort of wanting to play ball with her, but, ah, no. I'm not gonna play ball with her if it means that I have to cripple my life or my family's life.
>
> **Mediator:** So, the question, Roy, is do you have anything to give?

Roy: No, I guess I don't really have anything to give . . .
Mediator: I wonder about that. 'Cause really, I think that's the point that we're at now. You need to give something . . .
Roy: What's Jane given me?
Mediator: Well, actually, you may not like the proposal, but she came in with one. And we need to hear somethin'.
Roy: No, I can't do that tonight. No. 'Cause if I did, I would leave here feeling I've been railroaded . . . And I'm not gonna do that with Jane ever again, 'cause I've been in too many situations where I felt just like that. And I promised myself: No more. So, I'm sorry, you know, and I wish I did have something more specific. . . . So, what do you think, guys? Do you think I'm being pretty recalcitrant? You know, being kind of a pain in the ass? What's your honest opinion?
Mediator: It's necessary to give a little, generally. And one of the things that happens, that's tough, is you see when somebody comes in with a proposal laid out, and the other person doesn't have a specific proposal, the conversation tends to, uh, go at least in the format that, you know, whoever lays out the format tends to be a little ahead of the game. So, you need to put out a format. 'Cause now, in a sense, we're talking in Jane's terms. Until we see yours.

Notice in this segment the importance of the word *give*. In the four mediator turns, this is the hook they keep giving to Roy. In the context of their economic bargaining reality, this is their invitation for him to participate. A counterproposal is, in their social reality, the first, basic, preliminary act that anyone who engages in conflict must perform. His refusal is very perplexing to them. They do not hear it as a move, as a necessary act designed in his reality to prevent himself from being co-opted into Jane's familiar game. Instead, they conclude that he is irrational and out of control, as the following excerpt from their caucus illustrates:

Mediator₁: Do you think the guy's dumb? I think he's stone dumb. Either that, or he's so emotional that he can't see . . .
Mediator₂: It's emotional more . . . because he's jealous, he's hurt. And actually now I think he's hurt that she, I mean, he's getting revenge.
Mediator₁: and he's cutting off his nose to fuckin' spite his face at that . . . He's shootin' himself in the foot!

Mediator₂: Okay, he is, but love is blind.
Mediator₁: Don't you hear him? He's got another lover?
Mediator₂: Yeah, but love is blind.

The problem here is not that the mediators sided with Jane on the issues so much as they shared a big part of her social reality. By representing Jane's demands and suggestions to Roy, they became agents of her dominance and manipulation. By failing to hear his complaints as a manifestation of a deep social reality, they were unable to empower Roy, and they became agents of his withdrawal and inaction. In short, the mediation became a continuation and reconstitution of the pattern and made no progress in changing this pattern.

Ironically, although Roy quite clearly believed himself to be a victim of Jane's manipulations, he did not perceive the mediators' role in continuing the pattern. In our postmediation interview with Roy, he said that the mediators were just doing their job. Of course he was not privy to the mediators' private caucuses or their meetings with Jane and could not have know what they thought of the situation. We suspect that because of the institutional authority of mediators, disputants may not always recognize the subtle ways in which they can and do exert influence, even under the guise of nonintrusiveness.

This mediation failed for a variety of related reasons. Clearly, the disputants were unable to achieve coherence between their social realities. The establishment of a common reality or joint understanding would have been very difficult, if not impossible, in this case. Where the deep social realities of disputants diverge, conflict resolution becomes intercultural communication.

Managing Deep Differences

Seen from this perspective, the differences between the social realities of mediators and disputants may be dealt with in three ways. The first two aim to achieve common ground between the various realities involved. Mediators either attempt to assimilate the clients into the mediation game, or accommodate their approach to the realities of the disputants. The first solution seems to be the most desirable from the standpoint of traditional mediation, and much structuring work is designed to do just that (Burrell, Donohue, & Allen, 1990; Donohue et al., 1988). Clearly, in the case featured in this chapter, the mediators were unable to "train" Roy properly in the mediation procedures.

The second solution, accommodating to the realities of the disputants, is less desirable from the standpoint of mediation procedure and was not seen in this case and was, in fact, rarely seen in the eight case studies we conducted. In fact, the written guidelines and training for the mediation center expressly prohibited bending the standards or rules of mediation.

The third method of dealing with discrepant realities does not require achieving understanding among them, but coordinating them in such a way as to achieve an agreement irrespective of the varying meanings of that agreement. In brief, coordination involves the development of an interaction in which each person's actions seem appropriate to all participants, even though they do not necessarily have the same meanings for what happened. When coordination is achieved, each participant will feel that the outcome is appropriate and good, though the outcome may come to mean different things to each participant.

Given the problem of disparate realities in many mediations, coordination may be an important means to solution. Here the mediators would not try to develop understanding between the parties, but, recognizing the difficulty of that, would help each disputant understand issues and potential agreements from the disputants' individual points of view. This objective would probably be accomplished through reframing of some sort. For instance, the mediators might reframe issues and answers differently for each disputant, based on that person's social reality, or the mediator might create a meta-frame under which both realities could be subsumed.

How might coordination have been achieved in the divorce case? Certain common elements of the husband's and wife's realities could have been used as a meta-frame for cooperation. For example, the mediators could have used independence as an overall construct with which to develop an agreement. Within Roy's libertarian notion of conflict, independence would become a means of getting Jane off his back; for Jane's expressivist and egalitarian reality, independence would become a means of getting her share of common property so that she could pursue her potential as an individual.

If such a solution had been achieved, it might have satisfied both parties. Jane would have seen it as meeting some of her objectives and concerns, while Roy would have seen it as a means of avoiding subsequent interaction with Jane. This is not an interpersonally coherent solution, but it does illustrate how coordination can be used to reach an agreement.

Such a solution requires two practices on the part of mediators. First, they must be able to understand the deep structure of the conflict. That is, they must be able and willing to make interpretations of the parties' social realities on a deeper level than merely identifying surface issues and attributing the lack of movement to the psychological inadequacies of the clients. This kind of interpretive activity requires the mediators to become sensitive to the variety of social realities that disputants may bring to mediation and to communicate interculturally. It also requires them to move out of their own economic bargaining reality from time to time and to "think like a native."

More often, however, mediators expect clients to adapt to their own view of conflict and mediation. For example, Tan (1988) developed an assessment instrument to determine whether clients conform to mediation expectations and would therefore benefit from family mediation. The instrument is designed to measure in part: (1) whether client values match those of mediation, (2) whether they understand mediation in the same way the mediators do, and (3) whether they have the necessary skills to participate in the process. If deficiencies are found in any of these areas, various kinds of remedial strategies are called for, including values clarification, information, and skills training.

Second, mediators must be intrusive in suggesting new frames and possible solutions to the disputants. The most successful mediators we have observed in our case studies have been able to do this. The unsuccessful mediations we observed have led us to the tentative conclusion that rigid adherence to one method and one way of viewing conflict is an obstacle to mediating many of the kinds of cases encountered at alternative dispute resolution centers.

Perhaps the clearest finding in these studies has been that the practices of mediation can take on very different meanings as they interface with the social realities of various disputants. One way of looking at this phenomenon, of course, is to privilege the discourse of mediation, and view those who cannot rise to it, like Roy in our divorce case, as somehow deficient in communication or conflict-resolution skills. Another, however, is to recognize that the mediation of a dispute is part of a much larger life story and relational history of the participants and to acknowledge the legitimacy of the rich variety of social realities constructed within these personal histories.

How do disputant behaviors influence third parties' move-by-move interventions? How do mediators respond to parties' reactions during interventions? When do mediators complete or abort their intervention moves?

5

The Interactive Construction of Interventions by Divorce Mediators

David Greatbatch
Robert Dingwall

AS SIMMEL (1964) OBSERVED, conflict is one of the major positive forces in the construction of social relationships. In contrast with the purely negative force of indifference, conflict provides an incentive for interaction, whether to join or to oppose another's interest. In any specific relationship that endures there will be moments of agreement and moments of conflict. Although mediation may look toward the dissolution of a relationship in the long term, this can only be achieved by its preservation in the short term. Although each participant may be pursuing his or her own interests, all are subordinated to the general principles of mediation, much as Simmel argues that the law provides a framework of agreements within which conflicts can be managed. Each of the parties must defer in some measure to the others, if interaction is to be possible at all.[1] As any experienced mediator will recognize, were mediation to be marked only by conflict, sessions could not occur. Where there is no agreement on superordinate principles, the "frame" in Goffman's (1975) terminology, there can be no mediation. Similarly, where there is only agreement, mediation is irrelevant. All mediation balances precariously between the fundamental conflicts dividing the parties and their temporary agreement on the process by which they are seeking some resolution.

This process is necessarily accomplished through interaction. The mediator's relationship to the parties is constructed from the work that she[2] does with them, work conducted primarily through the medium of talk. It begins with their in situ socialization as she sets the frame, the explication of the foundational assumptions on which the session will proceed. It continues to the identification of the parameters of the dispute and to the step-by-step search for agreements. Finally, the session reaches some closure that, if not fully accomplishing its task, at least provides for the legitimacy of the work and the participants' respect for the frame. Each of these elements provides a context for what follows and may lead to the reinterpretation of what has gone before (Garfinkel, 1967). Our studies of mediation must reflect the interactive, sequential, and episodic character of the phenomenon itself.

In their review of methodological issues in the study of mediation, however, Kressel and Pruitt (1989a) emphasize the neglect of the interactive character of mediation:

> It is important to measure not only what the mediator does, but what *the parties* are doing when the mediator intervenes and what they are doing after an intervention. Mediation is a situation of reciprocal influence. Focussing exclusively on the mediator violates this reality. (p. 429, italics in original)

This is at least partly attributable to two of the specific methodological weaknesses that they identify: the reliance on self-reports by mediators rather than direct observations, and the tendency to assess mediator behavior by frequency counts of discrete mediator acts.

Although there has been a greater use of observational data since these comments were written (e.g., Cobb & Rifkin, 1991a; Dingwall, 1988; Donohue, 1989; Garcia, 1991; Greatbatch & Dingwall, 1989; Rifkin et al., 1991; Silbey & Merry, 1986), analyses of party behavior remain uncommon. The major exception is Cobb and Rifkin's (1991a) work on narratives in mediation. They show, for example, how parties who tell their story of a dispute first in a mediation session establish a privileged position in that the other party is then obliged to present his or her story as a response to the first. Without some positive action by the mediator, the second story becomes a subplot, a reaction to or revision of the first rather than a true alternative. This is an important finding, although not one that necessarily depends upon a discourse analytic approach: In his lecture on April 30, 1970, for example, Sacks discusses at some length the particular problems facing the tellers of second stories. Rifkin and Cobb's work, however, also exemplifies the methodological limitations of much discourse analysis. In particular, there is an uncertain relationship between the narrative and its interactional production and a reliance on stipulative interpretations of the data.

In Cobb and Rifkin (1991a), for example, the dispute between Kate, a school bus driver, and Frank, a boy accused of misbehavior on her bus, is presented almost entirely through the analysts' redescription. Although some passages from Frank's "second story" are reproduced, the transcript has been purged of important interactional information—hesitations, pauses, restarts, repairs, and so forth —that are crucial to the authors' arguments about the shaping of that story. This bowdlerization is particularly frustrating given the authors' own stress on the original incoherence of Frank's story (p. 81). The ascription of meaning and intention rests on the analysts' fiat:

> To identify a positive position, we look for instances in the text in which a speaker attributes good intentions or good characteristics to self or others. (The "good" is defined from within the narrative, according to the moral order established by the narrative.) To identify a negative position we look for instances in the text in which a speaker attributes bad intentions or assigns negative characteristics to other. (Cobb & Rifkin, 1991a, p. 78)

The methodology involves the observers' reading of the narrative to define its moral order and the projection of this understanding onto particular turns in order to establish their valence. It does not, however, establish that this was the understanding of the *parties*. That would depend upon a much closer analysis of the turns surrounding those in which the allegedly evaluative statements were made. In practice, Rifkin and Cobb are skillful analysts of interaction and it is highly likely that the result of trading upon their own competences, both technical and commonsense, produces something that approximates fairly closely to the order constructed by members. This would, for instance, explain why their analysis of first and second stories is persuasive, even if the adequacy of its documentation is contestable.

Our own work takes a slightly different direction because of its roots in conversation analysis (CA). This is a major branch of the research program of ethnomethodology—the study of the competences that underlie intelligible, socially organized interaction. Although CA began from the study of ordinary conversations, it has been increasingly applied to other forms of interaction, including medical consultations, courtroom encounters, and broadcast interviews.[3] A number of CA researchers have also begun to extend its principles to the study of visual conduct. Thus, in spite of its name, CA represents a general approach to the study of face-to-face interaction. Utilizing audio or video recordings of naturally occurring interaction, CA researchers aim to describe the procedures, rules, and conventions that speakers use in producing their own behavior and interpreting and dealing with the behavior of others. The modes of analysis they use are designed to exploit the fact that speakers "whether intentionally or not, implicitly display their understanding and analysis of what is happening as it happens" (Heritage, 1988, p. 129).

In our own work, then, we have preferred more detailed forms of sequential analysis to warrant our claim to be examining phenomena that have been interactively constructed by those taking part in mediation sessions. Although our characterizations necessarily acquire the status of second-order typifications (Schutz, 1962) from our own formulation and labeling, it is argued that these are grounded in analyses of interactional behavior that show that people must be orienting to features of this kind to generate the observable patterns of interaction. In a previous paper (Greatbatch & Dingwall, 1989), for instance, we described a procedure that we called *selective facilitation,* a way in which the choices available to parties during certain turns at talking were constrained by their sequential relationship to the mediator's construction of the previous turn. That paper was based on a single case study covering about 13 minutes of a mediation session in an independent British agency. The analysis showed how, at a series of critical points, the mediator shaped her talk such that one party's perspective was left unexplored, akin to Cobb and Rifkin's contentions concerning the neglect of second stories, and that certain turns were constructed in such a way that they could only be followed by concessions or retreats if the moral character of the designated next speaker were not to be seriously damaged. In one passage (Greatbatch & Dingwall, 1989, p. 632), for example, the mediator used a reference, by the husband to the position of his children, to propose that the husband's preferred course of action would involve taking their home away. If he were not to jeopardize his claim to paternal concern, he could only respond by giving way to his wife's preferred outcome.

This chapter represents the obverse of the analysis of selective facilitation. It is designed to respond to the challenge laid down by Kressel and Pruitt by examining the ways in which mediator behavior is influenced by party behavior. Mediators can also find their options constrained by their sequential relationship to a party's prior utterance. The occasions being considered here are all points at which there is a conflict between the mediator and one or both parties over the framing of the encounter (Dingwall, 1988, 1990; Dingwall & Greatbatch, 1990). Parties may be seeking to depart from the ascriptions of moral character built into the frame by attacking each other verbally; from the rules of relevance defining certain topics, like their emotional state, as inadmissible; or from the time orientation imposed on the session, by trying to introduce issues of past conduct rather than focusing on practical future arrangements. The mediators in these extracts are seeking to maintain the frame by sanctioning party deviations. Our concern is mainly with the effects of compliant or resistant talk produced by the parties in the context of these interventions. We shall, though, also comment on some of the more general implications for the study of client behavior and on the specific practice of co-mediation.

Data

The data are drawn from a bank of recordings of divorce mediation in England. The total set now amounts to about 120 sessions from 10 different agencies. This chapter concentrates on 9 sessions recorded in each of 2 agencies during 1990-1991. One agency is a probation service that uses mediation in the context of custody investigations.[4] The other is an independent service that recruits clients by referrals from lawyers or by self-referral. The agencies are situated in adjacent areas, allowing us to control to a considerable extent for socio-demographic or other environmental sources of variation, and are chosen to represent the main settings in which divorce mediation occurs in the United Kingdom. Although it is not a major theme in this chapter, the comparison between the two sites also addresses an important issue raised by McEwen and Maiman (1986) about the extent to which different forums are associated with different processes, a claim that has been strongly asserted by some U.K. mediators (e.g., Roberts, 1992).

Only one mediator, in the probation service, explicitly laid down a procedure for organizing the talk during the session, and this extended no further than getting each of the parties to relate their version of events at the beginning. A more open format followed. This mediator also showed some evidence of a more structured approach to co-mediation, although the illness of his partner meant that we only have one of three sessions in this format. Here the second worker acted as a consultant, only offering observations when invited to do so. In all the other co-mediated sessions both workers regularly intervened as they considered appropriate. In both agencies, the mediators mainly used a bargaining/task-oriented style of work.

> They neither reviewed the couple's relationship nor encouraged the release of feelings as a precursor to seeking agreement. When disputants raised emotional issues, the mediators normally moved quickly to focus attention back on the task of negotiating a settlement. (Dingwall & Greatbatch, 1991, p. 294)

The recordings from the probation service, which last between one half hour and one hour, cover eight cases and involve seven mediators (four male, three female). Six of the sessions involve co-mediation. In all cases, the probation officer with responsibility for writing a custody report is involved. The recordings from the independent agency cover five cases and involve eight mediators (four male, four female), all of whom are qualified social workers. Each session lasts about an hour and all but two involve co-mediation.

All of the recordings were made by the mediators, to minimize observer effects, with the knowledge and consent of clients. Most of the clients in this set come from working-class backgrounds. The samples were drawn by taking the first N cases where couples were willing to participate after an agreed date: We had hoped for 10 sessions from each site. Although this is not a random sample, there is no reason to anticipate any obvious selection bias, beyond that of client consent. In any case, the objective of the research is less to describe the prevalence of the phenomenon, where sampling would be critical, than to contribute to the development of a taxonomy of events, a language for understanding mediation. For this task, it is only necessary to be able to show that some behavior occurs with a sufficient degree of frequency to be worth identifying and labeling. Data of this kind can also be used within a Popperian logic of falsification to test certain general hypotheses, in this case, for example, that mediation sessions are driven by mediators.

The Influence of Client Talk
on the Development of Interventions

The relatively loose structures adopted by the mediators in this sample meant that while much of the clients' talk was directed through them, it was not uncommon for parties to speak to each other directly. Clients also frequently spoke while mediators were talking. Sometimes mediators abandoned what they were saying, giving up the floor or reacting to the clients' interventions. Sometimes they carried on, without appearing to acknowledge what had been said. On closer inspection, though, it is often possible to identify ways in which the mediators had in fact responded to interventions they had seemed to ignore. In this section, we shall illustrate this process by considering two sets of cases in which extensions of mediator interventions appear to be influenced by clients' responses. The first involve mediators extending their interventions more or less simultaneously with the initiation of responses by clients. The second involve mediators extending their interventions in the course of responses by clients.

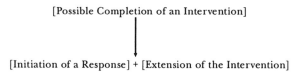

Figure 5.1. The Simultaneous Extension of Interventions and Initiation of Responses

The Simultaneous Extension of Interventions and Initiation of Responses

In cases with the simultaneous extension of interventions and initiation of responses, mediators extend their interventions beyond possible completion points by appending a syntactically coherent next utterance component or initiating a new syntactic unit. More or less simultaneously, however, clients begin to respond to their preceding talk. This configuration can be expressed as shown in Figure 5.1. In many of these cases mediators neither acknowledge the client's talk nor curtail their own intervention, preferring to complete the utterance they have begun. There are, however, observable differences according to whether the attempted response is compliant or resistant.

Resistant Responses

When clients produce resistant responses, mediators generally press forward on a confrontational footing. This may be thought of as the paradigm case of mediator control. For example:[5]

```
    (1) [Probation:1-1]
1  W:  But you (ought) to get in touch with Detective Sergeant
2      Jo:hnson hhhh at Dewsbury police station.
3      (1.4)
4  W:  He can tell you. .hhhh
5  M:  Wha- wha- what's he going to te:ll me:.
6  W:  He'll tell you why I- why I left him.
7  M:  But (.) that uh isn't important to me [(why he's)-
8  W:                                        [THAT IS IMPORTANT
       TO ME
9      BECAUSE OF- ME AND MY KIDS have suffer:ed.
```

```
10 M:   Yes I dare [say (you) have suff-
11 H:           [(              ) [bitch
12 M:                          [hey hey hey hey hey=
13 W:   =We've a:ll suffe:red.=
14 M:   =I'm sure you have but (.) [ at the-
15 H:                        [Keep Johnson out of it.
16 M:   at the end of the da:::y why you broke u:p
17      (0.6) is a matter for you and hi:m:, (0.2) isn't
18      i[t. Th- th- th- th- the- the truth i:s you=
19 W:   [.h We've all suffered in this.
20 M:   =are- you are no longer living together, (.) and you've got two
21      childre:n, (.) and some decision needs to be ta:ken about what's
22      going to happen to the childre:n.
```

At lines 16-18 the mediator attempts to check an argument between
the parents by proposing that the issue raised by W—why they broke
up—lies outside the framing of the session. The time orientation of
mediation is toward the future, not the past. However, as the
mediator begins to extend this intervention (line 18), W continues
to focus on the emotional issues that he is trying to exclude by
repeating her previous assertion "we've all suffered in this" (line
19). The mediator neither relinquishes the floor nor acknowledges
what W has said. Instead he presses on with the unit in progress,
or at least with talk that is formulated as its syntactic continuation
(lines 18 and 20-22).

Another example is located in the following extract where H tries
to resist the mediator by beginning to talk in a way that implies a
coming disagreement. Once again the mediator continues with the
intervention-in-progress.

```
    (2) [Independent:2/1-2]
1 H:   He says no matter what you do he says it's- it's just out of
2      devilment now.=
3 W:   =It's not out of devilment.
4      (0.2)
5 W:   I [said  [(it's not out of devilment).
6 M2:    [(Well [ ah-)
7 H:            [(Well how come your best mat[e said that.
8 M2:                                    [Yes but you have=
9 M2:   =to he[a:r w h a t - y o u h a v e to-
10 H:         [He said it's out of devilment.
```

```
11        (0.3)
12 M2:    =[We're-
13 H:     =[That I am not going to get them because I want them.=I am not
14        going to get them.
15 M1:    You're [not hearing Sue.=
16 M2:          [Yes but-
17 M2:    =you're not (0.3) what we're hearing (.) is what's in this
18        room Dave.
19 H:     Ye:[s.
20 M2:       [We're not interested in what anybody else has sa:id.
21 ( ):    .hhh
22        (.)
23 H:     Well I'm afraid I am.
24 M2:    (Yes but) [what we want to do is find out what Alison says=
25 H:              [(it- it all comes back to me).
26 M2:    =and what you sa:y.=
27 H:     =Yeah. It gets [back to me so much.=
28 M2:                   [And if-
29 M2:    =Yeah:.
30 H:     You know [so-
31 M2:             [So what do you think you could do: for Alison that
32        might help her: feel confident about
33 H:     Noth[ing to be quite honest. Because she's adamant that I'm=
34 M2:        [( )
35 H:     =not getting to get them.
```

As before, one party (H) is trying to bring the views of an outside
and absent person into the session. In concert with M1 (see line 15),
M2 tries to block this by invoking similar framing principles: that
what is important is what is said in this room between the parties
at this time (lines 16-18). H is not properly orienting to his partner's
talk. Just after H begins to respond (line 19), M2 launches into a new
negative unit (line 20). Notice that H's response "yes" acknowledges
M2's prior assertion, but does not indicate a willingness to go along
with it (as would, for example, "Okay," "All right," "Yes okay," "Yes
all right," etc.). This, combined with its tone, suggests that H may
be reluctant to accept the limits that the mediator is seeking to place
on the discussion. As in Extract 1, the mediator presses on with her
emerging intervention, completing the negative unit she has initiated.

Compliant Responses

When clients produce compliant responses, mediator interventions generally proceed along different lines. In these cases, mediators characteristically modify the emerging structure of their interventions by aborting or restarting the unit in progress and adopting a less (or non-) confrontational footing. In other words, even though mediators do not give up the floor or deal directly with the client's response, their talk is reshaped in ways that display sensitivity to the client's talk. For example:

```
     (3) [Probation:8-1]
 1  H:   But we have a:lways agree::d.
 2       (1.0)
 3  H:   I'm not gonnahhh
 4       (.)
 5  W:   We haven't [always-
 6  H:              [I'm not going to be .hh be er hh
 7  W:   No we haven't always agree[::d.
 8  (M):                           [.hhh=
 9  M:   =wu- We mustn't forget though it is about the children
10       isn'[t it.=It-
11  W:       [Yes I kno:[w.
12  M:                  [it's[:
13  H:                       [Yeah.
14  M:   it's no:t .hhhh (0.6) it's easier for me maybe to s- to
15       completely separate ou::t the- the children and their
16       intere:sts (0.4) u:hm
17       (.)
18  (W): hhhhhh
19       (0.5)
20  M:   from a statement that you must agree because (.) you obviously:
21       (0.6)
22  W:   There are lots of thi:ngs that [er:
23  M:                                  [Yea:h
24  W:   that I don't li::ke .hh abou:t the children and my husband and
25       lots of other things which I keep to myse:lf.
```

The intervention in question begins with the mediator sanctioning the parents after they start to argue about the feasibility of joint custody (lines 9-10). He seems set to extend this intervention with a contrastive structure that is common throughout our data. Having asserted what the session should be about (the children), he is now ready to state what it is not about (lines 10, 12, and 14: "It- it's: it's no:t"). If we compare this with lines 14-23 in Extract 6 and lines 5-10 in Extract 7, we could anticipate something that depicted the parents as preoccupied with their own interests rather than the well-being of their children. However, as the sanction at lines 9-10 reaches a possible completion point, W acknowledges and accepts the mediator's prior assertion (line 11). He restarts the extension (line 12), but W's completion is followed by H also producing an acknowledgment that implies agreement with the assertion at lines 9-10. Both parties have now endorsed the mediator's statement and undercut the second part of the projected contrast. Following this, the mediator again restarts the extension ("it's not") takes an inbreath (.hhhh), pauses ((0.6)), and then, instead of continuing with this negative line, initiates a line that not only opens in a less critical fashion ("it's easier . . .") but further downgrades itself as it unfolds (maybe to s- to completely separate): one that maintains the need to focus on the children, while now overtly acknowledging the difficulty of this for the parents (line 14, et seq). They are not to be blamed for their partial success at something that can readily be accomplished by a detached outsider. This has the effect of mitigating the sanction begun at line 9.

The mediator's acknowledgment of the parents' difficulties seems to react to their compliant responses, even though he constructs it as an extension of his turn at lines 9-10 rather than clearly linking it to their contributions. He has held back the critical second part projected by the contrastive structure and moved to a less confrontational footing.

We can see the same behavior in the following extract.

```
     (4) [Independent:4-6]
1  D:    And it's my opinion that he picked up a mental block about
2        school from you which (0.6) he is now getting over.
3  M1:   Well we're going- we're going back int[o
4  W:                                          [Yea:h.
5  M1:   arguing about er
6  H:    Mm[:
7  M1:      [Let's just (1.3) put Gerra:rd center stage: (.) can we?
8        Uh::m (0.3) can you- (1.0) because that's after all who we're
9        here to discuss (I think). (0.5) Can you just describe Gerrard
```

10   (0.2) for us Lucy.
11   (0.5)
12 W: He's (.) he's a ve:ry (.) gentle chi:ld...

As this extract begins, the parties have started to disagree over the reasons why their child is having problems at school. The mediator moves to check this sequence by sanctioning their behavior. As the mediator begins "into arguing" (lines 3 and 5), W produces an agreement token ("Yeah") in response to the sanction ("We're going back"). In other words, just as M1 is about to develop a critical elaboration of the initial proposition, that the parents are engaged in the out-of-frame activity of arguing rather than, say, negotiating, something is produced that implies assent. The mediator subsequently hesitates (line 5: "er"), restarting just after H has begun a response that implies that he is also likely to agree ("Mm:"). Again, the mediatior does not deal directly with the parents' responses. However, instead of continuing with the previous negative component, he starts a new unit; one that is still critical in tone, but less so than the one he has aborted. This time, he focuses on the positive (What we're *here to do*) rather than the negative (What you *are doing*). Now it is an activity that can involve all three of them, rather than one that has moved away from the mediator's framing and left him observing them playing a side game that is irrelevant to his work.

Once again a mediator appears to have withheld talk critical of the parents. In Extract 3 this involved redirecting a unit in progress: Here it involves the mediator curtailing a unit in progress and producing a new one. In both, however, the change of course follows favorable responses from clients. Projected negative components have been cut short or redesigned in the context of compliant responses. Although the mediators' subsequent talk is produced as if it were a continuation of an intervention in progress, its character has changed. The final shape has been modified in response to changes in the interactional environment.

The extracts considered here illustrate a general pattern when mediators start to extend their interventions more or less simultaneously with the initiation of responses from clients. In the case of resistant responses, mediators press on with, and on occasion upgrade, components that are critical of parents. In the case of compliant responses, mediators may observably change direction,

adopting a less (or non) coercive footing. Thus, although they do
not overtly acknowledge the clients' responses, they display an orientation to their character (see Figures 5.2 and 5.3). In the present
data there are a number of cases in which mediators *do not* observably modify their interventions in the context of compliant responses. In some of these the mediators press forward on a confrontational footing (in much the same way as they do in the context of
resistant responses). However, this generally happens where agreement components occur before the main thrust of an intervention
has been articulated or, alternatively, where they are produced by
a client who is not primarily the object of the sanctioning intervention. In other environments the compliant responses are followed
by talk that involves mediators moving to a less (or non) confrontational footing. For an example, consider the following case where
M1 begins to sanction W for getting back into the past instead of
looking at the present or future. The mediator designs the sanction
at lines 8-9 in the form of a question. W's agreements at line 10 accept
the thrust of the intervention.

```
      (5) [Independent:3/1-2]
      (Conclusion of "long" narrative)
 1  W:    And I thought that is it. No more:. (0.5) I've had enough. .hh
 2        If he wants the bachelor life he wants his big business he
 3        wants to .hhh I mean all his squash players and friends were
 4        (.) have their own businesses and they're all on the-
 5        businessmen on the way up the ladder.=And I thought well good
 6        for them. (.) It's the way to get business and that but (.)
 7        [quite a few of them have lost their wi:ves and
 8  M2:   [Do I feel a da:nger of getting back into the marriage
 9        again [Melanie in a [way.=And the-the question is abou:t how=
10  W:          [Yeah.     [Yea:h.
11  M2:   =much is- is- Chri[s f r e e : o f  y o u :
12  W:                      [Well this is what I'm frightened of [really
13  M2:                                                          [able not
14        to be jealous now isn't it. .hh And I just wonder how much you
15        feel that that's still around for you.=That he still
16        [is jealou:s.
17  W:    [Well you see there's nobody on the horizon at the moment
18        there's no: .hh there's no cars pa:rked outsi:de.
19        (0.7)
20  W:    [My hou:se?
```

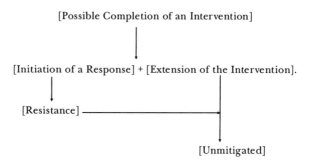

Figure 5.2. Resistant Responses

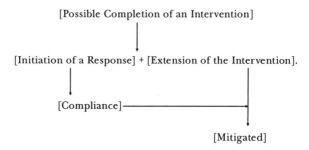

Figure 5.3. Compliant Responses

```
21  M2:  [So you don't kno:w.=
22  W:   =So I don't kno::w.
```

The mediator does not observably change direction at the first response implying agreement (line 6). The unit in progress is neither aborted nor observably redirected, although the mediator does conclude it with a qualifier tending to mitigate or soften the sanction ("in a way"). This can be compared with lines 14-16 of Extract 3 and the ways in which critical interventions can be downgraded. The process continues more obviously after the second agreement token. Here, the mediator further extends his intervention through an agenda statement, identifying the issue they should properly be focusing on. This is relatively benign in avoiding any direct criticism of either party. Here too, then, the mediator moves to a less confrontational footing following the client's compliant responses. However, in contrast to Extracts 3 and 4, the process does not involve any observable modification(s) of the structure of the emerging intervention.

The Extension of Interventions in the Course of Responses by Clients

In these cases clients again begin to respond at points at which mediator interventions are possibly complete and again their responses are overlapped by extensions of those interventions. In contrast to the examples above, however, these extensions are initiated in the course of the responses, rather than more or less simultaneously with their onset.

Here the configuration is as shown in Figure 5.4. It may appear that this configuration is ascribable to a speech-productional issue, namely the "pace" of the mediator's talk: A mediator pauses between components of an intervention and by the time she starts to produce the second component, a response from the client is already under way. Closer analysis, however, suggests that these extensions may again be related to the character of the emerging responses. All of the cases in our data are associated with resistant responses and occur at the point where the negative character of the unfolding response can be heard. For example:

```
     (6) [Probation:1-3]
 1  H:       She wouldn't like to be a part-time [mother?
 2  M:                                           [N o : :.
 3           (.)
 4  M:       Possibly no:t?=
 5  H:       =Let's see how she would like it if I [had them all week.=
 6  M:                                             [( )-
 7  M:       =But [y-
 8  H:            [.hhh And then she picked them up at five o'clock on a
 9           Friday [.hh and take them back on a su- (1.2) five o'clock=
10  M:             [But-
11  H:       =on a Sunday.=
12  M:       =But [a:ll
13  H:            [See how she wou[ld like it.
14  M:  1→                        [But you're talking about
15           what you wa:nt. What you fee:::l.
16  H:  2→   Yeah she won't put [herself out.
17  M:  3→   Yeah she won't put [And what she feels.=You're- [you know-=
```

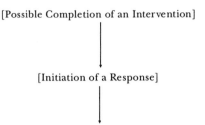

[Possible Completion of an Intervention]

[Initiation of a Response]

[Extension of the Intervention in the Course of the Response]

Figure 5.4. The Extension of Interventions in the Course of Responses by Clients

```
18  H:                                                          [(I)-
19  M:      =thi- this is- it's about you:::.
20          (0.4)
21  M:      I:'m talking about Tristan and Siegfried.=What about
            the:m? (.)
22          What do the::y fee:l being passed around like little pa:rcels.
23          Not knowing who they're going to be living with.
24  H:      They don't know where their own ho:me is.
25  M:      Ri:ght. Well what do they feel about it.=What are we going
26          to do about tha:t.
```

In this case H is talking negatively about the current situation and in particular about his wife. The mediator sanctions H for being preoccupied with his own interests and concerns rather than, by implication, those of his children (lines 14-15). In responding H resists the mediator's sanction by continuing to criticize his wife (line 16). Just after the point at which the potentially resistant character of his response becomes apparent, the mediator extends his intervention, adding a further sanctioning component (line 17).

Another instance is observable in the following extract:

```
    (7) [Independent:2/1-1]
1  M2:      That['s ri::ght.
2  W:             [But I mean he's never listened I mean [in all the ten=
3  M2:                                                    [If you could-
4  W:       =years we've been together he's never listened to me.
```

```
 5  M2:   1→  D'you think it might be possible for you- the two of you to
 6             think of yourselves as .h mum and da:d to the two
               children, .h
 7             and forget about the relationship between the two of
               [you.
 8  W:    2→  [No
 9             because some thi[:ngs
10  M2:   3→              [And sort out what['s best for the:m.
11  W:     →                          [I- I- t h i n k
12             (0.2)
13  W:        that the very fact of who we are and what we are:
14            (.)
15  M2:       Yeah.
16  W:        ha- has a lot to do with the wa:y (0.2) we see the children.=
```

M2 sanctions the couple for focusing on issues concerning the poor
state of their relationship rather than the welfare of their children
(lines 5-7). W resists this "request" ("No"), and then begins to provide
an account for her response ("because some things") (lines 8-9). In
the midst of the account, M1 extends her intervention with a further
assertion of the children's interest (line 10).

In both examples, then, we can see the configuration illustrated
in Figure 5.5. The mediators in the cases above may, of course, have
planned to extend their interventions before the clients spoke.
However, the current data set contains no comparable cases where
extension in this fashion follows a positive or compliant response.
This suggests that the occurrence and character of the extensions
is related to what the clients' talk is projecting: namely, an unfavorable
response, resisting the thrust of the mediator's preceding sanctions. The extensions seem to be designed to counter unfavorable
responses in progress, while appearing to ignore them. Had the
responses been leading in the direction of acceptance rather than
resistance, the extensions would probably have been withheld or
mitigated.[6]

The claim is made, then, that cases like these demonstrate mediators modifying their behavior in response to client interventions.
There are, however, a number of other ways in which the interactional environment can influence what mediators are doing, and we
shall now look briefly at two of these.

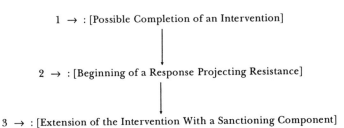

1 → : [Possible Completion of an Intervention]

2 → : [Beginning of a Response Projecting Resistance]

3 → : [Extension of the Intervention With a Sanctioning Component]

Figure 5.5. The Extension of Interventions in the Course of Resistant Responses by Clients

Other Factors Implicated in the Interactive Construction of Interventions

Thus far we have been concerned with the ways in which the occurrence of compliant/resistant talk from clients may have a bearing on the structure of mediator interventions. It is important to stress, though, that talk is not the only medium involved in the interactive construction of interventions. Moreover, interventions may be influenced not only by clients but also by co-workers.

Extensions Occasioned by an Absence of Vocal Response

The absence, as well as the occurrence, of talk by clients may have a bearing on the structure of interventions. For example, a lack of vocal response may result in silences that, in turn, may lead to further talk by the mediator. In the following case, the mediator acknowledges H's response to his prior intervention (line 5) and then goes on to further sanction the client's behavior, again through the proposal that they are not currently acting as responsible parents. This intervention is extended on three occasions (arrows "E") after clients withhold any form of vocal response (arrows "S").

```
    (8) [Probation:1-3]
    (continues Extract 3)
1  M:   I:'m talking about Tristan and Siegfried.=What about the:m? (.)
2       What do the::y fee:l being passed around like little pa:rcels.
3       Not knowing who they're going to be living with.
```

```
 4  H:      They don't know where their own ho:me is.
 5  M:   →  Ri:ght. Well what do they feel about it.=What are we going
            to
 6  M:      do about tha:tWhat are you as mum and dad going to do
            about
 7          your childre:n.
 8       S→ (1.0)
 9  M:   E→ Not what- what are you: going to do about the pai:n that you
10          feel or the pain that you fee:l.
11       S→ (.)
12  M:   E→ But what are you going to do about these poo:r (2.0)
               children
13          who are being deprive:d of their parents because they're so
14          busy fighting each other.
15       S→ (2.0)
16  M:   E→ [That's what I:'m concerned a[bout.
17  H:   E→ [I could say-              [I could say something but
            she
18          won't agree to it.
```

This process is found on numerous occasions in the present data: mediators extending their interventions after clients have passed up opportunities to respond. The absence, as much as the occurrence, of talk from clients can be a central factor in determining the shape that an intervention ultimately achieves. Certain components in any given intervention can be provoked by, and designed to deal with, the absence of response from the clients.

The Impact of Co-Mediator Conduct on Interventions

The majority of the sessions involve co-mediation in which both mediators actively relate to the clients. As noted elsewhere (Dingwall & Greatbatch, 1991), we have found that when one worker exerts pressure on clients to modify their behavior (or to accept proposals, etc.) co-workers often underline this by intervening either before or after responses from clients. For example:

```
    (9) [Independent:2/1-5]
1  M2:      We're not hearing about what- we're hearing that you both
            want
2          them to see each other. .hhh But uh- what I'm not hearing i:s
```

```
3            (1.0) how you're going to really make that happen.
4            (.)
5   M1:   → For them.
6   M2:      For them.
```

However, mediators may also collaborate in intensifying each other's interventions by furnishing agreements and agreement-implicative acknowledgments. In the following extract, M2 twice produces acknowledgment tokens that implicate agreement while M1 is sanctioning the clients for arguing. As M1 addresses the clients, M2 underlines the point(s) she is making:

```
        (10) [Probation:5-1(b)]
 1  H:       if we fail this time with these child[ren
 2  M1:                                            [M m :
 3  H:       and we [can't do better tha:n
 4  M1:             [Then you haven't got another cha::nce.
 5  H:       than=
 6  M1:      =No you don't have another cha:nce.
 7  H:       N[o:
 8  M1:        [The best- the only thing that'll actually help your
            childre:n
 9          (.) is to know (.) that mummy and daddy (.) have sorted their
10          life out and will go on and they can talk to either of you
11          about anything that goes wrong in the long te:rm, (.) and
            that
12          you will alwa:ys (.) have their interests in the front.
13          (0.2)
14  M1:      And that you will talk to each other abo:ut the children.
15  M2:   → Yes.=
16  M1:      =That is what your children need to know. .h And is the only
17            wa:y (.) that you're going to succeed with them.
18  M2:   → Mm=
19  M1:      =If you carry on like thi:s (.) you'll get nowhere.
20          (0.4)
21  M2:      Will you accept to bind it a bit further than that.=Will you
22            accept that (0.7) if they had the chance they'd have you back
23            together again.
24          (0.3)
25  H:       If they had the cha:nce [yeah.
26  M2:                              [Yes. Ri:ght.
```

Co-mediators engage in a variety of responsive activities during each other's interventions. It is emerging that such activities may lead to (1) continuations or extensions of interventions by coworkers; (2) the maintenance, and on occasion upgrading, of confrontational stances by coworkers; and (3) the suppression of response from clients, which may further enhance the likelihood of continuation by the co-mediator. It is becoming clear that, in the context of co-mediation, the activities of coworkers may be implicated as much as those of clients in the dynamic process of interaction through which interventions emerge.

Concluding Remarks

We have seen that mediator interventions can be influenced by the character or absence of response from clients and coworkers as they unfold. Any analysis of mediator behavior must, then, take account of the ways in which this responds to its interactional environment. That environment consists of phenomena that can only be located and analyzed via tape recordings of sessions *and* fine-grained transcripts. Video data might be useful in refining the analysis, particularly in considering the extent to which, for example, party responses may be elicited by shifts in the gaze of mediators; mediator interventions modified by changes in the expression or gaze of parties; silences are filled by nonvocal activities; and co-mediators coordinate their turns. Nevertheless it is clearly possible to achieve useful results from audio data alone.

The analysis presented here has particular implications for those types of study that treat mediator turns as the basic unit for classifying their communicative behavior. Mediator turns need to be located both as responses to preceding turns and as open to reconstruction in the course of their production. In sanctioning the conduct of clients, for example, mediators sometimes refer to the children's interests, sometimes not. Simple counts of these alternatives are, however, deceptive. Although some interventions begin by referencing the children's interests (e.g., extracts 3, 7, and 8 above), others do not: References occur only as the intervention unfolds. In the following example the mediator extends his intervention four times after clients have declined to respond (at least vocally).

```
    (11) [Probation:1-5]
 1  M:      And you i- i- i- ehuh- you have my permission (0.2) to
            beha:ve
 2          reasonably with each other.
 3      S→  (0.6)
 4  M:  E→  All ri:ght (.) you're not- you do- I'm not impre:ssed with y-
 5          you know by you:: (0.2) falling out with each other.
 6      S→  (0.7)
 7  M:  E→  And it would help the boys tremendously (.) no matter
            what the
 8          outcome of this is if you could cooperate with each other.
            For
 9          the:ir sake.
10      S→  (1.3)
11  M:  E→  It [really wou:ld.
12  W:         [((sniffs))
13      S→  (0.4)
14  M:  E→  You're not going to (0.9) you know you're not going to
            get back
15          together now: ( ) but you can still cooperate with each
16          [other.
17  H:      [( )
18          (.)
19  H:      I would like to.
```

The reference to the children's interests is not introduced until
the mediator is extending his intervention for a third time after what
(in interactional terms) are substantial silences. As such it would be
wrong to treat this in the methodology of workers like Donohue
(1989) as simply an intervention that sanctions a particular sort of
behavior by referencing the interests of the children and that in
turn has some specific effect. It is necessary to take account of the
way in which the intervention is built incrementally in the context
of an absence of response from clients. When viewed in these terms,
interventions of the sort shown in Extract 11 can be seen to be working
in a rather different way from those that set out by invoking the
children's interests.

    This analysis helps us to identify an important skill for profes-
sional mediator training. The various reactions to client interventions seem to have different sequential implications that may make
them more or less effective as a means of moving the session in a

positive direction. Mediators have various choices in the way they modify their interventions in the context of compliant responses. In Extract 3, for instance, the mediator, in moving to a less confrontational footing, formulates the clients' conduct as understandable (and thus, in the circumstances, not entirely unreasonable), while still pressing them to modify it. In Extract 4, by contrast, the mediator does not build in an acknowledgment of the parents' positions and seek to minimize the implication of fault on their part. These alternatives offer the beginning of a taxonomy of mediator choices that could lead into an evaluation of their effectiveness in particular contexts.

Mediators' responses to silence offer another example of the possibilities. In the present data, mediators employ a range of techniques when dealing with the absence of response from clients. At one end of the spectrum, they maintain a confrontational footing, often upgrading or strengthening the sanction, as in Extract 8 above. At the other end, they either move immediately to a nonconfrontational footing:

```
      (12) [Probation:7-1]
1  M1:       . . . We're concerned about (0.2) (that side), and not your
2            feelings on the subject.
3       S→  (0.5)
4  M1:  E→  Is there no: alternative to swimming. If- if swimming's a
5            problem because none of them can swim (0.5) is there no
6            alternative. Somewhere else you could take them.
7            (0.4)
8  H:        .hhhh (.) Well I take (them) on a Sunda:y
```

or confine themselves to soliciting a response:

```
      (13) [Probation:5-7]
1  M2:       The problem is that what you're saying is the children should
2            be put first and that's absolutely right I agree with that. But
3            I just have the feeling that what you might be doing at the
4            moment is fighting out your own battles.
5       S→  (1.9)
6  M2:  E→  Right,
7            (0.8)
8  H:        (What for what I want). . .
```

Again, further work on the effects of using these techniques in different contexts offers the possibility of helping practitioners identify effective solutions to a very common problem.

These data also throw some light on the possible consequences of co-mediator actions. An understanding of the ways in which co-mediators can affect the development of each other's interventions, as well as the behavior of clients, would help practitioners to make more effective use of this costly technique. In particular, there is a resource here to develop some recognition of the ways in which co-mediators can interfere with or promote each other's efforts. On some occasions, ill-judged co-mediator interventions can inhibit clients from responding and/or prolong the time spent on a confrontational footing. On others, the team collaborates to considerable strategic benefit.

At the end of the day, however, though this analysis should certainly caution us against underestimating the contribution of the disputing parties to the course of the interaction in a mediation session, it is not clear that it fundamentally compromises the growing view that mediation is a process that leaves far less autonomy to the parties than many of its advocates would claim (cf. Forester, 1992; Rifkin et al., 1991). Party interventions create the environment within which mediators have to work, but the real skill of mediation is the ability to take those interventions and to redirect them in ways that continue to progress the resolution of the underlying dispute. The mediator remains the "keeper of the frame," the architect of the short-term in situ agreements out of which a longer term unity can be built. In recognizing the contributions of the parties, we are also marking the profound improvisational talents of the skillful mediator, snapping up these trifles as the raw material of her work.

Notes

1. *Deference* is used here in Goffman's (1956) sense of an acknowledgment of the civil status of the other, rather than necessarily having connotations of super- and subordination.

2. Given the preponderance of women mediators in our database, we have used "she" to refer generically to mediators: where a particular mediator in a particular extract is male, we have adopted the masculine pronoun.

3. For a comprehensive review of recent literature on conversation analysis, see Maynard and Clayman (1991).

4. This is a traditional role for the probation service in England. Accounts of "court welfare work" can be found in Davis (1988), Davis and Bader (1985), Dingwall and James (1988), and James (1988).

5. In this and all following extracts, H = husband or male partner; W = wife or female partner; M = mediator. The transcripts use standard conversation analysis notation (Jefferson, 1984) and are edited to maintain the confidentiality of the sessions. The principal symbols used here are:

[A left bracket indicates the point at which overlapping talk begins.
]   A right bracket indicates the point at which overlapping talk ends.
(0.5)   Numbers in parentheses indicate the occurrence and length of silences in tenths of a second.
(.)   A dot in parentheses indicates a gap of less than two tenths of a second.
Word   Underlining indicates some form of stress via pitch and/or amplitude.
Wo::rd Colons indicate prolongation of the immediately preceding sound.
. , ?   Punctuation marks are used to indicate falling, nonterminal, and rising intonation respectively.
( )   Empty parentheses indicate that the transcriber was unable to hear what was said.
(Word) Parenthesized words indicate possible hearings.
(( ))   Double parentheses contain transcribers' comments or descriptions.

6. See Jefferson (1981) for a discussion of similar phenomena in ordinary conversation.

How do mediators use language and process to create third-party roles?
What images do mediators try to create for themselves during intervention?
How do these images help mediators develop settlements without having
formal institutional power to do so?

6

"Talking Like a Mediator"

Conversational Moves of Experienced Divorce Mediators

Karen Tracy
Anna Spradlin

WHAT DOES IT MEAN to talk like a mediator? What are the similarities
and differences? Why do the similarities and differences occur? In
this chapter we extend what has been learned through key ethnographic studies (e.g., Kolb, 1983, 1985; Rifkin, Millen, & Cobb, 1991;
Silbey & Merry, 1986) by analyzing the discourse of four experienced divorce mediators dealing with the "same" case. By comparing and contrasting the conversational moves among these mediators
we arrive at a deeper and more complex understanding of what it
means to "talk like a mediator."

In the first part of the chapter we focus on similarities. Mediation
raises an interactional difficulty. Mediators are expected to bring
disputing parties to a settlement but possess no institutional basis
of power (Silbey & Merry, 1986). To be effective, therefore, mediators
must talk in ways that give them interactional power—the assumed

right to influence and shape the final outcome. We show that the four experienced mediators used similar conversational moves to gain this interactional power. By displaying themselves to be expert and fair, they claimed the right to influence. They established expertise by labeling self as a professional and by referencing experience and knowledge; they worked to establish their fairness by implying they were fair people, by using referee-like conversational moves, and through the language they used to reframe disputants' face-threats to each other (Volkema, 1988).

In the second section we focus on differences and show how the conversational actions observed among the four experienced mediators extend, as well as challenge, past characterizations of mediator styles. Three conversational differences are highlighted—differences in language use, topic management, and interactional structuring. We demonstrate how the observed differences support and extend Silbey and Merry's (1986) characterization of the bargaining style but call into question their description of the therapeutic style. We begin with a description of the materials and method.

Divorce Mediation Materials

Background Information

In 1989 the Academy of Family Mediators (1989a, 1989b) created two 90-minute videotapes to assist in the training of mediators. The Academy produced the tapes to display various mediator styles for mediators in training. Three individual mediators and one co-mediation team demonstrated their individual mediation styles with the same case. The mediator sets included two men (Mediators A and B), a woman (Mediator C), and a man-woman co-mediation team (Co-mediators D). Additional members of the Academy enacted the husband and wife roles.

The case involved a divorcing couple who had been married for 22 years and whose divorce was complicated by parenting, property, and disproportionate earning-power issues. Each mediator set demonstrated two phases of the process: (1) the initial meeting, and (2) the property division discussion.

The videotapes seemed suitable materials to explore questions about mediator talk practices. The tapes involved experienced mediators drawing upon their experience to confront a new situation. Because the "new situation" was the same one for all four mediator sets, the tapes provide an especially good place for identifying differences in mediator communicative action. Although a simulation is lacking in some complexity encountered in regular cases, it does provide a way to untangle mediator style differences from mediation context differences. That is, much of the conceptualization of mediator differences arises from observing mediators in different organizational contexts (e.g., Kolb, 1983; Silbey & Merry, 1986). It would be valuable to see if the description of mediator style differences stands up when mediators face the *same* mediation context. It is also the case that past work (see, e.g., Silbey & Merry, 1986) does not allow us to rule out the possibility that observed mediator differences arose because the mediators possessed different levels of experience and skillfulness.

For this case we have strong implicit evidence that each of the four mediator sets is competent. Although the Academy may not agree with the specific procedures of any selected mediator, it is hard to imagine a professional group would select individuals they judge as novice or generally inept as training examples. It thus seemed warrantable to interpret differences as reflecting different underlying concerns as opposed to differences in the skillfulness of individual mediators.

The Case

The case involved a divorcing couple named Jane and Keith Summer. Keith, a medical doctor and professor at a medical school, had initiated a divorce from his wife, Jane, following 22 years of marriage. Jane had been a homemaker most of her life but recently had completed a master's degree in counseling and was in the process of seeking employment. The couple has two children, Samantha, 20, who was away at college, and Geoffrey, 17, a senior in high school. Jane was ambivalent about getting a divorce and preferred to stay married until Geoffrey has graduated from high school. Keith was adamant about completing the divorce as soon as possible. Both were concerned about property issues, especially what should be done with the house.

The first phase of mediation enacted by each of the four mediator sets was the initial mediation session. During this initial meeting the mediators met the couple to explain the purpose of mediation, typical procedures, and to get the disputants' initial formulation of the issues. The mediation was then "fast forwarded"; Sessions 2 and 3 were assumed to have produced agreements about parenting arrangements and child and spousal support. The training tape continued with Session 4 and the agenda of property division. For this session the husband and wife brought with them a financial statement containing asset and liability information. The mediators' aims in the second phase were to negotiate issues around property division and distribution of the marital property.

Analytic Procedures

We began by transcribing the videotapes. Transcription was done at a relatively broad level; exact wordings, filler speech ("you know," "I mean," "OK"), vocalized pauses (uh, hmm), and word repairs were transcribed but, except for a few instances, we did not attempt to capture vocal stress patterns, pauses, exact positioning of overlaps and interruptions, or gaze patterns. Several discourse analysts have noted (Coupland, 1988; Craig & Tracy, 1983) that there is no "right" level of transcribing specificity; the right level depends on the analytic purpose with a general trade-off between transcript specificity and amount of text examined. We opted for a less fine-grained transcribing of a larger amount of interaction.

Our goal in analyzing the eight mediation sessions was to identify similarities and differences in the conversational moves of the four mediator sets. In essence we approached the transcripts with an initial set of assumptions about the goals and purposes of divorce mediation and the kinds of differences routinely seen. These assumptions derived from past writing about mediation as well as mediation experience. In studying the transcripts we sought to identify which conversational actions could be understood as attentive to a specific purpose and which pointed to belief differences about the nature of mediation. Our goal was to extend past research by providing a more conversationally grounded sense of what general strategies (establish expertise) or style differences looked like. We see this goal as a desirable end in itself (Tracy, 1991) and also as a way to critique theoretical claims about mediation practice.

Divorce Mediator Similarities

All mediators face a similar interactional dilemma: they need to bring about a settlement but lack any formal basis of power to do so. Mediators deal with the lack of formal power by communicating in ways that build their interactional power. Through the ways mediators present themselves and their mediation program, they nudge people toward settlement. Silbey and Merry (1986) characterize the process this way:

> Claims to authority and by implication deference, are made as the mediators present themselves in their introductions and intermittently throughout the mediation session when they may offer advice, give information about alternatives and factual matters, or brandish language and symbols associated with the law or helping professions. (p. 12)

Kolb (1985) provides the most detailed description of how labor mediators accomplish this self-empowering process, a process she sees most mediators being only dimly aware of. Drawing upon Goffman's (1959) dramaturgical framework she identifies a set of conversational moves mediators use to create impressions of themselves as expert, friendly, and fair people. These impressions, Kolb argues, are expressive tactics used by mediators to influence parties to reach settlement.

Kolb's work gives us a good general characterization of similarities in the conversational moves of mediators. But because her work draws primarily upon interviews with mediators, we have a precise sense neither of what mediators say nor of the kinds of variation exhibited. Studying mediators' discourse refines the picture with regard to how mediators routinely establish their (1) expertise and (2) fairness.

Establishment of Expertise

Similar to Kolb (1985), we found the mediators doing interactive work to establish that they were experienced and knowledgeable practitioners of a complex process. For instance, consider what Mediator B said after initial greetings.

Excerpt 6.1

Okay, the reason I ask couples to come here for what I call an initial consultation is basically to cover, um, three main points and, uh, other things of course. But I've found over the years that, uhm, couples who are thinking about mediation, in considering using it, first of all I think they need to have an opportunity to meet with the mediator and interact and see how you feel. So I like to use this session for an opportunity to have the three of us just talk. And secondly since mediation is something that, while it's becoming more widely known, I think a lot of people would still have some questions about how it does work. Everybody does things a bit differently. And I like to take the time to explain exactly what I would do in the room to try to help the two of you.

In the opening monologue this mediator claims expertise by highlighting his experience. He does this by (1) emphasizing that he has been mediating for many years ("I've found over the years that . . ."), and (2) referencing his understanding of the typical viewpoint of couples approaching mediation. Note that such a viewpoint typification is only possible with experience. In engaging in an opening monologue like this, the mediator also conveys that he is in command of a process into which he will be initiating the couple. His references to experience establish him as a person who has a right to influence what happens in the situation.

Expertise was conveyed by two other conversational moves. One was a mediator's explicit statements about possessing technical kinds of knowledge ("I have a fair familiarity with business issues" or "I can tell you what the law says. . . . I can provide you some legal information"). Another way was by revealing facts the participants were unlikely to know ("It's actually fairly unusual for both parties to mutually decide to go ahead and get a divorce. That's fairly rare. Maybe about three-quarters of divorces one party decides or really initiates the process a lot more than the other.").

In addition to the above two kinds of conversational moves, documented for labor mediators (Kolb, 1985), the divorce mediators established themselves as experts by contrasting their work with that of other types of professionals. Consider how each mediator did this. Mediator C said:

Excerpt 6.2

I need to explain to you that I will not make the decisions for you and in that sense mediation is different from arbitration where you present sort of your case to somebody and somebody else decides. And mediation is also different from psychotherapy in that the goal here is to help you reach agreements rather than explore uh, either your own psychological issues or, uh marital issues which have created the kind of pain and conflict you've described. In that sense it's different. Also I'm not an attorney so I need to let you know among other things that I will not be giving you legal advice.

In this example Mediator C contrasts her role as a mediator with three others—arbitrator, psychotherapist, and lawyer—highlighting what she takes to be the noticeable difference. Mediator A makes a similar statement.

Excerpt 6.3

Let me quickly tell you that I'm, uh, an attorney and I'm also a social worker by training. But probably more importantly I'm going to be functioning as a mediator. So I'm not going to be working as either a lawyer or as a counselor for you.

Mediators A and C provided the most detailed contrasts, but all four made the contrast. Mediator B repeatedly stated he was not a counselor, and Co-mediator D indicated that mediation would not be involved with an activity highly associated with another forum and role ("We're really not here to psychoanalyze each other, to understand all of our underlying motivations.").

These characterizations establish the mediator as a "professional person." None of the mediators attempted to establish what they did as an extension of the kinds of activities people routinely do in their personal life; no one said "what we'll be doing here is similar to what you do when you try to help two friends work out a disagreement." Thus by comparing mediation with other more established professions, mediators put themselves in the broad category of *professional*—a category of people who know more than ordinary people and who deserve to have their suggestions followed.

Establishment of Fairness

Within divorce mediation a central obligation of mediators (and a central source of power) is to be neutral, to act as an "impartial third party," "unbiased," "fair," "balanced." Although we do not think each of these terms references exactly the same quality, we do see the terms as orienting to a constellation of interactional qualities that are essential for mediators. Unless mediators can establish their fairness, their chances of effecting a settlement are limited.

In the training tapes all mediators used three conversational strategies to establish their fairness: (1) they explicitly or implicitly labeled themselves as fair, (2) they engaged in referee-like conversational moves, and (3) they attempted to reframe disputant face-threats in less hostile or blaming language.

Explicit or Implicitly Labeling as Fair. The mediators sought to establish their fairness by stating explicitly or strongly implying that they were fair ("balanced," "neutral"). Mediator A was most explicit in this conversational action.

Excerpt 6.4

The other thing that I need for you to understand, my role as a mediator is, I'm not neutral. That sometimes surprises people . . . . My job is to be balanced. So if I do my job right in fact you'll both be convinced at some time or another that I'm really on the other person's side.

Although mediators can attempt to establish themselves as fair by self-labeling as Mediator A did, there are reasons to proceed in more subtle ways. It is often the case in everyday interaction that self-labeling occurs when a person feels threatened. Thus to label self as fair makes relevant that others would see self differently. Mediator A minimizes the potential negative implications of self-labeling by building a contrast between two presumably positive qualities (neutrality vs. balance). Each of the other mediators claimed their fairness more indirectly.

Co-mediator D establishes her fairness by recognizing and directing comments to each person in turn.

Fairness
by implication:
through action
active listening

Excerpt 6.5

First of all we're going to be sure each of you has a chance to explain
the situation as you see it right now and we'll be sure each of you has
an opportunity to ask the other questions if you have questions of
clarification. As you do that [Co-mediator's name] and I will be trying
to decide the major topics that need to be discussed and . . . Then
we'll look at those, at those issues, those items and try to understand
what's important to you [gaze directed to Jane] and what's important to you [gaze directed to Keith]. Uhm and how perhaps we can
come up with some options that will meet your needs [directed to
Jane] and meet your needs [directed to Keith].

By explicitly recognizing that each party has a story to tell and that
the two stories are not identical, Co-mediator D frames mediation
as a situation in which turn-taking will occur. By addressing each of
the parties in turn and mentioning that she will monitor turns, Co-
mediator D aligns herself with one important dimension of fairness—
that all parties get a reasonable turn. This framing strongly impli-
cates that Co-mediator D will be fair.

Mediators B and C imply their fairness by describing their goals
as mediators. Mediator B says:

Excerpt 6.6

And I'm trying to help you emerge from this room with a detailed
written agreement that you can say as you look at it, I understand what
it means, I understand what we did, ah, feels fair.

Mediator B implies that he will be fair in the mediation by saying
he will help the spouses produce an agreement they feel to be fair.
To help others create a fair document does not necessarily entail
that a mediator is fair but it is strongly implied. Similar to Mediator
B, Mediator C works to establish her fairness by describing the desired
outcome of working in mediation. She describes her role as to "help
you reach agreements, agreements that are mutually satisfactory to
both of you." Though we think the different language choices (fair
vs. mutually satisfying) are significant, of note here is the similarity
in how each establishes interactional fairness.

Referee-Like Conversational Moves. A second kind of conversational move used to establish fairness was to act like a referee. As in sports, mediators called disputants for violations of the rules of the game. In mediation this meant drawing attention to disputants who spoke for or interrupted the partner. Sometimes the rules of mediation were spelled out at the beginning as we see Co-mediator D do.

Excerpt 6.7

> This is not an easy thing and there are probably things we ought to agree on right from the outset about how we kinda conduct our business in here. Uh, that, that will help us. Let me just lay out a couple for you and see if you have any other thoughts about it . . . but we're going to ask you not to interrupt the other person.

But it was also the case that mediators did not always identify what the rules were until one was violated.

Excerpt 6.8

> One of the things that I like to do, that I think will help you reach an agreement is to ask you each to speak for yourself. [to Keith] You've said a couple times what's on Jo, uh, Jane's mind. [to Jane] You said that you clearly know why he left the marriage, and you're, Jane, telling me what, why he did things. I like to ask each of you to speak for yourselves.

Although it is possible to be perceived as an unfair referee, we would suggest that the mere act of refereeing is a significant part of the way mediators establish neutrality.

Reframing Face-Threats. In an analysis of divorce mediation cases, Jacobs et al. (1991) show that back-and-forth blaming and fault-finding often become the central conversational activities of disputants in divorce mediation. In this context, we saw the mediators establishing their impartiality to each party by diffusing negative comments of one party toward another (Rifkin et al., 1991). Consider how Co-mediator D accomplishes this in her response to a comment from Keith about Jane.

Excerpt 6.9

K: The fact is there really isn't a good time for divorce. It doesn't matter if you have new kids, or old kids or in-between. Uh, uh Jane knows my concern for Geoffrey and Samantha. Uh, uh I don't think she questions my ability to father or my love for the children uh but when she mentions this is not a good time for Geoff, for example in his senior year of high school, Good Lord is it a good time to see his parents separated? Or, or, or not really living together as husband and wife. I don't think, there's not a good time.

M: It sounds as though your major concern here is Geoff too, or at least one of them.

Co-mediator D's reframing takes the sting out of Keith's comment. Keith has implied that Jane is being highly unreasonable in her argument that the marriage shouldn't end until Geoffrey graduates. Through her restatement the mediator transforms Keith's criticism of Jane into an expression from Keith of his concern about his son, a concern that Jane also has.

Besides using reframings to delete information that portrays one of the spouses negatively, mediators also worked to apply potentially negative features equally to the spousal speaker.

Excerpt 6.10

K: ((we)) could probably work it out and try to resolve it but Jane is always emotional every time we sit down to discuss it

M: Oh alright but hang on now

K: and therefore uh that's why we're taking this route

J: Of course I'm emotional I don't want you making me into [the

M: [You both are emotional. Nobody goes through a divorce without both of you being emotional

In this segment, Keith has implied that Jane is the cause of their inability to work through the details of their divorce without seeking help. It is her "emotionality" that is the problem. Jane clearly responds to this issue of blame. While Jane never finished her sentence because of the mediator's interruption, a likely completion would be the following (I don't want you making me into the *villain* or the *bad guy*). The mediator attempts to head off this blaming segment by treating emotionality as normal and something that both participants must be experiencing. In doing so, he attempts to mitigate the criticism of Jane by treating emotionality as a characteristic that does not distinguish between the two spouses. Mediators establish their fairness when they successfully reframe. But reframings are not always successful; sometimes a reframing buys into one participant's view. When this happens it is likely that one party will feel that he or she has been treated unfairly. Consider what an unsuccessful reframing looks like.

Excerpt 6.11

J: There's some things that I don't understand very well and that's where I'm most uncomfortable.

M: That's important and it's important for me to know that and for you to let me know that. And let me say this to you again. I won't go any faster in mediation, I need to be very clear about it. It takes both people to understand, OK? We can come up with the best agreement in the world, I mean the most fair decent agreement but if one person doesn't understand then it doesn't help, right? There'll still be some resentment.

K: OK, but I hope there's not gonna be any stalling.

M: Well you know I appreciate that, I appreciate that concern. Jane you know

J: I'm not sure I understand what he means by stalling

K: Well if you don't want to get the divorce you can drag this out and go slow and pretend that you don't understand.

M: umm hmm

J: I'm not interested in playing games, Keith.

M: *Well OK I hafta take you both at your word at this point and I think you can both check each other, OK? And if you feel that's an issue you can raise it Keith. By the same token Jane I have no reason to believe either of you won't be permitted if you say, to do what you say.*

In this interchange the mediator has been unfair to Jane. Jane expressed concerns about being rushed; Keith expressed concerns about mediation going too slowly. Yet when we look at the mediator's final comment, his formulation is more sympathetic to Keith. The mediator frames his comment as if it has equal implications for both parties

("Well OK I hafta take you both at your word at this point") but within the ongoing sequence of conversation it does not. Jane has just expressed that she would not attempt to slow the process for her own strategic gains ("I'm not interested in playing games, Keith"). She is the only party who has given her word about how she intends to act. Because of this, the mediator's comment about checking each party's word is not equally implicative. If instead of what he did say, the mediator had said something like "Keith, if you think Jane is stalling you can bring it up; Jane, if you feel Keith is pushing an agreement too quickly for you to understand, bring that up," the framing would have been much fairer to both parties.

Reframings are perhaps the most routine and ongoing way through which mediators seek to establish, but sometimes call into question, their fairness. All four divorce mediators revealed similarities in the conversational moves they used to establish expertise and fairness. But while evidencing similarities, they also managed the interaction in some strikingly different ways.

Differences in Mediator Communication

It is a commonplace in mediation that there are differences in the way individual mediators "do" mediation. Attempts to formulate the nature of these differences have garnered considerable attention (e.g., Bernard, Folger, Weingarten, & Zumeta, 1984). Most typically, observable differences among mediators have been formulated as a matter of style. Mediator style differences have been described as differences in degree of directiveness (Blades, 1984), whether a mediator is an activist or passivist (Marlow, 1987), attorney-trained or therapist-trained (Gold, 1984; Marlow, 1987), a "dealmaker" or "orchestrator" (Kolb, 1983), task-oriented versus socio-emotional (Kressel & Pruitt, 1989a), or exhibiting a bargaining or therapeutic approach (Silbey & Merry, 1986).

Of these characterizations, Silbey and Merry's (1986) is the only study of family/community mediation that is based on extensive observation and detailed interactional differences. Silbey and Merry argue that mediators exhibited either a bargaining or therapeutic style. Our analysis supports and extends their description of the bargaining mode. Two of the experienced mediators (A and B) communicated in ways consistent with this style. The other two mediators' styles (C and D) only partially support their characterization of the therapeutic approach. Although the talk of Mediators C and D displayed therapeutic features, it also reflected a commitment to interest-based negotiation. Thus, if we are to retain Silbey and Merry's "therapeutic" label, we will need to redefine how it is expressed among *experienced* divorce mediators. In the following sections, we highlight mediator discourse differences. We show how examination of mediator talk both supports and challenges the bargaining and therapeutic style characterizations.

Silbey and Merry (1986) described the bargaining style as one where mediators: (1) claim authority as professionals with expertise, (2) define the purpose of mediation as reaching a settlement, (3) use a high degree of process structuring, (4) ignore emotional demands, (5) assume that disputants know what they want, and (6) focus on demands that can be traded off.

Mediators A and B, the ones we have identified as evidencing a bargaining style, engaged in conversational moves that accomplished these aims. These mediators established themselves as bargainers and distinguished themselves from mediators C and D in three primary ways: through their language use, topic management, and structuring of interaction.

Mediators' Language Use. Mediators differed with regard to the language they used to frame the goals of mediation as well as the root metaphors (Lakoff & Johnson, 1980) that informed their talk. Bargainers used a language that presumed a much more clear-cut world than that oriented to by the non-bargaining mediators. Contrast the comments of Mediator B (Excerpt 12) with those of Mediator C (Excerpt 13).

Excerpt 6.12

What's going to be most important to me about this mediation is that both of you have an opportunity to come to a, uh, *informed voluntary decision.* OK? And by that I mean that both of *you have all the information* that you need and you've basically considered all the options.

Excerpt 6.13

Basically mediation is a, a *cooperative problem-solving process* in which the goal is, uh, for the two of you to reach agreements about all the issues . . . my job is really to facilitate this process to assist you in understanding all the data that you need to look at and to understand what each of you feels about these things, *what your needs and interests are,* also of your children, and to help you reach agreement, *agreements that are mutually satisfactory* to both of you.

Consider the different view of mediation implied by describing the process as oriented to getting information so disputants can make fair, informed agreements versus reflecting on each participant's needs and interests so that agreements that are mutually satisfactory can be developed. The former language frames it as a relatively objective decision-making process. Although people may dispute for any particular case what is to count as fair, the assumption is that there is a socially shared standard of fairness that can be appealed to. The latter language does not presume this. Instead it points to a more complex process. It presumes that people do not start off knowing what they need; they need to reflect upon the "data." Furthermore, in describing the agreement as "mutually satisfactory" it frames the goal as one of reaching consensus rather than coming to know what is fair.

In addition to the language used to frame mediation, mediators evidenced different root metaphors in their talk. Root metaphors are ways of framing one activity in terms of another (e.g., Smith & Eisenberg, 1987). In contrast to the non-bargaining mediators who drew upon training and therapy metaphors, the bargainers used economic metaphors to describe mediation. In addition to labeling the family as a "business" and framing mediation as something that would restructure the couple's relationship, Mediator A repeatedly used language that called to mind economic decision making. In business, people are concerned about time and money, and take account of these factors in all decisions. In business, people use organizational charts to describe the relationships among people. In business, people work to clarify decisions, removing ambiguity and complexity. Mediator A did all of these things. He referred twice to the fact mediation costs money, something none of the other mediators did. In his opening statement he specifically mentioned he would provide information about "time, cost." He summed up a dispute between Jane and Keith about each person's contribution to parenting, saying "but the *bottom line* is that the two of you have done pretty good parenting, right?" His opening 20-minute interview is peppered with time-sensitive markers ("let me quickly" "very briefly" "I'm not going to dwell on") that remind us that time is money and one needs to ration time by task importance. He used a flip chart in the opening session to draw a diagram of Jane and Keith's family structure. He framed the choice the couple had at the end of the first mediation session in a sales-oriented way, "Now here's your choice and here's what mediation is all about, quick and simple." Through all of these ways of talking, Mediator A conveyed a view of mediation as an economic transaction.

In contrast to talking about mediation in economic language, Mediators C and D drew upon the language of training and therapy. They did this by frequent acknowledgment of feelings, their use of reflective listening, and their encouragement for each partner to check his or her understanding of the other's perspective.

By using language in this way, the mediators established themselves as bargainers or non-bargainers. The bargainers' language use pointed to a world of clear economic issues that could be assessed, a world where disputants could be assumed to know what they want, a world where the job of reaching a settlement could be approached in a relatively straightforward way. Style differences were also displayed through the mediator's topic management strategy.

Topic Management. Mediators are information gatekeepers, deciding what is or is not an acceptable topic of talk in mediation. A noticeable difference among the four mediators was the degree to which topics concerning emotions or participants' feeling states were acceptable. Mediators A and B explicitly marked emotional topics as outside the purview of mediation. Consider how this was done. Following Jane's expression of upsetness about her marriage ending, Mediator A comments:

Excerpt 6.14

You might understand Jane, I can't make Keith stay in the marriage, OK? What I can do is, if you need to go through this very hard time, is maybe give you an opportunity to maintain some kind of control of that. . . . I'm not really gonna dwell on, on, I know the feeling you both have and the relations, relationship issues are extremely important, and we'll talk about that from time to time. But I'm not a counselor, OK so that I can't uh, and won't be the person that helps you work that through.

Mediator A's comment has a "yes, but" structure, a typical way people express disagreement (Pomerantz, 1984). Mediator A indicates initially that feelings are important but then goes on to mark them as inappropriate for discussion in mediation ("but I'm not a counselor"). Mediator B makes several comments of this nature.

Excerpt 6.15

Uh, I don't know what went on in your counseling sessions but I am not here as your mediator for the purpose of continuing that counseling.

Excerpt 6.16

I'm sensitive to the emotions and feelings about why the marriage is ending, but my main focus in this room is to help the two of you arrive at a written parenting agreement for the care and exchange of your children.

Each of Mediator B's comments follows a comment from Jane about her feelings of distress about the marriage ending. Assuming that the mediator is adhering to expectations of conversational relevance (Grice, 1975), Mediator B's comments function as a rebuke to Jane for introducing topics inappropriate to the setting. Thus bargainers inform disputants that emotional topics are inappropriate to mediation by explicitly marking such topics as out-of-boundary when a person introduces them.

In contrast, the non-bargainer mediators did considerable work to acknowledge the legitimacy of feelings. Early in the process Mediator C said:

Excerpt 6.17

Well these are tough issues. The two of you are entering into a period that for most couples is a very difficult period. It's a lot of disappointment and anger and hurt and frequently a lot of issues get caught up in that and one of the purposes of mediation is to provide a forum for the two of you in which hopefully you can sort of identify and deal with all these issues in a way that makes you feel you've been heard in reaching some agreements. And I understand that it's a difficult process.

Emotions for the non-bargainers seemed to be cues to help guide the discussion toward uncovering what each party's interest was. Consider how Co-mediator D responded to an emotional flare-up:

Excerpt 6.18

K: [to Jane about her wanting to keep the house] It's a museum. It's got 5 bedrooms and there's only one kid home now. I mean why do you want a big house? Sentimentality. That she, I think it's just symbolic of uh uh, of uh uh uh not giving up the marriage.

M: [to Keith] I know you have some real decided opinions about what you think ought to happen but I'm really still trying to get *what's important about it for you,* what we do with the house

K: It's important for me to sell that house because there's enough equity in it so that we can both buy or at least put a substantial down payment on another house . . .

Thus, where the mediators using the bargaining style ignored emotional issues by marking them off-topic, the non-bargaining mediators legitimated such feeling expression and worked to use it to discover what interests it reflected.

Interaction Structuring. The bargaining mediators oriented to mediation as a much more structured process than was seen with the non-bargainers. This was interactively displayed most strikingly in the session focused on property settlement. Mediators A and B began the session by clarifying an inventory of monetary values associated with assets and liabilities within the marriage. Each mediator used a flip chart to write down the numbers associated with the monetary value of marital property items. Columns on the flip chart were labeled: "property item," "value," "Jane," and "Keith." Mediator A, in fact, had used written materials supplied by the spouses to fill in much of the chart before the session began. He explained what they would be doing this way:

Excerpt 6.19

The very first thing I'd kind of like to do tonight is I'd like to kind of see where we are in terms of an inventory and the assets. Alright? And then we can get some kind of a total picture. Then we're going to go through and refine these numbers and make sure we have final values, make sure our addition's right and so on when we put it together in the final property settlement agreement. The question will then be is what will be the principle of division you're going to use. How do you want to split the property? And then we'll look at who's going to get what property and put them in each column so that you'll be able to see how close you come to your principle of division as to what you both think makes sense for you in an agreement you can live with.

Mediator A's explanation and use of the flip chart suggest he has a clear sense of the steps divorcing couples need to go through in dealing with property settlement—the interactive process is knowable in advance. That the process is seen as having a predictable structure is implied by his willingness to formulate what the property issues are before discussion and his systematic laying out of the steps the three of them will use in working with the chart to help them reach a good agreement.

Contrast Mediator A's use of the flip chart with what Mediator C did. Instead of using columns, Mediator C listed the first property agenda item, the family residence, and began asking questions of clarification. After recording whatever figures were given by the participants Mediator C asked both parties, "From your perspective what are your thoughts about the house?" This process was repeated for each of the major property items. Concerns about each property item were surfaced through this format. In essence, Mediator C sought to identify the issues based on discussion. Her use for the chart was quite similar to what Co-mediator D did verbally.

Excerpt 6.20

As I understand it what we're here to do tonight is to look at your uh property and see how it can be divided in, a in a fair way, in a way that you can both see as being fair and will meet your needs. I mean there's some property that's marital, there's some property that's joint, there's some separate, but we need to look at all of it and see how it can be divided fairly. What are your major concerns about this property issue, how it's divided, what's divided, what's most important to you about this whole issue of property?

Mediators C and D did not presume to know what the issues were before hearing from the couples. In specifically questioning each party about how they saw things and what was most important to them, the interactional structure was treated as an emergent thing, something arrived at through the process of talk. From their vantage point, non-bargaining mediators seem to see mediation as an interactive process that must be controlled in a local ongoing way rather than by using a preestablished format to guide interaction.

Summary

Thus far we have demonstrated how Silbey and Merry's (1986) bargaining style is displayed conversationally. We have also suggested what the non-bargaining style looks like. Some of what we have described as the non-bargaining style is consistent with what these authors call the therapeutic style. As was evidenced in their therapeutic style, the non-bargainers did (1) sanction a greater range of emotional expression, (2) expand the discussion to explore feelings and past relationships, and (3) assume that disputants did not always know what they wanted at the outset. Missing from their description of this style, however, was a sense that there was a coherent rationale that undergirded the specifics.

For Silbey and Merry (1986), therapeutic mediators opened up issues but did not go anywhere with them. This characterization strikes us as missing an essential feature we observed—*Why* talk was opened up. Such a reason was strongly implicated in the talk of the two non-bargaining mediators. Mediators C and D were not just opening up communication, they were enacting mediation as a forum in which disputants had to articulate their interests before solutions and decisions could be considered. Their opening-up moves were directed to helping each member of the couple identify his or her needs.

The conversational actions of Mediators C and D reflected a strong commitment to interest-based negotiation (Fisher & Ury, 1981; Haynes, 1983; Moore, 1986). This commitment was hinted at in earlier excerpts but is even more visible in the Co-mediators' (D) management of the property settlement session. At the outset of the session Jane had argued that she should keep the house because her mother gave her the $25,000 down payment as a gift. Keith's position was that his working had paid for the house so it should be sold with the equity split down the middle. Both disputants were entrenched in their positions.

In the following excerpt, observe how the mediator works to uncover the underlying need behind Jane's position:

Excerpt 6.21

M: what you're doing right now, Jane, I I think is, is uh arguing for why you think the house ought to be credited to you in the in the terms of inheritance. Is that right?

J: Well yeah.

M: Tell me a little bit more about *what's really important to you* about the house.

Jane answers the mediator's questions with a lengthy emotional response that reveals her desire for some continuity and stability during this time of emotional disruption ("Right now everything else has been ripped out from under me." and "It's a home."). The underlying motivation in Jane's position would seem to be her need for some stability in her life.

Following an exchange in which Keith defends his positions, the other mediator also works to unearth Keith's interest behind his position about the house. In response to the mediator's question Keith states,

Excerpt 6.22

It's important for me to sell that house because there's enough equity in it so that we can both buy or at least put a substantial down payment on another house. One that more fits our needs now that Sam's grown and Geoff is going to graduate next spring.

Shortly thereafter we see one of the co-mediators reframing Keith's expressed need this way.

Excerpt 6.23

So, you want to get something of your own, you want, you want stability as well. You want something that is yours and is your house that you can live in. And that's what the equity represents. That's one thing. Is that correct?

Through the opening up of topics and exploring of emotional expression around the house we see Co-mediators D uncovering, or creating, a self-interest shared by both Keith and Jane—both parties want stability in their lives. Even though the training tapes were too short (20 minutes) to permit study of how this framed mutual interest was pursued, it seems likely that the end result of mediation conducted using this style would differ from the bargaining style mediation. This analysis suggests that if we are to retain Silbey and Merry's (1986) label for the mediation style that contrasts with bargaining, we will need to redefine it. Experienced *therapeutic-style* divorce mediators open up interaction but do so in structured pursuit of disputants' interests underlying initially articulated positions.

In contrast to Silbey and Merry's description we did *not* see the mediators either encouraging *full* expression of feelings and attitudes or operating out of an assumption that such encouragement would produce empathy with the partner, harmony, and ultimately consensus. Some therapeutic-style mediators may have these type of open-ended goals. The two experienced sets of mediators on this training tape did not. In sum, we suggest that a key feature that distinguishes experienced therapeutic-style mediators from bargaining ones is their commitment to interest-based negotiating.

Clearly our own position toward the two styles is not neutral: We favor the therapeutic style. We think mediation conducted with the therapeutic approach will produce more creative solutions and more deep-seated satisfaction among disputants than will mediation conducted using a bargaining approach. At the same time the advantages of the bargaining style should not be underestimated. We think bargaining mediators are often likely to take less time, cost less money, and have slightly higher settlement rates.

Conclusions

In this chapter we have provided a description of the similarities and differences in the conversational moves of experienced mediators. All mediators used a range of conversational tactics to display their expertise and fairness. As such, we would conclude that being seen as expert and fair are identities salient to all mediators.

Other aspects of identity were differentially valued by mediators. These differences have traditionally been labeled *style* differences. But labeling a difference a stylistic one minimizes a difference's significance. Not only does it treat it as relatively minor, it implies an ease with which actors can change. We find both of these implications questionable. In contrast, to frame mediator differences as differences of desired identities is to highlight that a value issue is at stake. That is, learning to "talk like a mediator" requires choosing between competing definitions of what mediation is about and who the mediator is to be.

Part Three

Contextual Influences
on Intervention

What cultural differences make a difference for third-party involvement in disputes? How do various models of mediation deal with cultural differences? How can mediators become more sensitive to cultural influences on disputes and third-party processes?

7

Communication Issues in Mediating Cultural Conflict

William A. Donohue
Mary I. Bresnahan

ON THE EVENING of November 4, 1991, in Lansing, MI, police dispatchers issued a general call that a Hispanic male was threatening people with a gun at a local motel. When police arrived on the scene, a man fitting this description stepped out of the shadows and leveled his gun at the police. In the confusion that followed, police claimed they heard the weapon discharge and responded with return fire including 26 pistol rounds plus a shotgun volley. It was later learned that the man was carrying an unloaded BB gun. The outraged Hispanic community demanded police accountability for what they perceived as excessive use of police force. The city's Human Relations Department was charged with negotiating a settlement between police and the Hispanic community. Two solutions resulted. First, the Human Relations Department sponsored three public meetings in which police and community members expressed mutual concerns about violence in the Hispanic community. Second, the mayor assembled a multiethnic special citizen's committee to recommend solutions for community tensions.

In this chapter we will examine factors of cultural insensitivity that caused these attempts at third-party intervention in the Torrez case to fall short. The chapter has two broad goals. First, we seek to explore the role of cultural differences in the genesis and management of conflict between members of the majority group and race-ethnic minorities in the United States. Second, we will examine the implications of these differences for third-party involvement. Knowledge of cultural differences that prompts individual behavior can assist mediators in understanding the nature of the conflict they are confronting as well as assist them in making strategic choices for empowering disputants to arrive at lasting solutions. We accomplish these goals by first exploring prior research focusing on key sources of intergroup conflict. Next, we probe sources of resistance to intervening in intergroup conflict. The chapter concludes by merging a model of cultural differences with models of mediation to provide mediators with guidelines for dealing with cultural differences in their work. Throughout this discussion, special emphasis is placed upon the importance of cultural factors in crafting an intervention/solution that is sensitive to disempowerment and other perceived indignities that minorities have experienced in their interaction with members of the majority community.

Sources of Intergroup Conflict

Intergroup community violence is a problem that, in the short term, is not going to go away. In a provocative essay on panethnicity in the United States, Lopez and Espiritu (1990) argue that even though all the major white ethnic groups have assimilated in some way, given the current climate that exists in the United States, assimilation is not possible for people of color. By *assimilation*, Lopez and Espiritu clearly do not mean Anglo-conformity, which they would see as an undesirable goal. Instead, they suggest that assimilation means complete access to political, social, and economic power. Lopez and Espiritu (1990) convincingly argue that "the question of ethnicity in the U.S. is increasingly a question of race. Recent and probably most future immigration will be dominated by non-whites.

It is important to emphasize that no non-white group has ever fully assimilated into American society" (p. 220). In contrast to assimilation, ethnic differentiation/pluralism is the opposing pole of the interethnic continuum (Feagin, 1991). *Panethnicity* is defined as "the development of bridging organizations and solidarities among subgroups of ethnic collectivities" (Lopez & Espiritu, 1990, p. 198). Lopez and Espiritu document that the development of panethnic liaisons among people of color has been prompted by ethnic and racial violence over the past decade. In the context of this hostile, exclusionary, and sometimes violent environment, people of color have tended to develop their own subcultures. Their insightful analysis suggests that future mechanisms for resolving intergroup conflict will emanate from coalitions of people of color. In the short term, intergroup hostility and tensions between members of the majority and people of color pose some real problems for community mediation. Better dispute resolution programs are needed to negotiate differences and both to manage the development of panethnic coalitions within minority communities and to empower mediators to negotiate harmonious, culturally sensitive settlements between minority and majority that will have some staying power. This is the challenge of third-party intervention for the growing diversity of the United States in the near future.

Creating such dispute resolution programs, however, requires understanding the key sources of intergroup conflict. According to Tajfel and Turner (1986), much of the early work on intergroup conflict focuses on intra-individual discrimination and aggression rather than group processes. They argue that intergroup conflict escalates when group members stereotype others based on group membership, have low access to other groups, attach a high level of opprobrium to those groups, believe in the necessity of radical social change, and view resources as being unequally distributed. The authors provide evidence to show how these conditions lead to ethnocentrism and outgroup antagonism that, in turn, facilitates aggression and even violence.

For example, Ronald Ebens justified his brutal attack on Vincent Chin with a baseball bat in 1982 by saying that he thought that Chin was Japanese. This explanation evokes media images of responsible Congressional office holders smashing Japanese cars and computers with baseball bats on the steps of the capitol. Tajfel and Turner

(1986) say further that these situations of unequal resources and ensuant antagonism provide opportunities for minority groups to take action to try to redefine a negative self-image that has been created for them by the oppressor. The dominant group might respond to this minority flexing of muscle with renewed efforts to enhance their own distinctiveness in the effort to further entrench the status quo. Tajfel and Turner indicate that there is no reason to assume that intergroup differentiation is inherently conflictual. On the other hand, impeding a group's expressed desire for positive distinctiveness tends to promote overt conflict and hostility between groups.

Feagin (1989), in a comprehensive study of racial and ethnic adaptation and conflict in the United States, identifies recurrent themes that underscore tension between majority and minority. These include social inequality, economic exploitation of people of color to profit whites, and the roles of class structure and law in the maintenance of racial and ethnic inequality. In a more recent study on discrimination against blacks in places of public accommodation, Feagin (1991) found that discrimination continued to range across Allport's (1954) continuum from avoidance action, to rejection, to verbal attack, physical threat, physical attack, and finally, to killing. Feagin claims that blacks are confronted not just with isolated incidents of demeaning treatment and aggression, but with a lifelong series of such acts of discrimination. Feagin worries that if discrimination is common in places of public accommodation where there is accountability, then interracial hostility on the streets can be expected to be much more severe because street sites are unprotected and anonymous. Bystanders who witness street violence are generally reluctant to come forward either to assist a victim or to testify against the aggressor (Feagin, 1991). If earlier predictions about diversity are realized, these points of conflict between majority and minority will be amplified as whites feel increasingly threatened by an expanding minority.

Blalock (1982) concurs that panethnic coalitions, which empower minorities to extract important concessions from the dominant group, have the potential for feeding conflict. These minority coalitions become particularly threatening, according to Blalock (1982), in times of persistent recession, which lowers the average standard of living (1982, p. 115). Blalock further suggests that although only a small segment of majority and minority populations are responsible for intergroup violence, the research shows that a much larger segment of both populations secretly, if not openly, endorses "retaliatory" acts between minority and majority. Even though intergroup violence regularly prompts escalating cycles of retaliation, Blalock concludes that moderate displays of violence by ethnic and racial minorities have symbolic import.

According to Worchel (1986) in early studies on interracial conflict, the contact hypothesis suggested that bringing disparate people together would foster convergence of attitudes. However, subsequent studies revealed that simple contact was also likely to escalate antagonism. A second suggestion for resolving intergroup conflict proposed in this early period was to ask leaders of opposing groups to collaborate in the negotiation of a settlement. Because they had to compromise to achieve settlement, leaders were often scorned and lost influence when they returned to their group. Threat of a common enemy was a third factor associated with intergroup conflict reduction. These coalitions generally were abandoned when the immediate threat was over. These issue-centric coalitions were clearly temporary and did not represent a lasting solution to conflict. Worchel (1986, p. 292) suggests that intergroup cooperation, which he defines as "the willingness to share both the work on a task and the rewards," is the way out of this dilemma. Worchel concedes that cooperative conflict management is much more likely when groups share equal status, the outcome is likely to be successful, and when interaction extends over a series of interdependent activities rather than a single event.

Factors of Resistance to Intervention in Intergroup Conflict

By understanding sources of intergroup conflict, mediators gain essential background information needed to manage this kind of conflict constructively. Managing intergroup conflict, however, is exacerbated by several points of resistance to third-party intervention. For example, an important challenge to cooperative problem solving among interracial groups can be found in the mistrust that minorities tend to have of institutional representatives in general, and the police in particular. Feagin (1991, p. 110) observes: "For most whites threatened on the street, the police are a sought-after source of protection, but for black men this is often not the case." In an interesting and provocative study on policing minorities, Smith, Visher, and Davidson (1984) found that even though there is a slightly greater probability of arrest when the offender is black and the victim white, the race of the victim has a greater impact on police decision making to arrest than the race of the offender. More specifically, the study found that black victims and other people of color receive a diminished police response compared to white victims. These researchers suggest that police are likely to be more responsive to white victims because they view people of color as more hostile to them and less deserving of legal protection.

The tension between police and minorities is clearly illustrated in the Torrez case. Police are generally more unsympathetic to minority group members, and blacks in particular. Arrests are more likely to occur in lower status neighborhoods because offenders in such contexts are seen as more deserving of arrest (Smith et al., 1984). According to Black (1984), when police are confronted with a violent dispute they have three decision options: (1) to separate the disputants, (2) to attempt to mediate the dispute, and/or (3) to arrest the person who is legally culpable. The first option is the easiest of the three because it requires the least amount of police involvement and follow-up. The other two options demand increasingly greater police commitment and involvement through conviction in the legal system after arrest.

In a second study, Smith (1987) observed that because blacks and other people who live in poor neighborhoods tend to behave with hostility toward the police, the police will be less likely to use mediation as a means of resolving violent disputes. They will also be unlikely to use arrest. Violence against nonwhites will in all likelihood be handled by simple separation. Black (1984) calls this separation-only option "avoidance style" because it requires the least possible effort and involvement by the police. Arrest is more likely to occur either when the disputant acts abusively toward the police or when the victim specifically requests that action be taken. There is also a slight statistical preference for arrest when the suspect is black and the victim is white. Smith et al. (1984) conclude that:

> differential responsiveness toward victims is a more invisible form of police discrimination. Proactive racial bias in policing directed against black suspects can be offset, in part, by prosecutors refusing

to fully prosecute such cases. Yet, if police are less likely to arrest in instances involving black complainants, the matter is closed. (p. 248)

Blalock (1982, pp. 112-113) observes: "In short, police violence in America is still a potent means of minority control. Needless to say, it also serves as a major irritant within minority communities as the number of minority demands for police accountability and civilian-review boards clearly indicates."

Negative encounters with established authority figures have taught minorities distrust, uncertainty, and disempowerment. A mediator, who is an institutional representative, could expect to encounter skepticism. The Torrez incident is illustrative. The Torrez killing set off an avalanche of protest in the Hispanic community. Like the Rodney King incident in East Los Angeles, the issue was whether the police had used excessive force. Police claimed that all of their officers had met strict standards for use of deadly force on the firing range. The Hispanic community wanted to know why had it taken trained sharpshooters so many shots to disable a suspect? Personnel in the Human Relations Department of the city government attempted to resolve this dispute between the enraged Hispanic community and the police. When the prosecutor's investigation exonerated the police, mediators from the Human Relations Department failed to anticipate the response in the Hispanic community and were at a loss for how to deal with the publicly expressed outrage. This outcome also confirmed and strengthened skepticism and anger in the Hispanic community and further alienated them from the police and the city authorities. Would the police and city officials behave so callously if the gunned-down youth had been upper class, white? This poorly managed incident illustrates the question that is the focus of this chapter. How should third parties adopt an intervention posture that can address the cultural needs of disputants?

Variant Concepts of Conflict

To address this question it is necessary to understand how various cultures deal with conflict. For example, a major distinction between East and West has emerged in the cultural conflict theory literature (e.g., Ting-Toomey, 1985, 1988). In Western-style cultures, individuals tend to view conflict as a healthy catharsis for anxiety as well as a positive mechanism for invigorating moribund relationships. The rules of fair play require that if you have a quarrel with someone, explanations are mandated. It is more honest to be open about resentment and to attempt to resolve disputes. In Eastern-style cultures, conflict-avoidance is the norm. Whenever parties approach a situation of potential conflict either the disagreement is ignored or an intermediary is called in to resolve the conflict before it intensifies. Part of one's personal goodness is measured by how well conflict is avoided and how adeptly the feelings of others are spared. In addition to different conceptions of the acceptability of conflict, Eastern and Western styles of conflict differ in the ways in which they organize and present information, demonstrate a willingness and ability to provide explanations for discrepant behavior, show solidarity and friendship, demonstrate a willingness to deliver reprimands, and demonstrate propriety and deference toward one another.

Alternate conflict resolution style is illustrated in a study on third-party intervention in the People's Republic of China. Wall and Blum (1991) identify the following features that characterize the 200 successful and unsuccessful attempts to mediate. Chinese mediators are known both to the community and the disputants. No one expects the mediation to be neutral. Mediation is mandated by the state. Before a case can go to court, the disputants must attempt mediation. Mediators tend to be older, trusted members of the community, and generally women. Mediators first conduct fact-finding and then they formulate a fair settlement. The mediators then attempt to persuade disputants to accept this settlement. A critical part of the intervention is the apology. Wall and Blum (1991) observe:

> Mediation to westerners is a social aberration. Seeking mediation is analogous to western medicine: The doctor is visited when someone is ill; a cure is administered for the patient's disease; and the physician, usually a stranger, is not seen until the next illness. If the cure does not work, the patient goes to a specialist. For the Chinese, mediation is integrated within their society. (p. 19)

In contrast, La Resche (1992) reports that the basic assumption of American mediation is that although conflicts can be disruptive, they may result in improved relationships between dysfunctional conflictants. Typically, mediators see themselves as process managers, helping disputants identify and sort through various settlement options. Mediators prefer to remain professionally detached while viewing their relationship with the conflictants as discontinuous. Mediators generally receive substantial training in procedures for conducting the mediation session and in creating a written, formal agreement by the end of the mediation. La Resche (1992) suggests that this model may not be productive for Korean-Americans. She indicates that they tend to see conflict as a shameful inability to maintain harmonious relationships with others. For them, conflicts are not just problems in communication, but indicative of lack of respect. As in the Chinese example, great care is exercised in selecting a respected member of the community as intermediary. The mediation is part of a continuous relationship. After extensive fact-finding, the Korean-American intermediary proposes a solution and allows the disputants time to find ways to bridge their differences. Apology signals that a settlement has been reached.

In view of these cultural differences, mediators need to be ready to make certain adjustments to their concepts about mediation. Depending on the cultural needs of the disputants, mediators can sensitize themselves to recognize that their preferred procedures for intervention might need some fine tuning or even major alterations. The client's cultural and ethnic identity must be considered. La Resche (1992) advises that if conflicts in multiethnic communities are to be handled effectively, third parties must, at a minimum, become knowledgeable about different conflict values and forums so they can respond flexibly and competently when persons different from themselves request assistance. For example, mandatory mediation programs face this very issue. Should these programs coerce people into a process that violates their cultural and ethnic values or embarrasses them? A deeper understanding of diversity is called for that goes beyond the customs that are readily manifested. Documenting an ethnic group's orientation toward interpersonal conflicts and methods for handling them is only the initial step in preparing a full complement of true alternative dispute resolution services.

For example, disputants from cultures that seek to avoid conflict are likely to be much more anxious and uncertain than mediators might normally expect. In many group-oriented cultures, the norm is to internalize anger and anxiety and never to express it publicly.

It is possible that conflict-avoidant disputants might not even overtly manifest the anxiety and shame that they are feeling in any recognizable way during the mediation session so that the mediator might incorrectly assume that the situation is normal. The resentment that these disputants feel for being put through such humiliation greatly increases the probability that they will deadlock or fail to comply with any settlement. Silence and absence of protestation can easily be interpreted as cooperation. In this context, silence is as likely an indicator of low communication satisfaction.

The Need for Cultural Sensitivity

When culturally diverse disputants are part of mediation, mediators might assume that they need to examine their own assumptions about the nature of conflict and how these conflictants need to be approached. This perspective is consistent with the philosophy of most mediator training efforts aimed at remaining sensitive to disputants' needs. In cross-cultural conflict, an appropriate starting point for mediators is not to see themselves as "settlement experts" but as students eager to learn about the tension between the disputants' underlying motives and the surface features of the conflict. Furthermore, it is likely that usual strategies for eliciting discussion and for engendering cooperation may fall short in such a mediation. It would be easy for mediators who adopt an "expert" approach to conclude that culturally different conflictants were being uncooperative and stubborn when they might be from a culture that discourages the open expression of problems as being overly individualistic and improper. Mediators must guard against making these unfavorable attributions, which will impair their ability to mediate. A documented parallel example for this context can be seen in jury behaviors. Jurors in the U.S. courtroom, for example, are similarly susceptible to this tendency of giving negative attributions to unexpected behavior of foreign-born defendants (Bresnahan & Kim, 1991).

In addition, the ethnicity and gender of the mediator plays a significant role in the conflict. For example, ethnic-minority disputants might find it difficult to work with mediators that appear middle-class, educated, and Anglo. More often than not, a legacy of unfair treatment has socialized racial and ethnic minority disputants to expect failure in every interaction with the dominant group mediator. Powerlessness is defined as the feeling that one is "controlled, manipulated, and trapped" (Hecht, Larkey, & Johnson, 1992, p. 215). Third-party mediators ought to be aware that their relationships with these disputants are much more complex than they might initially seem. Even though a mediator might work hard at professional detachment, the fact of his or her power status as a member of a historically oppressive dominant group will intrude on the mediation. This power imbalance inherent in the relationship between mediator and disputant can inhibit any attempts by the mediator to empower the disputants. It can also mute meaningful, constructive elicitation of dialogue between disputants. In many cases, the court-appointed mediator is clearly a gatekeeper for institutional power. Donohue (1991) observes, "This official, court-connected status gives mediators considerable power because they are inside the system that will ultimately decide the outcome" (p. 7). Even in community-based mediation when the mediator has no power as arbitrator of the dispute, the third-party mediator still represents authority.

Persons of color from the United States or another culture can be justifiably pessimistic about what mediation will mean for them personally. Learned helplessness often prompts them to expect that they will get the short end of a settlement. Handled poorly by mediators, these differences can transform into real barriers to a settlement. In the next section of this chapter we present a model that will elucidate some key factors that mediators might use as a starting point for understanding the significance of cultural differences for interaction. Although this model was designed to compare culture in organizations, we believe that the cultural factors it identifies can also offer insights in situations requiring third party intervention. Finally, Berg-Cross and Zoppetti (1991) caution that individuals often exhibit beliefs that are different from their cultural stereotypes. Berg-Cross and Zoppetti advise (1991) that "errors of stereotyping can indeed become more problematic than errors of cultural insensitivity. Cultural knowledge devoid of personal knowledge inevitably leads to stereotyping and an inability to relate empathetically" (p. 7). This is a delicate balance for a mediator to achieve.

A Model for Understanding Cultural Differences

We must first begin with a definition for *culture* that is sensitive to conflict. Nadler et al. (1985) define culture as "the system of socially created and learned standards for perceiving and acting, shared by members of an identity group" (p. 89). The key to this definition is its focus on identity groups. These groups set the standard for determining what counts as acceptable or unacceptable, cooperative or uncooperative communication. Whenever outsiders lack access to these standards, they risk miscommunication and expanded relational distance. An out-group member's inability to predict, anticipate, and interpret results in greater communication uncertainty (Gudykunst & Nishida, 1984). Further, Nadler et al. (1985) contend that culture impacts conflict in three ways: how it is conceived, how it is conducted, and how it is resolved. This conceptualization is particularly useful because it emphasizes that culture affects the way in which people interpret differences, how they communicate to manage those differences, and how they create options for resolving those differences. This chapter will use these three categories of culture as a framework for discussing how culture impacts mediation. Specifically, this chapter will merge Donohue's (1991) mediation models with Hofstede's (1989) model of cultural difference to create a new understanding of how culture relates to mediation choices. The impact will be discussed from Nadler et al.'s three-stage impact model.

Hofstede's Model of Cultural Differences

Power Distance

According to Hofstede (1989), the four main dimensions on which cultures can be differentiated include power distance, uncertainty avoidance, individualism, and masculinity. Power distance is a relational indicator that focuses on how powerless people deal with their status of inequality. This inequality can be based on a number of factors including physical and mental characteristics, social status and prestige, wealth, power, and law. Hofstede developed his power distance index by systematically asking three questions of thousands of people in 40 countries: Do you fear disagreement with people who have power over you? Do you think the people who have power over you make decisions without consulting you? Do you want them to make decisions without consulting you? Low power-distance countries value independence, loose supervision, consultative management, friendly disagreement, positive value of wealth and reward, and legitimate and expert power. High power-distance countries value conformity, close supervision, autocratic paternalistic managers, conflict avoidance, negative association with wealth, prefer coercive referent power, with more centralization and broader acceptance of authority. Predictably, Hofstede found that Euro-American countries tended to be low in power distance.

Uncertainty

Uncertainty is a well-documented communication construct that examines how people deal with situations of interactional ambiguity (Berger & Calabrese, 1975; Sanders & Wiseman, 1991). High uncertainty avoidance suggests intolerance for ambiguity. Countries have been characterized by their tolerance for uncertainty and their need to have rules. In high uncertainty-avoidance countries, change is seen as threatening, there is less achievement motivation, fear of failure discourages risk-taking, there are many rules that are observed, conflict is seen as undesirable, and competition is discouraged. Low uncertainty-avoidance countries welcome change, have high personal motivation to achieve, encourage greater risk-taking, are highly pragmatic, see conflict as positive, and feature high tolerance for ambiguity (Hofstede, 1989, pp. 132-133).

Individualism

Individualism is a broadly studied social construct that addresses concept of the self with respect to others. The relationship and obligation that we have to other people is referred to as collectivism (Bond & Forgas, 1984; Hui & Villareal, 1989; Triandis, Bontempo, Villareal, Asai, & Lucca, 1988; Triandis, Leung, Villareal, & Clark, 1985). Tension between primacy of the individual and primacy of the group is an insightful indicator of how conflict plays itself out. Conflict as a response can both protect and fortify individuality from undermining challenge (Ting-Toomey, 1985, 1988). It can strengthen self-esteem, but it can also be very destructive. Conflict is uncomfortable in situations of group primacy where individual goals ordinarily give way to group goals. Ting-Toomey (1988) posits that individualistic cultures use direct, dominating, goal-oriented conflict styles while collective cultures tend to prefer conflict avoidance. Leung and Lind (1986) similarly found that North American subjects preferred competitive, adversarial procedures while collectivist cultures advocated more passive, indirect, face-sensitive conflict resolution strategies. Trubisky, Ting-Toomey, and Lin (1991) observed that: "On a comparative basis, members of individualist cultures tend to stress the value of straight talk and tend to verbalize overtly their individual wants and needs, while members of collectivist cultures tend to stress the values of contemplative talk and discretion in voicing one's opinions and feelings" (p. 68).

Masculinity

Masculinity is a descriptor for a paradigm of interactive styles that are associated with socialized gender. The masculine paradigm includes behaviors that emphasize assertiveness, self-reliance, self-actualization, and give preference to instrumental tasks. The counterpart for masculine style is feminine style. Feminine style includes behaviors that are nurturing, affiliative, helpful rather than competitive, compassionate, and conformative. Expressive tasks are preferred in the feminine mode. Men and women from other cultures and ethnic and racial minorities in the United States do not necessarily value ambition, competition, and individual achievement in the same way that Euramericans value such traits. Strong goal orientation and desire for material rewards may not be the primary value. Masculinity will determine whether conflict orientation is seen as adversarial or cooperative.

Hofstede's (1989) method of differentiating cultures is useful for mediators because it provides a language for understanding cultural biases inherent in the various kinds of models mediators use to assist disputants. For example, mediators might encounter disputants who appear uncomfortable discussing differences, want the mediator to make the decision, express little interest in taking risks that might threaten group norms, and avoid competitiveness. The mediation model, however, might require disputants to communicate in ways that are inconsistent with these cultural orientations. The model might require them to confront differences, take risks, reject mediator decision making, and threaten group norms. If a mediation model contradicts or even rejects the disputants' cultural orientations, is it inequitable for them? To answer this question mediators first need to know something about the cultural biases inherent in their mediation models. To provide this information, this chapter will turn to a discussion of Donohue's (1991) models of mediation that include an assessment of how they function with respect to Hofstede's cultural dimensions.

Mediation Models

Mediator Control

In his assessment of the divorce mediation literature, Donohue (1991) offers four distinct mediation models that appear fairly widespread in practice. The first, labeled the mediator control model, has also been called the "med-arb model" (McGillicuddy, Welton, & Pruitt, 1987). In this model, mediators can become arbitrators if they believe that the parties have deadlocked and remain unable to create an agreement on their own. This model is most widely used in community mediation centers that are not court connected. The McGillicuddy et al. research comparing this model to straight mediation indicates that parties communicate more productively and responsibly when they know the mediator is evaluating their contributions for possible arbitration. In addition, they are more satisfied with the outcome when compared to straight mediation. The risk in this model is that mediators might turn too quickly to arbitration, thereby discouraging them from being patient and working hard with the parties to create and sift through a wide range of alternative solutions to the dispute. Nevertheless, the data suggest that these risks are minimal and that disputants are more satisfied with outcomes produced from this model.

This model exhibits some interesting cultural biases based on Hofstede's (1989) dimensions. First, people from high power-distance cultures might prefer this model because it takes a fairly autocratic approach to mediation, at least when it turns to arbitration. In fact, they would probably prefer that the mediator turn more quickly, rather than less quickly, to arbitration, particularly because they value conflict avoidance. People from high power-distance cultures look to a centralized authority to make a decision, As a result, they could be expected to gravitate toward arbitration and away from mediation.

Second, the mediator control model offers both comforting and troubling features to people from high uncertainty avoidant cultures. The troubling feature is that disputants are required to control agreements. This lack of structure, and the need to remain flexible in building creative solutions, creates a great deal of uncertainty about both the mediation process and outcome options. This issue is probably least troubling to people from high uncertainty-avoidant cultures with the mediator control model. At least if deadlocks occur, the process tightens up considerably when the mediator turns arbitrator. Arbitration offers more structure about how outcomes will be determined and thus might prove more attractive to people who shun uncertainty. As a result, people who prefer these cultures might choose not to participate in the mediation part and push to have the mediator turn arbitrator and make the decision.

On the other hand, mediation might offer a comforting aspect to people from high uncertainty-avoidant cultures. Much of the concern about uncertainty has to do with the effects of the dispute on the relationships between the parties. Uncertainty about the process leads to uncertainty about the effects of the dispute on the relationship. In this aspect people from high uncertainty-avoidant cultures might find mediation comforting because mediation focuses on forging a mutually acceptable and cooperatively achieved solution to a problem. It is probably this feature of mediation that most appeals to Chinese in their extensive use of mediation (Wall & Blum, 1991). Mediators might thus pay special attention to relational objectives when working with people from high uncertainty- avoidant cultures.

Third, the mediator control model conforms to valued features of collectivist cultural orientation, at least when the mediator is still mediating. In fact, the spirit of mediation centers around developing noncompetitive approaches to problem solving. The mediator advocates for the disputants so they are not forced to confront one another directly. Yet, the mediator control model also focuses on creating a specific solution to a specific problem with the emphasis on problem solving and not necessarily relational development. Mediators want specific solutions and would view a repaired relationship without an agreement as less desirable than the reverse. So, from that standpoint, the mediator control model supports an individualistic cultural perspective that is more aimed at achieving task goals with little emphasis on relational objectives. However, the primary emphasis in mediation focuses on generating solutions that are desirable for both disputants, which suggests more of a collectivist orientation.

Fourth, the mediator control model's emphasis on achieving task objectives suggests more of a masculine cultural priority. Feminine orientations value more expressive tasks. Yet, any mediation process aims at achieving the more feminine virtues of building a nurturing, affiliative, helpful communication context. But, the emphasis on solving the problem, particularly when the disputants know that the mediator can arbitrate or force a solution when deadlock appears likely, suggests the mediator control model to be more masculine oriented.

The mediator can address these cultural issues from a number of perspectives, most of which involve spending more time listening to disputants' concerns and perspectives. For example, if the mediator senses that the parties want arbitration without mediation, the mediator might lengthen the orientation session by talking about the need for mediation and cooperative problem solving. Gaining feedback from parties about this issue might prove difficult, but addressing it up front is probably more productive than not directly confronting the issue. To soften this discussion a bit, and to soften fear of change from uncertainty avoidance, the mediator might consider caucusing first with the disputants to learn more about their perspectives on the issues and on conflict as well. If parties value a more collectivist orientation that discourages face-to-face conflict, caucusing might prove particularly useful. Finally, the mediator can soften the competitive quality of the mediator control model by advocating more vigorously for clients who might feel reluctant to advocate for themselves. Mediators should be prepared to do this for any client, but clients who prefer a more feminine-oriented culture might find this advocacy particularly useful.

Interventionist

The interventionist model also emphasizes a fairly powerful mediation role. Developed mostly for divorce mediation, the interventionist model assumes responsibility for the best interests of parties not represented in the conflict. In child custody, visitation, and support-focused divorce mediation, the mediator typically assumes responsibility for ensuring that the disputants' discussions and agreements serve the best interests of the children. As a result, the mediator evaluates disputants' options, creates appropriate options, and otherwise "moves" parties in the "desired" direction. The mediator does not have the option of turning to arbitration in the event of deadlock. Yet the mediator exercises a great deal of control over the process and must guard against developing an adversarial role with disputants. Most evaluations of this model reveal fairly high user satisfaction with the process and fairly high compliance with agreements (Donohue, 1991). The high degree of satisfaction stems from the high degree of control the mediator exercises during the process. Parties are restricted from engaging in unproductive conflict because that kind of discussion distracts from forging agreements in the best interest of the children. Thus parties stay on task and get things done.

Many of the kinds of cultural biases associated with mediator control are evident in this model. The exception is the high power-distance feature of Hofstede's (1989) model. Lacking the option of becoming an arbitrator in the event of deadlock reduces the authoritative nature of the mediation process. The mediator cannot act paternalistically with respect to outcome control. However, the process control assumed by an interventionist posture plays into a high power-distance orientation. In that case, the disputants might look to the mediator to generate most of the options for settling the dispute; and they might even encourage the mediator to select options and create an agreement. Mediators might even appreciate this perspective because the parties would appear as quite compliant and "cooperative." However, the danger in taking the bait here is creating agreements that have not received sufficient input and buy-in from the parties. Is the agreement a legitimate outgrowth of resolving important issues and interests or an authoritative product of the mediator?

Handling this problem again requires an additional time commitment, both in the orientation process and in pursuing caucusing sessions. The mediator must ensure a full understanding of the mediator's role and a full hearing of the issues dividing the parties. Without these kinds of commitments, the mediator can never really know if the mediation solves the problems or creates more problems.

Disputant Control

In the disputant control model, mediators try to facilitate an agreement between the disputants that they control. Unlike the mediator control model, the mediator has no option for arbitration in the event of deadlock. And, in contrast with the interventionist model, the mediator has no interest in protecting anyone potentially affected by the outcome. The mediator simply helps the parties create whatever agreement they feel is appropriate. This model is used frequently in community settings, such as neighbor disputes, in which the agreement bears only on those parties with few others affected. Most of these mediations involve one-shot sessions, largely because mediators stick only to the issues in dispute while avoiding any relational or other problems that might arise during the discussion. Unlike the previous two models, this disputant control model is more neutral with respect to power distance. Because mediators are less focused on the quality of the outcomes, they communicate less power distance. Clearly they remain in charge of a process that encourages open conflict and finds its legitimacy from some kind of centralized authority. Yet the mediator remains less autocratic in controlling outcome. As a result, power distance biases are much less apparent with this model, even though many of the other cultural biases associated with mediation remain. This model still places parties in a context that promotes uncertainty because divisive issues are addressed openly and parties with a conflict-avoidant orientation might find this disquieting. In addition, the mediation process generally promotes individual goals over group goals, and it remains relatively masculine, competitive, and task oriented.

Relational Development

A relational development model focuses less on specific task issues and more on addressing such relational problems as trust, control, and affiliation. Typically mediators use this model as a preliminary step in support of some other mediation model that seeks to resolve nonrelational issues. Often times, disputants come to mediation unprepared to discuss legal issues because of relational animosity. Parties use the mediation to punish one another instead of focusing on the issues. These couples might be referred to a relational mediation process that resembles a therapy session. In these sessions, parties talk openly, in a fairly unstructured process, about the key relational problems they face. It is not uncommon in a divorce for one party not to want to cooperate during mediation, to hold onto the marital relationship. The relational mediator seeks open communication between the parties to explore the relational divisions and how parties might put them aside to focus on legal issues. This kind of support system is not particularly common for communities or courts to offer. Relational mediation might occur more frequently through churches or some other setting that helps parties in distress. These mediations end when the disputants feel that further progress is no longer possible.

The relational development mediation model is most likely to reduce power distance between the mediator and disputants. Parties seeking to communicate under these kinds of authoritative conditions should find this model the least satisfying. Typically, these mediators exercise little process or outcome control. They hope to conduct an open discussion of relational divisions while not even attempting to deal with legal or other substantive issues. Because it does promote discussion, however, parties cannot easily avoid conflict. As a result, some power distance remains. Compared to the other models that have been discussed, this model concentrates more on a collectivist orientation because it looks to maintain group relations as a first priority. By promoting relational development, this model also supports many of the feminine qualities of being affiliative, nurturing, helpful, and expressive. However, the model still promotes some uncertainty by openly addressing conflict and asking parties to take risks and change their relational behavior toward one another.

Mediating the Torrez Community Conflict

Which of these models might most productively address intergroup conflict such as the Torrez case? To answer this question, several issues must be addressed. First, and most importantly, the issue of culture is central to this dispute. The groups involved in the dispute are city and police officials, who are largely from the dominant culture, and the Hispanic community. Given this mix, it is generally best to adopt a model of mediation that is most empowering to the group holding the least power as a means of balancing power (Donohue & Kolt, 1992). From Hofstede's (1989) model, the traditional Hispanic culture demonstrates high power distance, uncertainty avoidance, and collectivism. This would suggest that they might not prefer to confront the conflict, particularly since it involved confronting the centralized authority of the city. Yet they value a relationally cohesive community that the conflict threatens. As a result, they would probably prefer an informal mediation process that is relationally centered, such as the relational development model.

In this particular dispute, however, the city proposed a solution aimed at relational development that involved city officials meeting with Hispanic community leaders, without a mediator, to discuss concerns. This session failed to mend police-community relations because it violated several Hispanic cultural orientations. Specifically, it caused militant Hispanics to oppose more compliant community leaders who had accepted the official finding and seemed to be knuckling under to pressure. The community had become polarized by this incident, violating a need for collectivism. Also counter to cultural orientation, the meeting increased uncertainty in relations between Hispanics, the police, and the city government. Growing uncertainty is illustrated by one mother who testified: "I'm here to hold all of you accountable. I have sons and I have a lot of fear that if my sons go out there and look the wrong way or dress the wrong way, they might encounter what Torrez encountered."[1] Power distance was also increased when the police asked a panel of minority leaders to examine the police and death investigation reports. Police dismissive response to recommendations made by this panel further aggravated power distance. Thus the solution was culturally insensitive on every count—the police were totally exonerated without so much as a reprimand, the killing was pronounced to have been warranted, the minority leaders appeared to be co-opted, the Torrez family was left angry and grieving, and the Hispanic community became factionalized.

The failure of this meeting suggests that insufficient planning was given to structuring the dispute resolution process in this case. As a result, the second issue associated with creating an appropriate mediation process for this dispute centers around the primary focus of the conflict, substantive, or relational issues. Clearly, the primary issues dividing the groups are relational. Members of the Hispanic community do not trust the city administration's sense of justice in this case. The Hispanic community feels unrespected with little opportunity to receive fair treatment. This lack of trust suggests that mediation ought to begin with a focus on this fundamental relational concern. Without addressing this key issue, it is unlikely that the groups would enjoy any success negotiating the extent to which the police overreacted in dealing with the Torrez case. Thus the relational development model seems like a good place to start with this conflict, given the dysfunctional quality of the relationship between the Hispanic community and city officials.

This recommendation suggests that a more controlling form of mediation might serve to escalate the conflict as opposed to de-escalating it. Hofstede's (1989) model provides some interesting insights into understanding this kind of relationally focused intergroup conflict. Power distance is illustrated both in Torrez's clash with the police and in the relationship of the police to the Hispanic community. The police were looking for an armed and dangerous Hispanic male suspect in a poor neighborhood. Smith et al. (1984) suggest that status of the neighborhood has a big role in police decision making about responding to a call and what level of police intervention is needed. As a result, police and official sources of power are often viewed as highly oppressive. Any attempt to draw upon a mediation model reinforcing the sense of oppression that the Hispanic community is experiencing would certainly serve to escalate relational tension.

Third, it is also important to understand that this mediation involves large community groups as opposed to individuals representing only themselves. The primary implication of this complexity according to Bercovitch (1991) is twofold. First, the selection of the mediator. According to Bercovitch the mediator ought to be someone who is very powerful and well respected by both sides. Typically, this person is a strong political leader with whom each side has worked in the past. Second, the mediator ought to work extensively with caucusing and other prenegotiation strategies to plan carefully how the mediation will be arranged to address the needs of both sides. Bercovitch stresses the importance of prenegotiation planning and communication to deal with complex relational issues. Donohue and Ramesh (1992) stress the need for prenegotiation in their examination of how to improve relationships during negotiation. The mediator ought therefore to be neutral, prestigious, and committed to preplanning and caucusing. Perhaps co-mediation with one member of each community present might also be considered in working with this case. Whichever options are selected, it is clear that the Torrez situation should have been handled much differently by all parties involved, but certainly by the city and the police department because they are the high power parties and primarily responsible for equalizing power in this dispute.

Conclusions

Mediating intergroup conflicts will become more challenging as we approach the next century and the United States becomes more ethnically, and thus relationally, complex. According to Lopez and Espiritu (1990), new immigration since 1965 has both facilitated and hindered the development of panethnic consciousness. Some segments of the majority have reacted to this transformation in immigration with violence. This violence has prompted the development of stronger panethnic coalitions. As we see from Worchel (1986), coalitions that develop in the face of violence and other threats tend to be short lived.

Blalock (1982) suggests that some minorities are seen as "middleman minorities." This is a minority group that shares features with the dominant group and that stands between the dominant group and more disadvantaged minorities. In times of prosperity, all is well, but "during periods of stress the middleman minority will serve as an ideal scapegoat to the degree that it is the apparent source of frustration, it is politically unprotected yet visible, and it appears similar to the elite group with respect to economic position and function" (Blalock, 1982, p. 84). The majority maintains the "middleman minority" both as a source of cheap labor and to perform necessary functions that are dangerous or marginally profitable (Yu, 1983, p. 36).

Mediators must remain current on issues of changing cultural diversity to function effectively. For example, mediators can make a judgment about the degree of stakeholding for conflictants based on several criteria. Is the culturally different conflictant a temporary sojourner or a permanent stakeholder? Is the relationship between disputants temporary or long term? Does the mediator have an option of making the decision, or is the role merely facilitative and consultive? What do both parties have to gain and to lose in the mediation? How critical is face-saving to disputants participating in the mediation? For disputants accustomed to conflict avoidance, the presence of an outsider is potentially stressful and embarrassing. In such cases, several possibilities are likely. The conflict-avoidant disputant will be likely to clam up and secretly decide not to comply with the settlement. Mediators should be wary that silence is not agreement. If parties refuse to participate, the mediator should slow the process down and caucus separately with both parties to learn their positions. Another possibility that might be encountered is that, pushed to the limit of endurance with an uncomfortable mediation, the culturally different disputant might cling to an extreme position that precludes compromise because all hope of face-saving is lost. The mediator should be aware that aggression and defensiveness can be early warning indicators that this extreme face loss is underway. Once again, an aware and sensitive mediator can intervene and stop this face loss before the mediation moves into deadlock. In all cases, the mediator must remain especially observant and attentive to individual needs when dealing with disputants from different subcultures. Finally, mediators express cultural sensitivity by carefully assessing their own intervention values to see whether they are appropriate for this conflictant and for this context of mediation.

Note

1. "Police chief: FBI investigating Torrez slaying." *Lansing State Journal,* November 13, 1991, pp. 1A & 2A.

Why is an understanding of how children interact in conflict critical in developing school mediation programs? What cultural and social factors need to be taken into account in peer mediation?

8

"Teach Your Children Well"

Recommendations for Peer Mediation Programs

Tricia S. Jones
Heidi Brinkman

IN RESPONSE TO increasing violence and unrest in American schools, educators are increasingly committed to confronting broader issues of social responsibility and adjustment. In elementary and secondary schools that interest is manifest in a variety of programs targeted at teaching children how to deal more effectively with conflict situations. Whether these skills are taught under the rubric of peace education (Swadener, 1988; Tabachnick, 1990), social skills training (Maag, 1990), law-related education (Hawaii State Department of Education, 1985), cooperative learning (Levy, 1989; Manning & Allen, 1987; Margolis, 1990; Slavin, 1991), or general conflict training (Harms, 1987), a key component has been the institution of mediation training and peer mediation programs.

Peer mediation programs are still novel and relatively untested. Incorporating current knowledge about how children understand and respond to conflict may improve the design and delivery of

159

these programs. This chapter presents several recommendations, based on social scientific literature, for administrators, teachers, and parents who are interested in maximizing the benefits of peer mediation for their students and children.

Overview of Peer Mediation Programs

The history of school-based mediation programs is brief, spanning less than three decades. Maxwell (1989) has chronicled their genesis in the form of the Quaker nonviolence project in New York City Schools and their progress through support of community justice centers, Educators for Social Responsibility, and the National Association for Mediation in Education. Recent estimates suggest more than 300 peer mediation programs (Brinkman, 1991) in operation.

Why the explosive and continuing interest in peer mediation? Initially, some programs were developed to decrease violence and antisocial behavior among children; especially among children "at-risk" of dropping out, becoming involved with substance abuse, gangs, or other forms of juvenile delinquency (Social Science Education Consortium, 1987). Others sought a mechanism to reduce disciplinary problems in schools and free teachers to spend more time teaching (Burrell & Vogl, 1990). Some programs reflect educators' beliefs that conflict is an important aspect of students' socialization and maturation and should be addressed as such (Koch & Miller, 1987; Maxwell, 1989).

Underlying all of these motivations for program development lies a common perception that school children encounter conflict but do not know how to handle it productively. Children have more conflicts with schoolmates than any other group including siblings (Venkataramaiah & Kumari, 1975, 1986). And, in general, children rely more on antisocial (coercion and manipulation) than prosocial (reasoning and discussion) conflict strategies (Krappmann & Oswald, 1987) that often lead to strong feelings of guilt and unhappiness (Venkataramaiah & Kumari, 1975, 1986).

Cycles of antisocial strategy use and resultant displeasure can engender poor relationships between classmates in which peer rejection motivates disruptive classroom behavior, negative affect in the classroom, and negative attitudes toward other students (Johnson,

1981). Even more seriously, this cycle is related to higher drop-out rates, more juvenile delinquency, and a greater risk of mental health problems (Callias, Frosh, & Michie, 1987). The key to breaking this cycle is to teach children more constructive means of dealing with conflict. Mediation has been suggested as one such technique. Peer mediation programs in the schools train children to act as neutral third parties to intervene and assist other students in the resolution of their disputes. However, there is no simple template for these programs. They vary in terms of target population, nature of training, and formality of mediation.

Peer mediation programs have been attempted in elementary, middle, and high schools (Lam, 1988) with targeted grade levels encompassing kindergarten through senior year. However, the majority of elementary school programs limit involvement to third through sixth grades (Kaufmann, 1991).

Generally, training involves a two-pronged effort. First, a general conflict skills training program (that may involve just students in the targeted grades or expand to include the entire school community and parents) teaches basic conflict management concepts and techniques, usually in 15 to 20 hours of instruction (Davis & Porter, 1985; Lam, 1988), including problem solving, assertiveness training, interpersonal communication skills, critical thinking, and listening skills (Hutchins, 1990).

More specific mediation training is provided to students who are selected or volunteer as student mediators. In addition to the information and instructional formats discussed above, peer mediators are instructed to use a simple mediation process such as the following (Brinkman, 1991, p. 9):

1. introduce yourself and ask if mediation is desired
2. get agreement to ground rules (no interrupting, no name calling, honesty, agreement to solve the problem)
3. ask each party for a description of the problem
4. paraphrase what you have heard
5. ask each party what he or she could do
6. ask each party what he or she needs the other to do
7. restate
8. generate ideas with parties

9. ask each party what is best for them
10. restate
11. ask if resolution is fair and can be carried out
12. congratulate the parties

Training may be conducted by external parties (Salfrank, 1991), teachers, or a combination. In most cases external consultants train teachers who then train students and other members of the school community (Kaufmann, 1991). Student mediators are usually selected by teachers and/or administrators with attempts to represent a cross-section of the student body (Davis & Porter, 1985; Lam, 1988).

Initially, the application of the peer mediation program was to "playground" or "lunchroom" conflicts. In this informal model, mediators, usually working in teams of two, survey the playground or lunchroom watching for erupting conflicts or arguments that have not developed into fights or physical violence. The mediators then ask disputants whether they are interested in having their dispute mediated. If the students are amenable, mediation occurs.

However, some programs, such as the Milwaukee Public School System program that was pilot tested in elementary, middle, and high schools, use a more formal system (Burrell & Vogl, 1990) in which conflicts are referred to mediation by students, teachers, or administrators. If participants mutually agree to follow the peer mediator's procedures for the interaction, mediation takes place in a private and confidential setting.

There is surprisingly little research on the efficacy of these programs, possibly because more energy is currently invested in establishing programs than in evaluating them. The preliminary results, based largely on anecdotal evidence and qualitative assessments, suggest that peer mediation programs reduce incidents of violence (Social Science Research Consortium, 1987) and incidents of conflict (Davis & Porter, 1985), improve students' attitudes toward conflict (Lam, 1988), and increase student mediators' self-esteem (Kaufmann, 1991).

Recommendations for Peer Mediation Programs

A basic principle of any form of intervention is to tailor the activity to the person(s) involved. Peer mediation programs can protect the social learning opportunities and increase the positive benefits of conflict if they are designed to be sensitive to the developmental stage and social context of the children involved. The following sections review some key research and theory on children and conflict in order to derive sound, specific recommendations for the design and delivery of peer mediation in the schools. Although children differ from adults in their perception of and reaction to conflict, they are not naive social actors. Children use conflict to produce social organization, create political alignments, and negotiate their practical interests in a changing set of social relationships (Maynard, 1985a, 1985b). Conflict interactions may also function to increase autonomy and independence in non-peer, and especially child-adult, interactions (Kuczynski & Kochanska, 1990; Kuczynski, Kochanska, Radke-Yarrow, & Girnius-Brown, 1987).

Adjust to the Children's Developmental Stage

The most important insight from the social scientific literature is that children operate at different levels of competence with regard to conflict. As they age and develop cognitively, they understand and respond to conflict differently.

Piaget argued that social conflict among peers reduces egocentrism and stimulates differentiation (Aboud, 1981). Initially, a child (until age 6) is very egocentric, unable to distinguish self from other, resulting in a focus on self-needs and self-fulfillment. The child then learns to conform to social norms (until age 10-11), at first rigidly (from ages 5-8) but later more because of the desire to cooperate (from ages 8-11). As the child enters early adolescence, he or she differentiates self from other, recognizing the needs and interests of each and attempting to reconcile these interests in ongoing interaction.

In addition to cognitive development, children also undergo a process of moral development (Colby & Kohlberg, 1981; Colby, Kohlberg, Gibbs, & Lieberman, 1983). As children grow older, they are better able to integrate diverse points of view on moral conflicts and are more likely to assess and appreciate contextual/situational factors when responding to moral conflict.

Working with an appreciation of both cognitive and moral development, Selman and his colleagues have contributed significantly to our understanding of children and conflict. Selman (1980, 1981) posits three underlying dimensions of cognition that change with development: temporal orientation (from here-and-now to the future), focus of conflicts (from physical acts to people as psychological beings to the relationship itself), and conceptions of relations (from unilateral to bilateral to mutual). Based on this theory, Selman and Demorest (1984) created a four-level model of interpersonal negotiation strategies (INSs) used by children.

In *Level 0,* the lowest developmental level (usually lasting until age 3), children operate from momentary and physicalistic orientations. This level is typified by *primitive fight-or-flight reactions.* Conflicts are resolved through physical force or by halting interaction. Prototypical INSs at this stage are described as follows. Other-transforming strategies include: verbally drowning out the other, grabbing impulsively, or forcefully/physically repelling the other. Self-transforming strategies include: taking flight, using automatic affective withdrawal, or responding with robotic obedience.

Level 1 (operating at ages 3 through 6) adds the feature of an appreciation of the subjective and psychological effects of conflict. However, these effects are seen as only applying to self, not other; thus, conflict is not yet understood as a mutual disagreement. At Level 1, conflict orientation is best described as *win-lose or competitive egocentrism* and involves other-transforming strategies such as orders and threats; while self-transforming strategies include: making weak or tentative initiatives, accommodating to the other, acting victimized, or appealing to external parties.

In *Level 2* (during ages 7 to 12), conflict is seen as bilateral but not mutual. Children realize that one must get agreement from both parties, but they don't understand that these must be mutually satisfying agreements. Thus, children are involved in *strategic cooperation to protect self-interest.* Level 2 other-transforming strategies include: using friendly persuasion, seeking allies for support of own ideas, and impressing the other with one's own talents and abilities. The self-transforming strategies at Level 2 involve: asserting self-needs but making these secondary to other's needs and confronting marked inequality.

Finally, at the highest development level, *Level 3* (usually beginning between the ages of 12 and 15), conflicts are seen as residing within a relationship, and thus, only mutually satisfying solutions are acceptable, requiring truly *collaborative negotiation.* There is no distinction between self- and other-transforming strategies. Instead, due to the integrative developmental orientation, the child anticipates and integrates possible reactions by the other, balances a focus on relationship with a focus on individual goals, and negotiates with a view to relational consistency over time. Selman and Demorest (1984) stress that children may use strategies representative of their highest level of development as well as strategies representative of lower levels. However, they cannot intentionally use or understand strategies that are more advanced than their current level of socio-cognitive development (Selman, Beardslee, Schultz, Krupa, & Podorefsky, 1986; Stone, 1981). Indirect support for this model comes from studies of children's persuasion and compromising strategies. The level of persuasive strategy usage (more or less adaptive) (Delia, Kline, & Burleson, 1979) and the frequency of persuasive appeal usage increases significantly with age (Finley & Humphreys, 1974), thus improving chances for more sophisticated resolution of conflicts (Eisenberg & Garvey, 1981). Similarly, children use compliance-gaining strategies more frequently and more adaptively (Haslett, 1983) and demonstrate a greater tendency to compromise (Clark, O'Dell, & Willihnganz, 1986; Levya & Furth, 1986) as they age.

In addition to describing developmental levels of conflict competence, an important goal of this work is to foster adolescent social competence, or "the ability to create negotiation strategies which meet the mutual, shared needs of self and other(s); and . . . support the formation of lasting, stable, constructive interpersonal relationships in young adulthood" (Brion-Meisels & Selman, 1984, p. 291).

Assessment instruments have been created to evaluate operative levels of INS functioning and to design intervention strategies to promote higher level functioning (Yeates & Selman, 1989). These instruments have been used in observations of classroom interaction (Brion-Meisels, Lowenheim, & Rendeiro, 1982) and to study how children respond to teacher and peer criticism (Adalbjarnardottir & Selman, 1989) or handle conflict in classroom meetings (Selman, 1980).

The INS model has also informed the design of school curricula and intervention programs to improve children's interpersonal conflict competency. The individual competence analyses provide a baseline assessment of the students' interpersonal awareness and functional skills. Intervention efforts are then matched to the students' level of competence (Brion-Meisels, Rendeiro, & Lowen-heim, 1984; Selman & Glidden, 1987; Yeates & Selman, 1989). Clearly, children's conflict orientation and behavior is a function of their developmental level. Because developmental level is generally age-specific, this information suggests three basic recommendations for peer mediation programs.

First, peer mediation programs should be targeted at appropriate grade levels. Even simplistic models of mediation assume that mediation is most effective when the participants to the process can understand and appreciate integrative orientations. Some would even argue that real mediation cannot occur without disputants who have achieved this level of competency. Most mediation scholars agree that if the disputants are not capable of collaborative orientation and behavior, mediation is less beneficial for them and probably less effective in achieving resolution to the dispute (Moore, 1986).

Developmental theory indicates that children in early elementary grades have probably not achieved integrative conflict competency. Even assuming the inexact and general nature of age parameters given for the developmental levels, most children are not ready to comprehend and implement truly collaborative strategies until the end of elementary school or the beginning of middle school.

Some peer mediation programs have targeted children as young as kindergarten, however, and the majority operate in elementary schools with children from Grades 3 through 6 involved as peer mediators. Expecting children in kindergarten through second grade to understand and undertake mediation efforts is probably not realistic. Even involving children from third through fifth grades is questionable according to age parameters already discussed.

An alternate approach is to introduce basic conflict skills training at early grade levels (listening, communication, and critical thinking skills) and reserve mediation training and activity for later grades. This design enables all students in the school to have a basic understanding of constructive conflict management and helps ensure that mediation will have the most developmental benefits.

Second, training packages for general conflict skills training as well as peer mediation program training should be developed and tested in light of developmental levels. A quick perusal of available training materials (Kaufmann, 1991; Kriedler, 1984) suggests that adjustment for age-related competency is rare. Given time, age-specific training materials can be developed that enable peer mediation programs to maximize learning potential per grade level. Exercises, instructional curricula, and training formats should be evaluated for developmental appropriateness prior to use.

Finally, participants' INS levels could be assessed to evaluate better the impact of peer mediation programs and to improve selection of peer mediators. Assessing initial INS levels would provide a confirmation of the level of instructional material needed and mark a baseline from which change can be measured. Empirical verification of the developmental enhancement of peer mediation and conflict skills training activity may encourage more concrete support of these programs.

Likewise, assessment of INS competency could serve as a criterion for selection of peer mediators. Assuming maintenance of representativeness criteria, this addition would ensure that students placed in these positions are capable of understanding the process and more effectively modeling it for fellow classmates.

By tailoring peer mediation and conflict skills training programs to the developmental competency of students, all parties win. Program supporters will have increased the likelihood that program goals will be achieved. School administrators may see more effective use of resources and be more willing to dedicate scarce time and money to continuation of such programs. And most importantly, the children will have the maximal opportunity to increase their interpersonal conflict competency.

Appreciate the Influence of Social Context

Children's conflict does not exist in a vacuum. Rather, children are influenced by social contexts that dictate normative behavior, consequences for its violation, and latitudes for change within larger social structures. At least two aspects of social context are important to consider when designing peer mediation programs: (1) cultural context, or the social sources of rules children use to identify and remediate conflict, and (2) institutional context, or the influence of educational institutions on peer mediation efforts.

Cultural Context

Conflict is a communication event in which rules for interaction are culturally and contextually embedded. Those rules determine what kinds of events become conflictual, how the relationship between the disputants alters conflict strategies and tactics, and how broad cultural factors influence conflict behavior.

Children have conflicts for different reasons, usually because they perceive a violation of some regulation, cultural custom, or moral guideline (Much & Shweder, 1978). Cultural factors influence which rules children use to judge their own and other's behavior. And, children's conflict strategies vary depending on the type of rule being violated. For example, as Much and Shweder (1978) found, when a regulation is broken, children use legalistic reasoning and argue about competing rules that may apply to the situation, placing the focus on whether the rule itself was valid under those conditions. However, when a moral rule is violated, children discuss the extent to which the actions in question constitute a clear violation of the moral. The moral is not debated, only the extent of its violation.

Children also develop a sense of "rule conception" or sophistication that enables them to judge which rules should be privileged in certain situations. Shantz and Shantz (1982) suggest four levels of rule conceptions roughly equivalent to Selman's levels of INS competency. The levels progress from all rules being given equal weight, to judgments based on consequences for the actors, and finally to recognition that moral rules are more salient than conventions or customs. Children who have more advanced rule conceptions are more likely to have successful conflict outcomes and are less likely to resort to verbal aggression (Jose & Hennelley, 1987; Shantz, 1984).

Children are also sensitive to relational context when determining the propriety of conflict behavior. In the simplest sense, a child's perception of the relationship will determine his or her willingness to be cooperative. Children adopt more prosocial or constructive conflict strategies when the conflict involves a good or "best" friend. Children not only have fewer conflicts with friends than nonfriends, they use more negotiation strategies with friends and more "standing firm" strategies with nonfriends and achieve more equitable outcomes with friends than nonfriends (Hartup & Laursen, 1987, 1989; Hartup, Laursen, Stewart, & Eastenson, 1988; Krappmann & Oswald, 1987; Ladd & Emerson, 1984; Nelson & Aboud, 1985; Sancilio, Plumert, & Hartup, 1987).

Because rules are culturally determined, children's cultural backgrounds and influences should be considered when understanding their conflict behavior. By *culture*, we mean the broader sense of the term, an identity group, which includes racial, ethnic, religious, class, and gender influences.

Culture may influence a child's conflict orientation, personal constructs used to initiate or resolve conflict, or conflict strategies (Nadler et al., 1985). Some cultures are generally conflict avoidant rather than engaging. If conflict is engaged, cultural training may predispose a child to adopt competitive rather than cooperative behaviors. Children's conceptions of personal constructs such as fairness, trust, and power—that mitigate perceptions of operative social rules and concomitant response—are also culturally influenced. Likewise, cultural norms for expressiveness and acceptable levels of physical involvement may differ significantly and even contribute to the incidence of cross-cultural conflict (Brenneis & Lein, 1977; Kochman, 1981; Lein & Brenneis, 1978).

Social class can affect children's conflict behavior (Shantz, 1987a). Children of lower social classes quarrel more than those of upper classes (Venkataramaiah & Kumari, 1975, 1986). Children who fight more often appear less likely to concede, are more likely to employ multiple conflict strategies, use more physical aggression, and are disliked more by others than children who fight infrequently (Shantz, 1983).

Gender differences have been found in children's compliance-gaining strategies, use of violence, and perspective-taking abilities. Boys are more likely to start or initiate a conflict, to use heavy-handed persuasion tactics, and to use aggressive, confrontational tactics than girls (Camras, 1984; Guerra & Slaby, 1989; Miller, Danaher, & Forbes, 1986). Girls are more likely to avoid conflict, are better able to take the perspective of the other (Stalcup, 1981), and use more varied conflict resolution strategies than boys (Peirce & Edwards, 1988).

All these cultural influences are channeled primarily through socialization that occurs initially in familial interactions. Children do not come tabula rasa to schools and do not cease to be influenced by their families once they begin schooling. As research clearly indicates, children learn their conflict attitudes and behaviors by modeling their parents and immediate family members (Acock, 1984; Cummings, Iannotti, & Zahn-Waxler, 1985; Hranitz & Eddowes, 1990).

When children receive instruction in school that challenges cultural or normative practice in the home environment, the child faces potential resistance and disapproval from both sources. Depending on the degree of difference in expectations for behavior, the resulting tension can range from mild to severe.

How does appreciation of children's cultural context enhance the design and delivery of peer mediation programs? It suggests the need to understand operative cultures, integrate instruction that is context-sensitive, and inform or involve families about the purpose of the peer mediation program.

Understanding the operative cultural context is easily advised and less easily achieved. The key is for educators to realize that not all students in their schools have the same orientation to conflict or the same understanding of appropriate conflict behavior. This realization will help target students for involvement in the program, suggest situations where mediation may not be workable, and necessitate revision of instructional materials or timetables.

Some students are going to be more resistant to the approach suggested in peer mediation training; some may even actively ostracize others who become involved in the program. The chances for these reactions seem higher for at-risk children, the very population initially targeted for the benefits of peer mediation. Proceeding in a flexible, informed, and patient manner will help children feel more comfortable with the education and will enable modifications in instructional materials or the mediation model to fit the cultural context.

Mediation cannot be used to solve all peer problems. As the literature on rules conceptions suggests, violations of certain rules are more serious than of others, approximating conflicts of value rather than interest. In these situations, the potential for a peer mediator to help resolve such conflicts is limited. Educators should recognize common rule violations leading to conflicts in their student populations, identify those that are not amenable to mediation, and establish alternative resolution procedures for those cases.

The involvement of children's family members, especially parents, is an important goal. As an initial step, parents should be informed about the nature and purpose of conflict management skills training and peer mediation. When their children begin to use these behaviors at home, a receptive parent is more likely to reinforce than punish aberrant action. If possible, training opportunities should be provided to parents, even to the extent of using parents as program assistants. If parents can model the behaviors at home for the child, or indicate through their support of the program that these behaviors are acceptable, the child's learning progress will be greatly enhanced.

Institutional Context

Schools, as institutions, are traditionally authoritarian and hierarchical (Bamburg & Isaacson, 1991). Teachers and administrators are affected by this culture that may inhibit critical support for peer mediation programs (A. M. Davis, 1986; Davis & Porter, 1985).

Davis and Salem (1985) argue that elementary and high school teachers tend to camouflage conflict, avoiding controversy in the classroom whenever possible. Teachers may be uncomfortable with conflict because they wish to restrict students' control over their situations (Araki, 1990), perpetuating what Johnson (1981) calls an "adult centrism." In school environments, most legitimate student-student interactions are limited to extracurricular activities. Instructional strategies emphasize teacher lectures and individual work by students. Most student conflicts are "resolved" by intervention from a teacher or staff member. Given the norm, it is understandable that if students begin to take control over conflicts and challenge situations, some teachers may fear that the challenge will extend to their authority.

Yet, teachers should let students handle problems by themselves. Children are more likely to learn and use collaborative strategies in peer conflicts than when interacting with an adult (Levya & Furth, 1986). Peer context is seen as more favorable to an equal exchange of ideas and makes students more confident that their views may be heard. In addition, children learn self-control more effectively when they are given the opportunity to solve their own conflicts rather than depending on a teacher to solve them (Brophy, 1983).

Moreover, if teachers are to instruct students in conflict skills, they should be able to model effective conflict resolution for their students (Brophy, 1983; Cochrane & Myers, 1980; Commanday, 1985; Garabino, Scott, & Erickson, 1989). As Kriedler (1984) says, "If students are to learn self-control and how to use their own power responsibly, they must see someone model the constructive, responsible use of power" (p. 33).

Ultimately, the success of peer mediation programs will depend upon the commitment of teachers and administrators. Peer mediation programs should not be forced upon unwilling participants. If there is questionable support, the better strategy is to go elsewhere or begin with a smaller program limited to a particular class or group where the commitment of the immediate teacher or support person (perhaps a counselor) is sufficient to sustain the program. Any program, and especially a full-fledged effort, should attend seriously to teacher training. If teachers are not going to train students, their training will still provide them with information about the students' educational experiences and may help them become better models. If teachers are going to provide first-line instruction to students, their training should be comprehensive and experiential as well as substantive.

Emphasize Experiential Learning and Application

Originally, educators assumed that providing children information about conflict and allowing them an opportunity to participate in basic exercises was sufficient to teach then to alter their conflict behaviors. However, studies in pedagogical effectiveness of general conflict and negotiation skills training (Callias et al., 1987; Fleming, 1977; Taylor, 1986) and persuasive skill enhancement (Burke & Clark, 1982; Clark, Willihnganz, & O'Dell, 1985) challenge these assumptions.

Evaluations of peer mediation programs confirm that children need relevant, experiential involvement to improve their conflict skills. In their field experiment, the Social Sciences Research Consortium (1987) found that the objectives of decreasing violence and antisocial behavior, teaching new conflict and communication skills, effecting positive attitudes toward conflict resolution, and preventing attitudes that lead to delinquency were only obtained when students were able to engage in mediation of disputes relevant to their daily lives. Training in mediation concepts without the inclusion of a peer mediation program does not alter children's behavior (Johnson, 1988). Furthermore, children who act as peer mediators in a peer meditation program benefit the most from the experience (Benenson, 1988).

The message is clear. Children learn more by doing. The previous discussion of developmental theory suggests that children learn more sophisticated ways of approaching social conflict by applying conflict skills in interaction, especially with peers. Earlier we argued that peer mediation training was not appropriate for early elementary grade levels. However, the existing research suggests that the opportunity to act as a peer mediator produces the most significant developmental progress. For earlier grades, general conflict training should be geared to as much experiential learning as possible to maximize effect. At higher grades where peer mediation programs and activities are more appropriate, the emphasis should be on providing as many students as possible the opportunity to act as mediators rather than restricting the opportunities to a select few.

Conclusion

Peer mediation programs are still a relative novelty in education. They seem to be a good idea at the right time. Few would argue that some improvement is needed in the ways our children are dealing with social conflict. The notion of peer mediation programs, borrowed from peace education and the alternative dispute resolution movement, provides a compelling philosophical and practical grounding.

This chapter suggests that our knowledge of children and conflict can be incorporated into the design and delivery of peer mediation programs to improve their impact. Specifically, peer mediation programs should be designed to be consonant with the developmental competency of the children involved. Although conflict training is workable in early elementary grades, peer mediation activities should be targeted at highest elementary and middle school levels. Instructional materials should be age-specific, and assessment of developmental competency as baseline and change measures should be encouraged.

The social context of children's conflict should be considered. The issues that become conflictual and the ways children deal with those disputes are dependent upon a number of cultural and contextual factors. Educators should attempt to understand the perspective of the child and the cultural or familial reinforcements of that perspective before assuming that change is simple or appropriate.

The institutional culture of schools should also be considered a potentially powerful influence in the progress of peer mediation. If teachers and administrators fail to support the program or model the behavior, peer mediation instruction is unlikely to be effective.

What factors influence managers' involvement in disputes within organizations? What influences the way disputes get framed as they are addressed by third parties in organizational settings?

9

Managerial Third Parties

Intervention Strategies, Process, and Consequences

Rekha Karambayya
Jeanne M. Brett

THIRD-PARTY INTERVENTION has traditionally been used to describe the behavior of a neutral intermediary invited to help resolve a conflict that the disputing parties have attempted to resolve without success. Managers frequently find themselves resolving disputes (Mintzberg, 1975), often acting as third parties to disputes among colleagues and subordinates. However, unlike other third parties who practice dispute resolution as a profession—such as arbitrators or judges, or even community mediators—managerial third parties may find themselves in a role with few defined boundaries and for which they have little or no training or motivation (Sheppard, 1983, 1984).

Professional third parties typically have a well-delineated role that prescribes the limits of their authority. Managers, in contrast, exercise considerable discretion in choosing when and how to intervene in disputes (Kolb, 1986, 1989; Sheppard, 1983; Sheppard,

Roth, Blumenfeld-Jones, & Minton, 1991). Managerial third parties differ from professional third parties in a number of other ways as well. Professional third parties are typically invited to intervene in disputes; managers may insinuate themselves into them. Managers also are not strictly speaking neutral third parties. They have relationships with disputants that extend beyond the dispute context. Sometimes they have hierarchical power over the disputants, sometimes social relationships with them, and often vested interests in the outcome of the dispute (Kolb, 1986, 1989; Neale, Pinkley, Brittain, & Northcraft, 1990; Sheppard, 1983; Sheppard et al., 1991). Perhaps most important, managers may have a personal stake in the outcome of the dispute.

How managers enact their third-party role affects the outcome of the dispute and the perceptions of parties to it (Karambayya & Brett, 1989; Karambayya, Brett, & Lytle, 1992). Thus, managers who take on third-party roles have the opportunity to influence organizational outcomes, long-term relationships among the parties involved, and their own future relationships with the disputants and the organization.

Research on managerial third-party intervention offers the opportunity to explore the process by which third parties resolve conflict under conditions that are more complex and less restrictive than those facing professional third parties. It can help us understand how dispute resolution processes emerge and the long-term implications of third-party intervention for organizations and disputants. Such research may also offer insight into new third-party roles that occur naturally in the organizational context but are prescribed in other institutional environments where third-party roles are formalized. It can inform us about the effectiveness and consequences of managerial third-party behaviors and form the basis for training in organizational conflict resolution.

This chapter proposes a process model of managerial third-party intervention. We explore the nature of the antecedents of third-party behavior from within the organizational context. We identify the implications of managerial third-party behavior for the outcomes of the dispute and the resolution of similar disputes that may arise in the future. This is a preliminary conceptual model that reflects the nature of organizational contexts, contextual influences on the enactment of managerial third-party roles, and the direct and indirect implications of those roles.

The model is descriptive rather than normative, in that it attempts to map the processes through which managers adopt and act out third-party roles, create or facilitate resolutions, and are evaluated by disputants. Although most existing research explores the relationships among a small set of variables, either focusing on the antecedents of third-party intervention or on its consequences, this model conceptualizes disputes, and those who participate in their resolution, as embedded in organizational contexts. Managers, acting as third parties, may interpret the context in unique ways, respond to the situation as they see it, and eventually change the context through their enactment of dispute resolution processes (Kolb, 1989, 1986). Each dispute may affect perceptions of, and responses to, future organizational disputes. We also explore the implications of the model for future research and for the practice of managerial dispute resolution.

In the following sections we review research linking various combinations of the elements of the model. Although we do not attempt a comprehensive review of the literature, we present existing empirical evidence from our work and that of others, as and where available and relevant. Although the components of the model appear differentiated and well defined, our discussion of it suggests that these factors are interdependent and interpretive. Organizational disputes and their resolution emerge through a dynamic interaction between the context and the participants. The dispute and its organizational context are experienced and interpreted by those involved in the dispute, be they disputants or third parties. Disputants and third parties may see the context somewhat differently and base their behavior and evaluations of success and failure on their unique perceptions of what the dispute involves.

The process by which parties to the dispute arrive at their unique understanding of the dispute, and begin to develop a shared view of it, may be more important than any one element in the model. We refer to these interpretive processes as "framing," and accord them a central role in third-party conflict resolution. Although there is little empirical evidence on how framing effects work, and what role they play in the adoption of third-party behavior, we offer our own admittedly speculative views on what these processes might contribute to our understanding of managerial third-party behavior.

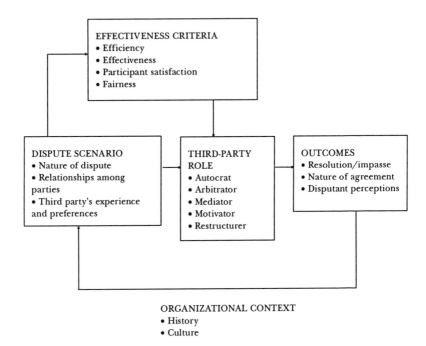

Figure 9.1. Third-Party Intervention: A Process Model

A Model of Third-Party Intervention

The major elements of the proposed model and their inter-relationships are presented in Figure 9.1. These elements are defined and their interrelationships are explored, using the results of prior research to support the proposed pattern of relationships.

In explicating the model in Figure 9.1, we relied heavily on the studies of managerial third-party behavior. These studies use a variety of samples and research methods including experimental simulation (Karambayya & Brett, 1989; Karambayya et al., 1992; Lewicki & Sheppard, 1985), ethnography (Kolb, 1986), surveys (Lissak & Sheppard, 1983; Neale et al., 1990), and interviews (Sheppard, 1983, 1984). Some investigate antecedents, some consequences, and some the behavior of third parties in organizational settings. They do not always use the same terminology to describe third-party behavior, yet their results are reasonably consistent and provide the basis for our model of third-party intervention.

The Dispute Scenario

The dispute scenario refers to the nature of the dispute and the characteristics of the setting in which resolution is being attempted —factors that may be expected to have a direct impact on the role played by the third party. The dispute scenario may also influence the implicit or explicit choice of criteria used to evaluate the resolution and thereby indirectly affect the third-party role.

Three groups of elements of the dispute scenario may influence the way third-party managers intervene in disputes. The first, referred to here as the nature of the dispute, encompasses considerations such as the number and nature of issues over which there is conflict, deadlines or time pressure, and the significance of the dispute. A second group consists of the nature of the parties involved and the relationships among them. A third group of elements refers to the characteristics of the third party. Although most existing research has explored the effects of one or a few of these factors, these characteristics of the dispute scenario may act collectively or interactively to influence the nature of the third-party role enacted and the criteria used to judge the outcome and process of dispute resolution.

Kolb (1989) points out that organizations have a tendency to avoid or ignore conflict. As a result, the existence of a conflict and the nature of issues involved may neither be openly acknowledged nor discussed. Under such conditions, managers may experience ambiguity about whether a conflict exists, about what issues are central to the dispute, and about how serious the dispute is. Disputes in organizational settings then may be particularly open to individual interpretation. Other concerns, such as whether the parties to the conflict are likely to interact in the future, and the hierarchical relationship between the third party and the disputants, may be a function of organizational structure and less susceptible to framing influences.

Nature of the Dispute

Time Pressure. Lewicki and Sheppard (1985), using a set of organizational simulations with a sample of 100 managers, found that the third party was likely to assume control of the decision when the dispute was characterized by time pressure. Neale and her colleagues (1990), using a mixed sample of managers and graduate students, reported similar results. They found that managerial third parties were less likely to avoid the conflict, and more likely to exert control over the outcome and impose a solution, when the dispute involved time pressure.

Importance of Issues. Managerial third parties try to maintain control over the outcome of the dispute when the dispute has wide-ranging implications for the organization and for organizational members other than the disputants (Lewicki & Sheppard, 1985). In addition, when the issues in dispute are important to the organization, third parties are more likely to focus on the underlying causes of the dispute, rather than on the more superficial facts of the particular case in which they are currently involved (Neale et al., 1990).

Relationships Among the Parties

Future Interaction. Organizational disputes may involve parties who are engaged in long-term relationships. The dispute resolution process and outcome may affect the nature of future interaction among those involved, a factor that managerial third parties appear to be sensitive to.

When the parties to a dispute are likely to have to work together in the future, the third-party manager may elect to let the disputants create a solution. Such a strategy may be used to help disputants learn to resolve future disputes, to develop ownership over the outcome, or facilitate implementation of the decision (Lewicki & Sheppard, 1985). When future interaction between the disputing parties is likely to be minimal, managerial third parties engage in behaviors that would end the dispute rather than resolve it (Neale et al., 1990).

Hierarchical Power of Third Party. Unlike professional third parties, such as arbitrators, mediators, and judges, managers may have social or authority relationships with the disputants that extend beyond the dispute setting. Those relationships may be a source of power over the disputants and could determine the behavior of the third party and the response of the disputants. Managerial third parties with formal authority over the disputants, by virtue of their hierarchical position, use that authority to impose solutions on the disputants, an option that is not available to all third parties (Karambayya et al., 1992; Neale et al., 1990). Third parties with hierarchical power are also less likely to avoid the conflict and more likely to engage proactively in conflict resolution (Neale et al., 1990).

Third Party's Relationship With the Disputants. The history of the relationship between the disputants and the third party may also influence behavior of managerial third parties. Neale et al. (1990) found that managers were more likely to initiate third-party involvement and work at resolving the underlying causes of the dispute, and less likely to maintain control over the dispute, when they had good relationships with the disputants. Managerial third parties who had poor relationships with disputants tried to end rather than resolve the dispute, by limiting interaction between the parties to it.

The Third Party

Unlike professional third parties, managerial third parties have neither standardized roles nor training in dispute resolution. Thus they may differ in their approach to third-party intervention. Kolb (1986), in an ethnographic study of ombudsmen, found that they used three major third-party roles. Some, who saw themselves as investigators, looked for and presented relevant information. Others acted as advisors, facilitating the process and advising the disputants. Some managerial third parties used their organizational authority to restructure interactions among the parties to the dispute. Kolb (1986, 1989) proposed that managers' definitions of their third-party roles and their subsequent enactment of those roles may be strongly influenced by their background and training.

Exploring the behavior of informal third parties, Sheppard, Blumenfeld-Jones, and Roth (1989) suggested that the frames that third parties impose on the dispute influence what criteria they use to evaluate the resolution and how they behave. In an empirical investigation of the effects of the antecedents and consequences of frames, Sheppard and colleagues (1991) found that third parties used four dominant frames: a right-wrong frame, perceiving one disputant as right and the other as wrong; a multidimensional frame, recognizing the legitimacy of some of the interests of each party; a

stop conflict frame, attempting to end the conflict; and an underlying conflict frame, recognizing the current dispute as a symptom
of a larger conflict.

Sheppard et al. (1991) conceptualized frames as a cognitive interpretation of the conflict. Third parties were assumed to engage in
a rational decision process in which the frame provided the diagnostic tool used to assess the type of intervention that would be
most appropriate, given the circumstances. In Sheppard's research,
framing is portrayed as a choice among a set of commonly used
interpretations of the dispute that takes place prior to third-party
intervention. Kolb (1986), on the other hand, has a more dynamic,
interactional view of framing processes. She suggested that managers
bring a unique set of experiences and perceptions to the third-party
role that colors their interpretation of the dispute and involvement
in it. According to this view, frames emerge and change during the
process of dispute resolution as a result of interactions between the
third party and the context.

We presume that at the point at which a third party becomes
involved in a dispute the disputants each have their own interpretation of the dispute, and the third party quickly acquires one. The
dispute resolution process, then, may involve explicit or implicit
negotiation over frames as well as interests and positions. The frames
in which a dispute is held may be expected to be dynamic, changing
through the course of interaction among parties to the dispute.

Our model proposes that the organizational context, factors associated with the dispute scenario, and the criteria used to evaluate
the effectiveness of resolution all contribute to the parties' interpretations of the dispute. Those interpretations then affect third-
party roles adopted, which in turn have implications for the outcomes
achieved. Thus our perspective differs from the conceptualization
of frames as cognitive strategies in that we presume that external
factors interact with each other, and with individual preferences,
to influence frames. Frames may be neither as rational, nor as static,
as these approaches assume.

Nothing in our model presumes that there is agreement among
the parties to the dispute about what the dispute involves or how
the outcomes should be evaluated. Indeed, we assume that in order
to resolve the dispute, the disputants must reach some accommodation of interpretation, if only of the meaning of the outcome and
their roles in implementing it. We hypothesize that if this accom-

modation is not reached, implementation of the decision may not be successful and the dispute may recur. Yet we do not assume that in order to reach agreement disputants and third parties need agree as to the issues in dispute or the major criteria of effectiveness. It is perfectly reasonable that the parties have concerns about different issues, and the decision reflects some, rather than all, of their concerns. Likewise, a third party playing the role of a mediator may have to navigate among different perceptions of the dispute scenario, and different effectiveness criteria, in order to arrive at a resolution.

We find two aspects of the discussion of framing in the negotiation and dispute resolution research to have useful implications for managerial third-party intervention. First is the recognition that the meaning of the dispute is interpretive and may be influenced by the context in which the dispute occurs. These interpretations may not be shared by the parties involved in dispute resolution. Secondly, simple frames can act as diagnostic tools to direct behavior. Both of these points have practical implications for managerial third parties.

We hypothesize that, assuming that it is possible to develop a comprehensive typology of frames used by third parties, the choice of a frame may result from an interaction between the third party's sense of the context and people involved in the dispute. The third party's prior managerial and dispute resolution experience may be particularly important in the shaping and enactment of frames.

The professional training and expertise of the third party influenced the choice of the dispute frame, which in turn affected the behavior of the third party in Sheppard et al.'s study (1991). Third parties who framed the dispute in either right-wrong or underlying conflict terms were more likely to exert control over the decision than those who saw the dispute as multidimensional.

We proposed that, if durability of the resolution and satisfaction of the disputants are valued (Karambayya et al., 1992), managerial third parties may learn with experience that facilitation of the resolution process may be more effective than imposition of a solution. In our study, managers with considerable supervisory experience used a facilitative role more often than those with less experience, even when they had the formal authority to exercise direct control over the outcome of the dispute.

Effectiveness Criteria

The goals or objectives that the third party wishes the dispute's resolution to achieve are called effectiveness criteria in our model. Managerial third parties may display concern with a range of criteria that go beyond simply resolving the dispute and arriving at a settlement. Lissak and Sheppard (1983) focused attention on a variety of criteria used by managers and nonmanagers to evaluate dispute resolution procedures. They found that in both groups getting at the facts of the case, reducing the likelihood of future disputes, and effecting a successful resolution were rated as most important. Two other criteria that emerged as important were airing of the problem and speed of resolution.

Since Lissak and Sheppard's study, there have been quite a few studies investigating the nature of the criteria that managerial third parties use to evaluate outcomes and procedures, and their implications for third-party intervention. Instead of attempting a comprehensive treatment of all types of effectiveness criteria, we have elected to focus on some areas of commonality across studies.

Four categories of criteria emerged from previous research: efficiency, effectiveness, participant satisfaction, and fairness. These criteria are not intended to represent mutually exclusive categories.

Efficiency reflects a cost-benefit approach and could include concerns such as getting the dispute resolved quickly, controlling the costs of dispute resolution, and minimizing the disruption caused by it. Four studies (Neale et al., 1990; Sheppard, 1983, 1984; Ury et al., 1988) reported that efficiency appeared to be an important criterion to third-party managers.

Effectiveness involves taking a longer term perspective on the dispute and its consequences. Previous research has focused on some of the forms it could take, such as the quality of the solution, its durability (Sheppard et al., 1989), prevention of the recurrence of similar disputes, and the costs of the implementation of the solution (Ury et al., 1988).

Participant satisfaction includes the acceptability of the solution, disputants' perceptions of the third party, and concern for the future relationships among the parties to the dispute. It has emerged as an important consideration in a number of studies (Neale et al., 1990; Sheppard et al., 1989; Ury et al., 1988)

Fairness reflects a concern for the distributive, procedural, and interactional justice perceptions of the parties. Prevention of bias in the solution and the procedure and fair treatment of the disputants by the third party are also in this category. These concerns were raised by participants in some studies of managerial third-party intervention (Neale et al., 1990; Sheppard et al., 1989). These criteria are interdependent rather than independent. Some are compatible with others; for example, compromising on participant satisfaction may be ineffective in that it could lead to implementation problems and to the recurrence of the dispute in the future. Some of the other criteria may be inherently incompatible, requiring implicit or explicit trade-offs among them. For instance, pressures toward efficiency may favor a quick resolution, rather than the development of durable, effective solutions.

Dispute Scenarios and Effectiveness Criteria

Third parties may assign higher priority to one or another evaluation criterion based on their perceptions of the dispute scenario. When the dispute has serious implications for the organization, the endurance of the solution may appear more important than how quickly the solution is arrived at. When the parties to the dispute are expected to have a long-term working relationship, criteria such as disputants' satisfaction with the resolution and disputants' perceptions of third-party fairness may be seen as important (Neale et al., 1990).

Sheppard et al. (1989) proposed a rational decision perspective as a model for third-party intervention. They suggested that third parties make a rational choice of how to intervene in a dispute based on an analysis of their intervention goals and the dispute context. Their empirical results indicate relationships among characteristics of the dispute, effectiveness criteria, and managerial third-party intervention. They found that disputants' satisfaction was stressed as a goal when the dispute was complex and important and when there was considerable interdependence between the disputants. Fairness was emphasized when the third party had formal authority, and de-emphasized when the dispute was seen as a personality clash.

These results reflect empirical relationships among characteristics of the dispute and effectiveness criteria chosen by the third party. A rational decision-making process was proposed as the explanation for the pattern of relationships. The study did not test whether the third parties actually used a rational decision-making process.

In fact, we have little empirical research that explores how third parties assign relative priority to alternative effectiveness criteria. Sheppard (1983, 1984) has speculated that managers may be socialized by organizations into according most priority to efficiency or expediency. Alternatively, professional training and experience may encourage a personal preference for one or the other criterion (Kolb, 1986). Given a particular dispute scenario, framing processes may be the mechanism through which contextual and personal preferences influence which measures of effectiveness are considered most appropriate.

Third-Party Roles

"Roles are standardized patterns of behavior" (Katz & Kahn, 1966, p. 37). Third-party roles are the patterns of behaviors adopted by third parties during their intervention in disputes.

Research on the role behaviors of managerial third parties has relied heavily on Thibaut and Walker's (1975) characterization of third-party roles in legal settings. Thibaut and Walker (1975) identified third-party roles in terms of two dimensions: decision control, reflecting third-party control over the final solution or agreement, and process control, the extent of third-party control over the presentation of evidence.

We briefly summarize research on managerial third-party roles and provide a map between role and typical role behaviors. We chose to include in our model five of the third-party roles that have been identified in multiple studies: autocrat, mediator, arbitrator, motivator, and restructurer (see Figure 9.1).

The autocrat, often referred to as inquisitor, has control over the decision and the process, including the presentation and interpretation of information relevant to the dispute. Four different studies (Karambayya & Brett, 1989; Karambayya et al., 1992; Neale et al., 1990; Sheppard, 1983, 1984) report that managerial third parties frequently behave autocratically.

The arbitrator controls the decision, but not the presentation and interpretation of information relevant to the dispute. Arbitrators may enforce the rules of presentation, but they do not intervene in the presentation. Two studies (Neale et al., 1990; Sheppard, 1983, 1984) report that managerial third parties sometimes act like arbitrators. The mediator does not have ultimate control over the decision to resolve the dispute, but could exert considerable influence during the dispute resolution process. Mediators may give advice about how they think the dispute might be resolved. They may set and enforce the rules of presentation of information relevant to the dispute and ask the disputants questions about the substance of the dispute. Four studies (Kolb & Glidden, 1986; Karambayya & Brett, 1989; Karambayya et al., 1992; Neale et al., 1990) suggest that managerial third parties sometimes do mediate.

Sheppard (1983, 1984) found that managerial third parties used an additional form of control that he labeled "motivational control." It involves offering positive or negative incentives to get the parties to agree to a resolution. These incentives could be coupled with a directive to resolve the dispute without the third party's further intervention. We labeled this third-party role the motivator. In our simulation research (Karambayya & Brett, 1989; Karambayya et al., 1992), third parties who were provided with resources often used those resources to help resolve the problem.

Kolb's (1986) research identifies one unique managerial third-party role: the restructurer. The third party taking this role makes arrangements for the disputants to be reassigned, so that they will not have to interact in the future. Neale et al. (1990) also identify a similar behavior pattern directed toward ending the dispute rather than resolving it. The restructurer may be assuming that disputes are interpersonal and that by changing the people who must interact, conflict will disappear. Organizational disputes, however, are often structural, arising out of differences in time and goal orientations and uncertainty associated with different management functions (Brett & Rognes, 1986). Changing the personalities will not make structural conflict disappear, and the restructurer may be surprised to find the same disputes recurring between new parties.

Although the advisor and investigator roles identified by Kolb (1986) may be clearly differentiated among ombudsmen, these roles share behavioral elements with the mediator role and so are not distinguished in Figure 9.1.

The procedural marshal role identified by Karambayya and Brett (1989) is a behavioral pattern that has some overlap with the roles of the autocrat, the arbitrator, and the mediator. The procedural marshal sets and enforces the rules or norms for disputants' behavior in the dispute resolution process.

Neale and her colleagues (1990) point out a managerial third-party role that had not been identified in prior research: the conflict avoider. This role consists of behaviors engaged in by managerial third parties who do not want to become involved in the dispute. Ury et al. (1988) point out some of the merits of conflict avoidance. Neale et al.'s (1990) identification of the conflict avoider role may indicate that at least some managerial third parties choose their battles, avoiding involvement in some disputes.

An extension of the control framework proposed by Thibaut and Walker (1975) helps distinguish these managerial roles. Managers, by virtue of their organizational authority, appear to have more control options at their disposal than professional third parties. Although the autocrat or inquisitor may control both the process and the outcome, the arbitrator relies on control over the outcome, and the mediator on control over the process. These roles are similar to the third-party roles in legal settings investigated by Thibaut and Walker (1975).

The motivator and restructurer have no parallels in legal settings. In each role, the managerial third party uses organizational authority that exists outside of the third-party role. The motivator uses control over resources or rewards to move disputants toward a settlement. The restructurer, on the other hand, uses authority over task allocation and structure to remove the disputants from the conflict setting.

Even though these roles are often portrayed as alternative behavioral options, in reality the behavior of the third party may represent a combination of these roles. Our research (Karambayya & Brett, 1989; Karambayya et al., 1992) suggests that the behavior of the third party may change during the process of dispute resolution, as the third party tries one role, gauges response to it, and then moves on to another. Managerial third-party intervention is likely to represent shifting patterns of behavior that first look like one role and then like another or a unique combination of behaviors representing more than one role. Those patterns may be expected to mirror the underlying interpretive processes taking place during dispute resolution.

Effectiveness Criteria and Third-Party Roles

Choice of a particular evaluation criterion, or the relative priority assigned various criteria, may affect the behavior of the third party. Sheppard (1983, 1984) has pointed out that an emphasis on efficiency may lead the third party to act as an autocrat, retaining control over the decision in order to ensure an expedient resolution. On the other hand, concern for effectiveness and participant satisfaction may trigger mediation, which allows the disputants to maintain ownership over the agreement and leads to a more enduring resolution and better implementation (Karambayya et al., 1992).

Managers have been found to be more willing to get involved as third parties when participant satisfaction is a major concern (Neale et al., 1990). Sheppard et al. (1989) found that emphasis on participant satisfaction as an intervention goal led third parties to engage in diagnosis and clarification of issues, and procedures that involved less control over the decision.

Fairness, as an evaluation criterion, led third parties to spend time on fact finding and to attempt to go beyond the current conflict in order to address the underlying problem (Sheppard et al., 1989; Neale et al., 1990). In contrast, concern for efficiency and an expedient resolution led to greater third-party control over the decision (Sheppard et al., 1989).

Outcomes

Whether or not the dispute is resolved, two types of outcomes may ensue. First-level outcomes arise directly out of the dispute and reflect the results of the type of third-party intervention: whether the dispute is resolved, and what kind of resolution was achieved. Second-level outcomes reflect the longer-term implications of the intervention and may arise out of perceptions of first-level outcomes and dispute resolution processes. Second-level outcomes may have implications for the resolution of future disputes in the organization. Examples of second-level outcomes include disputants' evaluations of the fairness of the procedure or outcome, harmony or tension in the relationships among the parties to the dispute, and implementation of the resolution and its durability.

Although first-level outcomes reflect the issues on which settlement has been reached, second-level outcomes represent a subjective evaluation or interpretation of those outcomes. Our research has shown that, given the same agreement, disputants and the third party may arrive at different assessments of who benefits from the outcome, whether the settlement is fair, and whose ideas were adopted (Karambayya et al., 1992). Retrospective rationality and self-serving biases may play a role in these framing processes, so that parties to the dispute may display a tendency to overestimate their own role in the resolution of the dispute and how much the resolution appears to benefit them. Such positive frames may be necessary in order to facilitate implementation of settlements and prevent recidivism.

Second-level outcomes are likely to have an effect on disputants' perceptions of the third party, highlight the costs and benefits of reliance on third parties to resolve disputes, and could create or change organizational norms around third-party intervention. In effect, these outcomes may have a precedent-setting value for future managerial third-party dispute resolution processes.

Third-Party Roles and Outcomes

We have found that mediation that eschewed reliance on decision control was more likely to result in compromise decisions. Autocratic third-party behavior, in contrast, was more likely to result either in outcomes favoring one or the other disputant, or in impasses (Karambayya & Brett, 1989; Karambayya et al., 1992).

Consistent with research on third parties in legal settings (McEwen & Maiman, 1981; Pearson, 1982; Roehl & Cook, 1989), we found that when managerial third parties allowed disputants control over the decision, the procedure was rated higher on fairness than when third parties made the decision to resolve the dispute themselves (Karambayya & Brett, 1989; Karambayya et al., 1992).

Disputants' assessments of the fairness of the dispute resolution procedure and that of the third party could affect under what circumstances disputants would seek out third-party intervention and whom they would choose to act as third party in the future. Satisfaction with the outcome of the dispute could influence disputants' willingness to follow through with implementation. Perceptions of the process of dispute resolution could also have long-term effects on the relationships among the parties to it, either aggravating an already strained relationship or building a foundation for a more supportive one. Although there is limited evidence supporting these proposed relationships in legal settings, there have been no studies following organizationally based disputes to determine the long-term effects of different third-party roles.

The Organizational Context

The organizational context includes elements reflecting the history of how disputes like the one in question have been resolved in the past and the organization's culture for disputing and dispute resolution. The existence of strong organizational norms regarding disputes and their resolution could encourage the creation and reinforcement of collective frames regarding the nature of disputes and the appropriate effectiveness criteria and third-party roles.

For example, Kolb (1986) described an organization in which there was a persistent pattern of dispute avoidance. Managers failed to confront differences over budget and project authority and put off dealing with problems until they became crises and the president would step in and make a decision. Kolb offered two explanations for this disputing pattern. First, the organization's decision-making structure was highly centralized; second, the cultural background of the president and senior management stressed the appearance of harmony, avoidance of confrontation, and deference to authority.

Avenues for Further Research

The implications of organizational dispute resolution go far beyond the dispute at hand. Although the dispute and third-party involvement in it may unfold in stages each stage is inextricably interwoven with those that preceded it, and with the organizational context in which it occurs. Focusing exclusively on one or the other stage, as much of the research has done, leads to an oversimplification of the nature and consequences of managerial dispute resolution. The most obvious limitation of the research is its focus on short-term outcomes at the expense of the long-term implications of third-party intervention. Prescriptions from this research for what is effective third-party behavior may be biased toward criteria such as efficiency, rather than preventing recurrence of the dispute, simply because our short-term focus does not allow an assessment of whether the dispute recurs.

In addition, restricting study of third-party intervention to one particular dispute may not reveal organizational or third-party learning that may be central to the choice and evaluation of third-party roles. In offering suggestions on third-party dispute intervention derived from studies of single disputes, researchers may have focused too much on whether and how the third party resolves the dispute, when a more appropriate long-term outcome may be whether the disputants have learned to reach agreements without a third party. In order to study how third-party roles are enacted, researchers ought to track behavior and organizational responses across disputes.

Research on dispute resolution in organizations may have to pay explicit attention to the particular features of the organizational context in order to explain choice of effectiveness criteria, third-party behavior, and types of resolutions achieved. We could explore how much of managerial-third party behavior is context-specific by studying similarities and differences across organizations.

Finally, the inclusion of framing as an important element in organizational dispute intervention raises a basic question about how and when social or task interaction gets framed as a conflict in the first place. We know little about the circumstances under which managers recognize a conflict, and either seek third-party help to resolve it or attempt to resolve it themselves.

Part Four

Practitioners' Perspectives

Can mediation help build and maintain community? What can researchers and theorists gain by considering mediation's community-building potential?

10

Why Do We Mediate?

Carl M. Moore

THE INTEREST IN MEDIATION has grown exponentially in the past 10 years. Why? It is not the common explanation, that mediation is used because the courts are unable to handle all of the demand for its services. It is implausible that mediation is used so widely merely because it is a means of *alternative* dispute resolution. Much of its use is fully independent of the legal system, and when it is connected to the legal system—that is, court-based programs—I prefer to believe that ADR stands for *appropriate* dispute resolution.

My argument is that mediation is the *appropriate* means of dispute resolution because we are unhappy with our communities the way they are. We believe they can be better and would like for them to be better. We know, at some level, that although resolving differences is key to living in a better community, some means of dispute resolution are more likely to enable community and others are more likely to jeopardize community. Mediation is becoming increasingly popular as a means of dispute resolution because people figure out that it is a preferable way to enable us to live in better communities.

The way I will support the argument is to explain that our unhappiness is due to a malaise in our culture. The best I am able to do is offer indications that the malaise exists and speculate about what are some of its causes. *Habits of the Heart* (Bellah et al., 1985) caught the imagination of many people and had a widespread influence because its essential argument resonates with our lives. We live during an age in which people have become increasingly individualistic—putting their own growth and advancement ahead of almost all other considerations—but we find, paradoxically, that we need others to find ourselves. *Habits of the Heart* argues that it is through community—the meaningful interaction with others whom we know—that we make sense of our own lives. In order to support this view, that increasingly we are turning to community, this chapter will describe what I mean by community, explain why there is an interest in community, and then illustrate why mediation is preferred to litigation as a way to encourage community.

What Are Indications That People Are Unhappy With Their Community?

Whenever I ask audiences, "How many of you are happy with your community the way it is?", very few people raise their hands. And everyone raises their hand when I ask, "How many of you believe your community could be better than it is?" "*Harper's* Index," a regular feature of *Harper's* magazine, provides a numerical window on our society. The following are a few highly selective indicators that something is wrong in America.

> One out of three high school seniors cannot locate Latin America on a world map.
>
> In 1989, 710 NY City public school teachers were assaulted on the job.
>
> The United States has the highest per capita prison population of any country in the world. The prison system is the fastest growing sector of U.S. government employment.
>
> In 1976, ½ of 1% of Americans held 14% of all private wealth in the United States. In 1986, that same percentage controlled 24% of the wealth.

In 63% of the American families living below the poverty line, at least one member is employed. Chances are one out of three that a homeless American holds a full- or part-time job.

Most Americans—60%—live in areas where the air does not meet the standards of the 1970 Clean Air Act.

One-third of all U.S. coastal waters are too polluted for commercial shellfishing.

There are traces of PCB in the milk of 87% of the nursing mothers in North Carolina.

In 1988, 619,565 cosmetic surgical procedures were performed on Americans. Cosmetic surgeons remove 200,000 pounds of fat and implant 60,000 pounds of silicone and collagen each year.

In 1990, $52 billion was spent on private security forces in the United States.

Our culture, and much of the rest of the world, appears to have adopted patterns of behavior that are obstacles to community:[1]

Extreme individualism on the part of many citizens, producing isolation, separation, and alienation.

Intense nationalism—and related "isms": racism, ethnocentrism, anti-Semitism—yielding hatred and a strong tendency to "scapegoat" outside groups.

Widespread reliance on bureaucratic social structures, stressing hierarchical distinctions, specialization, and centralized authority.

Rampant consumerism, with its emphasis on the accumulation of things over the pursuit of interpersonal connections.

Popular indulgence in the "alternative realities" presented by the mass media.

The fast pace of life, in which individuals rush about to fill their lives with activity.

Emphasis on professional success above all other considerations.

What Is "Community"?

Before I make my case for why people are beginning to turn from individualism and to community,[2] I will define the term. *Community* is the means by which people live together. Communities enable people to protect themselves and to acquire the resources that provide for their needs. Communities provide intellectual, moral, and social values that give purpose to survival. Their members share an identity, speak a common language, agree upon role definitions, share common values, assume some permanent membership status, and understand the social boundaries within which they operate.

All communal forms have a political nature. For any collection of persons to live together over time there must be an ultimate appeal to some kind of finality, authority, or power.

> There can be no such thing as civilized living in the absence of etiquette and law. Even if one has a well-developed intuitive feeling for the moral point of view and manners, one cannot navigate through civilized society by social instinct alone, or by mere reliance on one's human nature. (Martin & Stent, 1990, p. 245)

Commitment to a community is likely to exist if there is a communal return, if people derive a sense of belonging, recognition, or acceptance from being part of the community. Communal membership must be satisfying on many levels of experience and must involve emotional and physical investment and returns. One form of communal return is that community provides the "stage" on which the individual may achieve integration. Community is the context in which the person is viewed as complete.

Conflict is essential in creating and recreating community. If there were no differences between people, there could be no community. But differences alone do not make a community. Community is forged out of a struggle by people to determine how they can live together.

One of the critical requirements of any community is to invent the processes of interaction that allow people to live together. Mediation is one such process.

A community is larger than the most personal components of a society, such as couples, groups, and families (even extended families), but smaller than the most complex components of a society, such as a large city, a region, or a state.[3] Some theorists make a distinction between primary (strong, primitive) communities and secondary communities. The state or the country is an example of a secondary community.[4]

Community exists when people who are interdependent struggle with the traditions that bind them and the interests that separate them in order to realize a future that is an improvement upon the present. There are some groupings within our culture that are often referred to as communities but do not meet one or more of the important criteria implied in this definition. These pseudo-communities may lack identity, commitment, commonality of place, differences, or the motivation to struggle with their differences.

Why Is There an Interest in "Community"?

There are many signs that the idea of community is currently of great interest in American society. "Community" was the principle theme of the successful campaign of President Clinton. President Clinton recently announced a new initiative called "empowerment zones" and claimed that it was needed for the same reason as a number of his other initiatives, to help build "community." The media has used the notion of "community" to explain why selected professional athletes have chosen to remain with their current team rather than opt to move and make more money with a new team. There has been a substantial amount of writing about the notion of community by important scholars and commentators (e.g., Etzioni, 1993; Gardner, 1992; Kemmis, 1990; Lasch, 1991; Rouner, 1991) and there is an influential journal called *The Responsive Community: Rights and Responsibilities.*

There are many reasons why people concern themselves with "community." The first is most basic. People instinctively gather together. Humans have never lived alone. We live according to evolving social norms. We are curious about the social forms we live in, about why they exist, and about whether they serve us well. The discipline of sociology was created to explain the changes that were taking place in society as a result of the Industrial Revolution. Most classical sociologists—Max Weber, Emile Durkheim, Karl Marx, Georg Simmel—have given significant attention to the theme of community in light of the changes they observed in social patterns.

The changes that resulted from the Industrial Revolution, particularly the need for a concentration of people to work in mechanized industries, resulted in the dislocation and isolation of people. The seeming paradox discovered by early sociologists and psychologists was that the larger the population, the more people became isolated as a way to protect themselves. Two of the most marked changes in society are the evolution away from family (extended kinship groups) and the migration away from the traditional village to the city. Driven in upon themselves, people seek environments that are more "communal." They are acting to regain something that has been lost because they do not want to end up naked and alone.

Neighborhoods were created within cities to enable people to live in smaller—more community-like—environments. People built towns and "suburbs" (sub-urban) that were close by but apart from the city. It is clear that we have invented living patterns that attempt to create community in the shadow of the city.

Technology has expanded our contacts but has caused the quality of contacts to suffer. It is within the smaller aggregate of the community that people can improve the quality of their lives by finding relationships that are meaningful.

Complementing the belief that change is always possible is the uniquely American view that growth can solve any problem. Primarily due to our "frontier mentality," Americans have always seemed to believe that things will be better over the next horizon. What is new is that the potential for change seems to have closed in on us. We have been warned for some time that we are entering the Age of Retrenchment. We can no longer assume that change as we have known it in the past—more space, new frontiers, more money—can solve our problems. If there are no additional resources, we will have to solve problems by doing more with what we have. We will need to be better, more efficient. Such a change necessitates working directly with people, rather than making decisions for them. If such a change is to occur, it will have to occur at the level of the community.

A popular theme in intellectual circles is the "end of modernity" or "post-modernism." The argument goes something like this: For the past 350 years, approximately since the time of Descartes, people have believed that it was possible to discover rational solutions for any problem. We have come to realize that complex human problems cannot be solved by rational thought alone. Experts do not know enough, can never know enough, and, ultimately, are not responsible for the outcomes that follow from their advice. It is the people with the problems who must determine what solution is right for them. They can benefit from expert advice, but that is an insufficient basis for making decisions.

Why Is Mediation Preferred to Litigation?

I do not doubt there always will be a need for both adversarial and collaborative means of resolving differences (Mansbridge, 1983). But my purpose here is to explain why there is an increased emphasis on the less adversarial form called mediation. Eli Sagan (1985), in *At the Dawn of Tyranny,* explains that:

> Human society changes and develops by bringing back the energy of what has been repressed and using that energy to transform social forms. The great growth of individualism in the last three hundred years, for example, has been achieved only by the repression of the human need for community, and this age of individualism will cease only when the energy in the repressed need for community becomes viable again. (p. 370)

We are living in an era when the previously repressed need for community is becoming viable again. And to continue with Sagan's argument, the energy of the change will transform social forms, such as the means used to resolve disputes. Litigation, as a social form, is especially suited to an age that favors individualism, because it is an effective device for ascertaining the limits of individual rights. But, because it is effective at that, it is not as useful for preserving relationships that are critical for creating and sustaining community.

In their analysis of the limitations of law as a way of understanding interdependence—the common good—the authors of *The Good Society* (Bellah et al., 1991) explain why the emphasis on rights conflicts with the values of community.

> The legal order sustains a moral commitment to righting particular injustices, but it does not encourage consideration of the common good or of justice in more general terms. . . . To cast a social question in terms of rights tends to make the answer to it an all-or-nothing affair, and to prevent precisely the consideration of how one choice is interdependent with other choices. . . . A right is absolute, and once legally established, must be assured regardless of cost or consequences . . . casting complex moral or social questions in rights language

. . . restricts our understanding of them. . . . we end up with rigid protections of a limited number of social goods that are understood as inviolable individual rights, with no way to attend to broader questions about our common future. . . . The most troubling problem with "rights" is that everyone can be said to have them, and when rights conflict, the rights language itself offers no way to evaluate competing claims . . . the language of rights cuts off debate, polarizing society politically. . . . The individualistic language of rights at the heart of the American legal tradition is a way of talking about the common good that inadequately addresses the kind of interdependence that is crucial in a modern society. (pp. 127-130)

When I reflect on the contrast between mediation and litigation, in light of my definition of community, I conclude that: Mediation is one of the processes of interaction that has been invented to allow people to live together.

If community exists when people who are interdependent struggle with the traditions that bind them and the interests that separate them in order to realize a future that is an improvement upon the present, then community is in the struggle. And it can be achieved and preserved only if we find the right ways to struggle with others who are unlike us. Mediation is preferred to litigation as a way to struggle because it is more likely to preserve relationships.

Mediation is more likely than litigation to provide a communal return. It can provide people with a sense of belonging, recognition, or acceptance as being part of the community. That is especially true when the mediator is a fellow citizen, rather than a robed priest of the law.

Whether the "human need for community" is encouraging the use of mediation or whether mediation is one of the tools we have stumbled upon that allows us to become more community oriented again, I believe our use of mediation has a good deal to do with the desire to live in an improved community.

Notes

1. These ideas come primarily from George Cheney, University of Colorado, Boulder, and are from his participation in a dialogue on community sponsored by the Lyndhurst Foundation in September 1990.

2. My beliefs about "community" have been influenced substantially by Scherer (1972). A slightly fuller explication of the ideas presented here can be found in Moore (1991).

3. Aristotle considered "[5,000] too large for satisfactory communal existence . . . [because] to have a community of such size, living as a leisure class would require a territory the size of Babylon, therefore it would cease to be a *polis,* and, we may infer, also cease to be a community. The best *poleis* are relatively small; this is in accordance with the general proposition that 'law is order, and good law is good order,' but a great multitude cannot be orderly . . . there is therefore a limit to the size of *poleis,* as there is to other things, plants, animals. . . . [I]f there are too many [citizens], it is not a *polis,* but an *ethnos* (nation). And to maintain order in such a one would be work of 'divine power' (*Theia dynamis*)" (Friedrich, 1959).

4. Smith (1989) explains that

> this "secondary community," the nation, is a superstructure of ideas and ideals, of common aspirations sustained by "the mystic chords of memory" which binds the primary community into a larger national community. The symbols of the secondary community are crude and highly simplified summaries of those of the primary communities, for the life of the primary community is concrete while that of the secondary community is abstract; it is from the primary communities that the secondary communities draw their life and meaning. (p. 28)

Do innovative theoretical perspectives frustrate mediation practitioners?
How can research and theory have a meaningful impact on practice?

11

The Practitioner's Dilemma

Janet Rifkin

ONE INTERESTING FEATURE of the dispute resolution movement is the extent to which it has been the subject of investigation by a broadly based research community. Since the early 1980s, researchers have been involved in evaluation efforts of specific programs and in the development of a critical analysis of the field that has focused on the social, philosophical, and political implications of informal justice (Abel, 1982). Although theoretical accounts and research studies encompass a range of perspectives and findings, much of this work embraces conclusions that are critical of contemporary mediation practices, raising concerns about power and neutrality (Cobb & Rifkin, 1991b), coercion (Northrup & Segall, 1991), and justice (Auerbach, 1983), concerns that mediators themselves debate and worry over.

Yet, despite the fact that both researchers and practitioners share angst about the social implications of the field and about the micro-dynamics of good practice, there has been remarkably little ongoing interaction between them. Mediators, for example, flock to sessions at national meetings where research presentations are made that might inform or perhaps challenge practitioners to rethink some of their practices. But these types of exchanges are primarily limited to formal professional meetings and the impact on practice is superficial. The tensions between researchers and practitioners certainly reverberate in other professional arenas beyond mediation. But these tensions present particular difficulties for mediators.

In the contemporary organization of the dispute resolution field, mediators gain entry into the mediation world by completing a training program that, depending on the state, runs from 30 to 40 hours. These courses are run by professional training consultants who have mediation experience, or in-house staff of mediation programs. For most mediators, these trainings constitute their initiation into the field, orienting trainees both to a way of thinking about the mediation process and to a structural approach to practice. This initial introduction indelibly shapes mediators' understanding of both how they should be mediating and how they should be thinking about mediation. Both their ideological view of mediation and their strategic interventions within their practices stem from their initial training experiences. Yet, for the most part, these training programs are devoid of explicit theories of practice, emphasizing instead skill building through role playing, implying that the hallmark of good practice is mastery of technique.

The impact of the initial training experience is profound for would-be mediators as it attempts, like legal education, to embed knowledge and a perspective into the trainee's formative processes in the learning of mediation and in developing professional self-images (Pipkin, 1993). In general, however, these programs are devoid of an explicit theory of practice, and it is only when practicing mediators occasionally meet up with the research community, concerned with constructing a theory of practice, that they are confronted by critiques of their work and their world, which they are often unprepared to defend, as ideology is denied as a foundation of mediation practice. The critiques and perspectives of scholars and researchers steeped in varying paradigmatic traditions stun and occasionally stimulate mediators who have not been prepared to think of themselves as engaged in a theory of practice as they mediate disputes.

Thus, as theories of mediation practice are generated, such as those found in this volume, practitioners are confronted with a dilemma: to grow as mediators they are asked to recognize and acknowledge some of the theoretical tenets that informed their practice and shaped their training; they are urged to examine and reject many of these principles as problematic for good practice; they are counseled to reframe their understanding and approach to mediation in accordance with different theoretical traditions; yet too often they are not given guidelines that assist them to conform to the admonitions to think differently and transform their practices.

The call to think and act differently that reaches some practicing mediators is generally not directed to or heard by the community of people and programs who train new mediators. Whereas there are some, albeit few, advanced workshops for experienced mediators relating to some of these issues, new mediators are constantly being trained in what is becoming routinized and skill-oriented approaches to practice. The critical theoretical and research perspectives such as those found in this volume have little likelihood of affecting the training and initiation process for mediators entering the dispute resolution world.

For mediators it is sometimes unclear who they should be listening to and learning from. If they are guided by the theoretical perspectives that inform some research studies, they may undermine their chances for professional advancement. They risk losing the desirable goal of becoming trainers within their programs, for example, if they alter its format, content, and perspective. In this context researchers must question what their obligation is once they have identified and put forward a critical analysis of practice that calls for a rethinking of the way that practice is conceptualized and conducted. Practitioners generally want to know from researchers what to do differently. Yet practitioners are often let down by scholars who offer a critique and few recommendations for the transformation of practice, which they argue goes beyond the boundaries of what they set out to do. There have been too few opportunities for researchers and practitioners to collaboratively explore the practical implications of research studies. As a result, the work of researchers often is ignored or met with cynicism by practitioners, and the orientation of practitioners remains unaffected by findings and perspectives of researchers that offer provocative and exciting insights about practice. This dilemma is well illustrated by many of the readings in this volume that call for a new discourse, a reframing, and a reformulated perspective on mediation practice.

The conclusion in several of these chapters is to call for a new theory of mediation, as each highlights differing problems within the current landscape of dispute resolution. Practitioners will undoubtedly benefit from these analyses. But many will ask what they should do differently in their practices. How should they modify their current approaches? What tactical interventions should they continue? Which should they discard? As Cobb (this volume) suggests, how can they "materialize" these emerging theoretical perspectives? But perhaps even more fundamentally, it needs to be asked whether the call for new paradigms of mediation can be understood by practitioners who have been and continue to be shaped by the professional training of their primary disciplines.

Although the picture of who constitutes the contemporary mediation community is not totally clear (Harrington & Rifkin, 1989), it is increasingly evident that a significant proportion of practicing mediators have law backgrounds. For example, much of the current teaching about ADR takes place in law schools where most law programs offer at least a course in this area and where some have infused a problem-solving perspective into the entire curriculum (Pipkin, 1993). In this context, would-be mediators are trained to think about mediation practice as an adjunct rather than as an alternative to formal law work. It is unlikely that the critiques emerging in these and other studies would sway this group of would-be mediators who are, as a result of their law training, more likely to be tied to a status quo theory of mediation rather than to an approach that advocates transformation and change.

There are additional reasons why there is likely to be resistance to the idea of innovation and change and to some of the theoretical approaches discussed in this volume and elsewhere. Mediation is becoming professionalized. The ADR field is well into its second decade, and tensions are emerging as part of its evolution as professional practice (Pipkin & Rifkin, 1984). The main professional organizations are preoccupied with the setting of standards for practice, with the regulation of trainers and the promulgation of ethical codes. The tensions stem from the fact that there is not a consensus among practitioners as to what constitutes good practice. Within the practitioner world, some of this discussion reflects a move to begin to control or even restrict entry into a field in which there is a high demand to participate but a low demand for services. As the competition for access increases, it is likely that the debate about standards of practice will intensify.

It is in this context that practitioners will understand and react to the studies in this volume. The research accounts that call upon practitioners to reevaluate and redefine their practices offer pivot-al opportunities to shift and improve their process. At the same time, however, these research accounts create dilemmas for mediators, who by modifying or repudiating the approaches to mediation imparted in their trainings, may suffer the consequence of not advancing within the mediation field, driven by a culture that many of these studies critique. In drawing upon differing aspects of communication theory, these studies critically assess the work and orientation of the majority of practicing mediators, suggesting that current constructions of practice are problematic and perhaps flawed. Furthermore, they urge practitioners to reassess their theory of practice as well as their strategic interventions within their practices. Despite what will undoubtedly be the appeal of these approaches for many mediators, they will wonder how to implement these critical perspectives without having the support structure to guide them in their attempts to operationalize new models.

Practitioners need to be retrained. As the studies in this volume suggest, new orientations to mediation that incorporate communication perspectives offer practitioners a theory of practice and the possibility to alter and perhaps improve their strategic interventions. However, although more experienced mediators may benefit from critical research, new mediators continue to enter the field through training programs that remain impervious to these critical assessments. Without changes at this point of entry into the field, it is likely that most mediators will be stymied by the practitioners' dilemma; they will want to follow the way of thinking that is advocated in these research studies but they will not know how. Mediators who are attracted to these theoretical arguments may find themselves alienated from and perhaps rebuffed by their mediation community. As they further their understandings, researchers need to reach not only practicing mediators but, perhaps more fundamentally, they need to find ways for their work to be absorbed into the training, education, and initiation process for would-be practitioners.

How do practicing mediators present themselves to parties as professionals and experts? How are differences in parties' and mediators' perceptions of morality, conflict, and justice played out in complex disputes?

12

Mediator Communication and Influence in Conflict Management Interventions

A Practitioner's Reflections on Theory and Practice

Christopher W. Moore

THE STUDY OF MEDIATOR communication patterns, means of influence, and interaction dynamics with disputing parties has been an area of increasing study by communication and dispute resolution researchers. This knowledge can increase intervenors' self-awareness of what they do to assist parties in dispute and help plan future interventions with greater clarity and intentionality. I will examine two aspects of several of the authors' analyses in more detail and show how their findings apply in practice.

Building Credibility and Means of Influence

Mediators have an unusual relationship to parties with whom they work. Although possessing no institutional basis of power that would give them legitimate authority to influence the attitudes and behavior of parties, mediators are expected to, and do, significantly motivate parties to move toward settlement. This is an interesting feat in that, at least in Western "professional" mediation, the intermediary may have had no previous relationship with the parties nor will she or he be tied into the parties' relationship network in such a way that personal reputation could play an influencing role.

Tracy and Spradlin's (this volume) research on "mediator talk," based upon an analysis of transcripts of family mediation videotapes, identifies a number of ways mediators build parties' perceptions of the intervenor's expertise and fairness: identifying themselves as professionals, referencing experience and knowledge, talking in ways that demonstrate fairness and impartiality, acting as a referee between the parties, and using reframing to diffuse or mitigate disputant's attacks that could cause them to lose face.

Parties' acceptance of a mediator as a viable helper or "expert" is generally critical if the intermediary is to assist the disputants to move toward agreement. In most Western and developed societies, expertise is viewed as knowledge that is not widely held, which is often learned through an extended course of study or practice. Expertise is generally closely associated with the concept of professionalism, which may also imply a particular formal relationship between intermediary and clients and ethical standards of behavior. In the West, credibility is most easily gained by having parties perceive the intervenor as a professional and expert, for these cultures have a commonly accepted norm of turning problems over to experts for assistance. Witness the common acceptability of doctors, lawyers, therapists, social workers, scientists, and so forth, who actively and influentially intervene in people's lives.

So how do mediators go about the business of presenting themselves to parties as professionals and experts? Although Tracy and Spradlin stress specific communications patterns found during the opening statements of mediation sessions, the process of image building has probably begun much earlier with the initial contacts between the parties and mediator. Early contacts usually involve verbal, nonverbal, written, symbolic objects, and even spatial forms of communications, which build the mediator's image of professionalism. These are generally reinforced throughout the process of the intervention.

Initial contacts are often made by telephone, and parties frequently have a number of questions they ask of mediators. The latter may also provide information without being asked as a means of increasing his or her stature and influence. Mediators often talk about their years in the field and extensive experience in the general area of the disputants' conflicts ("I've been in practice for twelve years and have mediated a number of commercial cases").

They may also describe issues and dynamics of past cases, where appropriate and without breaching confidentiality, and outline specific areas of substantive knowledge ("Yes, I've handled a number of environmental cases involving water and stream flow, with similar technical issues, such as the protection of endangered species, similar to the case you are describing"). Academic training and professional background, often linked to another status profession (which I call "piggybacking"), may also be stressed. For example, "I'm trained as a mediator, and also have a doctoral degree in science" or "I was trained by Alpha Associates, which is one of the oldest and most experienced mediation organizations in the country." Associational influence may also be used by identifying colleagues with whom he or she works, for example, "I work closely with Dr. Clifford, who is an expert in this field"; and where appropriate, references to former clients who, because of their prestige or satisfaction with the intermediaries' services, will testify to his or her expertise ("I've worked for the Beta and Gamma Corporation, and they have been very pleased with the series of mediations that we have conducted. They said the process saved them thousands of dollars in contract claims"). All of the above communications are generally reinforced once the parties meet face to face in the first session.

In addition to the above verbal communications, mediators often use a number of symbolic objects to increase their image as experts. These include business cards, brochures, prospecti of services, lists of colleagues (with appropriate and widely respected degrees), former client lists, framed diplomas or certificates (university degrees, certificates of mediation training, or socially respectable awards), and professional-looking offices (preferably with lots of bookshelves with appropriate titles and professional journals!). I remember a case of a divorcing couple who had been mediating a financial settlement in one of my organization's small conference rooms. The room had some comfortable chairs and floor lamps and looked much like a living room or therapist's office. One day, the room was double scheduled and the couple's session had to be moved to the building's law library. The wife looked around the room, noted the large conference table and law books and said, "This is more like it! Now we can get down to business!" They did, and settled some difficult financial issues that had been blocking movement for the last two sessions. One wonders how much the setting played a role in creating an image of expertise, professionalism, and serious "business" that contributed to the dynamic of settlement.

Beyond developing an image of professionalism and expertise, mediators also try to develop an image of fairness. Common synonyms for *fair* include *equitable, impartial, unbiased,* and *unprejudiced.* In general, fairness can refer to the mediator's attitude and behavior toward the substantive outcome of a dispute, the process used to arrive at an agreement, and consideration for the psychological needs of parties. Fairness in the context of Western culture and mediation generally refers to equitable procedural and psychological treatment.

A perception of the mediator's fairness, as described by Tracy and Spradlin (this volume), was developed in three ways: (1) the intermediaries' verbal stress on their "neutral" or "balanced" role; (2) "referee-like conversation modes" to equalize the parties' communications; and (3) attempts to "reframe disputant face-threats in less hostile or blaming language." Mediators often comment that "seeing (or experiencing) is believing" when it comes to parties accepting that a mediator is fair and impartial. Procedural and psychological perceptions of fairness are generally demonstrated by a number of behaviors: (1) the mediator introducing him- or herself in an equal manner and performing equal nonverbals such as handshaking; (2) addressing the parties in a similar manner, demonstrating both equal respect and status (both by first names or more formally Mr., Ms., Mrs., Dr.); (3) sitting an equal distance from both parties and providing them with chairs of equal height and status; (4) describing a process that each considers reasonable and that provides each with a turn to describe the situation as they see it, identify their issues and interests, and jointly participate in problem solving; (5) establishing fair discussion guidelines, such as rules about interruptions; (6) maintaining equal and periodic eye contact with both parties, even during times when only one is speaking; (7) demonstrating an equivalent amount of interest in what each party has to say through eye contact, verbal acknowledgments ("uh-huh"), and questions; (8) allowing similar amounts of time for each to speak; (9) restating each party's issues, interests, and concerns; and (10) summarizing the statements of each. Mediators create an image of substantive fairness by: (1) describing, or framing, the problem or task to arrive at a solution that both parties will consider fair and reasonable; (2) assisting parties to identify mutually acceptable standards and criteria that they can jointly accept as frameworks for the agreement; (3) identifying past practices that parties might consider to be fair and reasonable; (4) identifying commonly accepted legal mandates, rules, or social standards against which parties can measure a possible agreement; (5) helping to develop trade-offs of items valued differently, the sum of which parties believe will be fair; (6) assisting parties to obtain an advisory opinion by experts whom they believe to be fair; (7) asking the parties to identify what they *feel* (i.e., in their gut) to be fair; (8) asking parties to identify solutions that would be acceptable in the future, that would minimize unacceptable risks or costs to each of them (especially if they evaluate the probability of future events or risks differently); and (9) suggesting mechanical means of arriving at fair and equitable decisions (splitting the difference, alternating selection or satisfaction of interests, tying an agreement to an external factor such as the Consumer Price Index, etc.).

Framing and Reframing

Framing the way a communication, problem, or situation is conceptualized, described, and articulated is often a critical factor in the dispute resolution process. The individual framing of a problem by disputants or the mediator can often determine whether the parties will reach an agreement or impasse. Framing can be applied to a number of situations, problems, or conditions (Moore, 1989). Framing can be used to describe:

- A general situation
- An issue or topic for discussion
- A position or preferred solution to a specific problem
- An interest or underlying need—substantive, procedural, or psychological—that a party wants to have addressed or satisfied as a result of interaction (negotiation)
- Timing for a specific act or performance

■ Consequences or threats that will result or be carried out if something is done or not done
■ A feeling, attitude, or judgment

Because the framing of a problem or situation is often critical to its negotiability or to parties' receptivity to communication, reframing is often required to change or modify the original frame and make it more acceptable. Reframing involves redefining or interpreting a communication, description of a problem, or situation in such a way that problem solving is more feasible and the communication is more acceptable to the receiving party. The act of framing or reframing can involve both content and process, that is, changing the substantive content of the message or modifying the way that it is delivered by changing words, syntax, tone, or pace. Let us examine framing and reframing in more detail.

Littlejohn, Shailor, and Pearce (this volume) focus on the general framing of the parties' reality and how their framing interrelates with that of the mediator. For these authors, framing of issues, and that reality about which the parties are negotiating, may be on the surface, where parties have similar views of reality; or may be much deeper, when parties fundamentally differ over their views of morality, conflict, and justice. They use these three realities—moral, conflict, and justice—to develop a framework that can be used to compare how parties and mediators define conflict situations. The compatibility or incompatibility of frames is often a significant determinant as to whether negotiated solutions are possible.

The moral reality, or philosophic principles held by an individual or group about the proper conduct of life, can be divided into four somewhat overlapping moral stances found in American society (Bellah et al., 1985). These include: (1) "the biblical or *authoritarian,* which is based on scriptural direction or divine authority; (2) the *republican,* which involves the idea of civic duty and public service; (3) the *utilitarian,* which seeks the fulfillment of individual interests by negotiating agreements with others; and (4) the *expressivist,* which calls for the pursuit of individual rights and free expression" (Littlejohn et al., this volume).

In general, conflict realities refer to parties' definitions of conflict, views about how it is appropriately handled and managed, and attitudes or values regarding the roles of third parties. Parties may see conflict as healthy, normal, functional, and useful, or dysfunctional, abnormal, unhealthy, and to be avoided or prevented. Conflict may be appropriately responded to by accepting and maintaining it but preventing its negative aspects; bargaining, to share gains and losses and reach compromises; imposing solutions, as in a power model in which the strongest side wins; creating coalitions, forming alliances so that the outcome is determined by the largest alignment of forces (such as in an election); or by building consensus, in which parties engage in cooperative problem solving and strive to address or satisfy as many interests as possible.

Littlejohn et al. identify two modes of reliance on third parties, the *adjudicative* and *authoritative*. Both models support a decision by a third party. The former is based on the weight or quality of argumentation, while the latter applies a cultural or religious standard to arrive at a conclusive answer. (Interestingly, the authors do not include a category of third-party assistance that focuses on process assistance, the basis of mediation, even though this is common in Western societies—such as counseling or therapy.)

Justice realties refer to principles by which parties determine if a proper or fair outcome has been achieved. The authors identify three types of justice reality: (1) *retributive justice,* in which wrongdoers are punished; (2) *competitive justice,* in which parties compete to maximize gains and minimize losses; and (3) *distributive justice,* in which resources or benefits are distributed according to one of four standards: (1) entitlements (gender, race, rank, role, or class); (2) equality (equal distribution regardless of consideration of other factors); (3) equity (according to some jointly acceptable principle of fairness); and (4) social welfare (promotion of the broader or common good).

The three broad categories or frames—moral, conflict, and justice—shape how individuals define broad conflict situations. Coordination between the parties' and mediator's realities is generally achieved by one of three means: (1) one participant (including the mediator) persuades the others to accept his or her definition of reality; (2) the parties jointly develop a mutually acceptable definition or frame; or (3) a situation is created in which the different framings are irrelevant to the settlement of issues in dispute. Let us examine how this process of framing and reframing works in real life. The following case illustrates both how parties frame a general conflict situation and how these frames are translated into specific issues to be discussed and negotiated.

In late 1992, the Alaska Board of Game, after several years of studies and deliberation, announced that the agency planned to implement a program of wolf control, systematic extermination of a specific number of wolves in selected areas to manage predator-prey among wolves, caribou, moose, and human hunters. Wolves are not a threatened or endangered species in Alaska as they are in the lower 48 states and, in fact, exist and reproduce in fairly large numbers. In spite of this fact, there was tremendous opposition to the proposed plan by a significant number of environmental and animal rights groups, which initiated a letter-writing campaign to public officials and launched a tourist boycott against the State until such time as the plan was reversed. The hunting communities, both sports and subsistence, were generally in favor of the plan because they believed wolves had seriously depleted herds in some sectors of the State. They began to put pressure on the Governor and the Board to implement the plan as soon as possible. In response to the surfacing of this serious public conflict, Governor Hickel convened a Wolf Summit, a large conference attended by representatives of all interest groups, to air views and determine if there were any areas of consensus as to what should be done. More than 1,500 participants and observers ultimately attended. Intermediaries, conflict managers from CDR Associates, and the staff of the State Ombudsman's Office were secured to design and facilitate the process and manage the meetings.

Although there were many groups involved in the meetings, they basically coalesced into four groups: (1) the State, including the Governor and the Board; (2) environmentalists and animal rights activists; (3) hunters; and (4) the facilitators and intermediaries. A critical task for the parties and intermediaries was to arrive at some common frames for the meeting that would allow for productive dialogue and exploration of possible areas of agreement. This was not an easy task given the range of frames for the situation and issues to be discussed.

The State framed the situation and its responsibility in terms of a combination of republican and utilitarian morality. It was the State's civic duty to find a just solution involving trade-offs that would satisfy the broadest range of interests. The State viewed conflict as normal, but believed that it was destructive to some of the key interests in the State. The State assumed that the decision should be made by elected or appointed authorities based upon the weight of the argumentation of concerned parties. A just solution for the State would be a combination of competitive and distributive justice that would ideally be based on a broad consensus of equity that would be best for the people of Alaska.

The hunters had a number of diverse views of reality depending upon whether they were sportspeople, subsistence hunters, or Native Alaskans. Generally, they viewed the situation in expressivist terms. Hunting was part of their individual self-concept and many of them had moved to Alaska, a state perceived to be less controlling of individual rights, to exercise their freedom. Native Alaskans saw hunting as a tradition and part of their culture. Many of the hunters viewed the people opposing the State's plan as "foreigners," "people from the lower 48," or "folks from another country, the U.S.A." (Some of the hunters belonged to the Alaskan Independence Party, a strong State's rights group.) Although some of the hunters took an adjudicative view toward the role of third parties, others cast their reality as God-given rights or the cultural heritage of Native Alaskan hunters. The hunters' view of justice ranged from a competitive approach, in which they struggled to get the plan implemented at the expense of other groups, to an entitlement approach advocated by Native Alaskans who wanted their traditions and culture to be protected.

The environmentalists and animal rights activists, although generally in the same interest group, had a range of realities that shaped their framing of the situation. Their moral realities were defined variously in authoritarian, republican, and utilitarian terms. They almost unanimously objected to the anthropocentric worldview of the hunters and the State. Some individuals in this group argued that it was morally wrong to kill animals, while others argued that it was the civic duty of the State and its citizens to develop a democratic solution to the problem that addressed all parties' (including the wolves') interests. For some members of this group, trade-offs were possible while, for others, a win/lose outcome was the only possible solution. This group viewed conflict as being normal and was familiar and comfortable with adversarial and adjudicatory means of arriving at decisions. They argued, by presenting the results of a poll, that the majority of the Alaskan population opposed wolf control and that this factor should be factored into the Board's decision. For many members of this group. a just decision would be one that was equitable and fair (especially to the wolf population), and that took into consideration the welfare of specific interest groups, including people in the lower 48 states and future generations that wanted to experience the wilderness and Alaskan wildlife. The facilitators, who were actually performing mediating functions, generally held a moral view that was a combination of republican and utilitarian. They viewed conflict as normal and potentially beneficial as a motivator to find better solutions. They viewed the role of third parties in neither adjudicative nor authoritarian terms, but preferred to view third parties in facilitative roles. The adjudicative process was seen as a backup system if the parties couldn't reach a consensus or find acceptable trade-offs. The mediators' concept of justice was distributive in nature, in that they valued equity (for both people and diverse populations of animals) and finding a solution that met the broader social welfare.

Given these diverse views of reality, how could the parties participate in a meeting to discuss the issues, how should they be framed, and what kind of process would be acceptable? The State had designed a preliminary agenda with broad time blocks and activities over which the facilitators had only minimal control. The facilitators, in conjunction with a "process design committee" composed of respected representatives of all major interest groups, worked to design procedures within this framework that would result in some convergence of frames and the greatest substantive, procedural, and psychological satisfaction possible for meeting participants.

The first part of the meeting was structured to allow participants to present some of their broader realities and worldviews and to identify issues or concerns raised by the Board's plan for wolf management. A balanced group of representatives of all interests was selected to participate in a series of panels to present their views, build a common base of understanding of the problems and issues, and raise relevant points for further discussion. An "open mike" was used to augment these presentations with the views of a broader range of participants. This session brought out the range of frames, issues, and interests of all concerned parties. All participants accepted this process as a way to begin, although they did argue about the amount of time allocated to individual speakers representing diverse interest groups.

The second part of the meeting was originally planned to include a 3-hour group plenary session in which participants would talk with each other about the interests to be met and components of a satisfactory policy and plan, using a rotating member "fish bowl" format. The facilitators hoped that the information shared by speakers and participants earlier in the day, and the participants' desire to talk about the issues, would result in a productive dialogue. It was here that the parties' concepts of acceptable dispute resolution processes and the facilitators' process realities diverged. The parties, who were familiar with and had an adjudicatory framing of the situation and processes, wanted to use the forum to make position statements as they would in a public hearing, even though a formal adjudicatory body was not convened to take their testimony and make a decision. The facilitators tried to encourage the group to use a more dialogue-focused problem-solving process, and some parties took this opportunity, but the majority wanted to have a more adjudicatory public hearing. Realizing that the parties' framing of the situation required them to make position statements before they could discuss the issue further, the facilitators restructured the agenda into a traditional public meeting format. Ultimately, this change of format performed an additional information exchange function, made participants aware that they could influence the dispute resolution process, and after positions were firmly and publicly stated, allowed them to move forward and discuss in detail some of their underlying concerns and interests in some small group sessions.

The third part of the meeting was a series of facilitated small groups, composed of a balanced mix of representatives from the interest groups. The groups were asked to explore whether there were any areas of consensus that they could recommend to the Board, and to come back with a report that would be presented to the Governor, the Board, and all participants. This task in itself imposed the moral and procedural realities of the State and the facilitators on some members of the group that were more comfortable pursuing a totally adversarial and adjudicative approach to conflict resolution. (Some of these groups viewed their role at the meetings to be completed once they had made their public position statements.)

Given the range of realities in the meeting, the facilitation team had to develop a framing for the purpose and tasks of the small-group sessions. They also had to frame the issues to be addressed; to allow the parties dialogue, not reach an immediate impasse; and to reach some areas of agreement. Framing issues involves the definition of specific topics that parties want to address. Parties often frame issues in a manner that is unacceptable to others. In this event, either the mediator or another party would have to try a reframe until a mutually acceptable definition is found. The possibilities for deadlock due to the diversity of frames of the broad reality and specific issues were immense. Some animal rights activists framed the situation and issue as "How to stop the killing of wolves." Some environmentalists framed the issue as "How can we implement ecosystem management, to place animal interests on a similar level as humans?" Hunters, from an expressivistic perspective, framed the issue as "How can we as Alaskans make our own decisions without interference from outsiders?", while Native Alaskans framed the issue as "How can I continue to exercise my God-given and traditional practices to hunt and preserve my culture?" The State's framing, though never directly articulated in these terms, was "How can we manage the animal populations to maintain a sustained yield of game, satisfy the various concerned publics, avoid costly and destructive conflict, and maintain our political viability?" Ultimately, the facilitators developed a proposal for multiple substantive and procedural framings of topics for the small groups to discuss that allowed for the diversity of participant views of reality and the diverse issues and interests that these implied. These included:

- What should the long-term objectives be for the State wolf management policies and practices?
- Are there any circumstances when wolf control is/is not appropriate?
- If wolf control were to occur, what are the appropriate methods for meeting wolf control objectives?
- What are the procedures by which wolf management policies should be set and implementing practices adopted?

The framing of issues was done in the form of questions that minimized either/or solutions, elicited more information on the parties' underlying interests, generated a range of options that might address the constellation of concerned interests, and encouraged the parties to develop their own consensus-based solutions rather than rely on an adjudicatory process. Although all participants were not satisfied with the framing of the issues, the large majority of parties accepted the framing and the process, grappled with the issues, explored interests, and developed more than 50 recommendations that received the general support of the group. These recommendations were presented to the Governor and Board for consideration.[1]

Conclusion

The ways mediators interact with clients are often major factors in the success of a dispute resolution initiative. Procedures intermediaries use to create credibility and promote an image of fairness are critical for initial entry and for increasing parties' acceptance of the mediator's assistance and influence. Reframing is a critical skill to redefine parties' situations, issues, interests, and emotions so that dialogue is more feasible and productive. All of these interventions and skills can be learned so that intervenors are more effective in working with clients and parties will have a greater opportunity to reach settlements.

Note

1. In public disputes of this type, parties do not always have final authority to decide issues. This authority rests with legally elected or appointed bodies. However, consensus-based solutions are strong recommendations that elected or appointed bodies generally take very seriously.

Epilogue

Toward Furthering Dialogue Between Researchers and Practitioners

ALL TOO OFTEN the links between scholarship and practice are ignored. Even in clearly applied arenas such as third-party intervention, productive dialogue among researchers and practitioners is surprisingly rare, especially in published forums. For researchers, this means that many good insights are not translated into practice. For practitioners, it means that research may seem irrelevant or even threatening—researchers may appear to be studying and analyzing without clarifying implications for practice or suggesting workable alternatives.

We would be disappointed if the ideas in this volume fail to contribute to the development of improvements in third-party practice. The communication perspective, as revealed in these chapters, provides an eminently "practical" understanding of mediation. It can be a cornerstone on which the mediation process is built, leading to effective and possibly new ways of conducting the process, training mediators, evaluating outcomes, and institutionalizing programs.

Our last effort in this volume is to further current dialogue that attempts to bridge theory and practice. In this sense, our ending is more appropriately intended as a beginning. We offer a springboard for dialogue by revisiting themes that underlie these chapters and detailing some of their practice implications. As with all beginnings, this one is necessarily selective and is therefore incomplete. However, by exemplifying how practitioners can draw from the communication perspective to impact practice, we trust additional insights will be available to those who draw from chapters in this volume.

Acknowledging the Contextual Influences on Mediation Practice

Throughout this volume several authors have echoed a key assumption of the communication perspective—that comprehension of context is key to understanding the nature of effective mediation. Several theorists ask us to recognize that mediation is not a context-free process; rather, it is shaped by and shapes the organizational, social, and interpersonal arenas in which it occurs. In much the same way that words are dependent on multiple levels of context for interpretation, conflict intervention processes such as mediation are interpreted differently depending upon the contexts in which they are enacted.

Taking this principle to heart means grasping the essence of operative contexts and appreciating their intermingling. Authors in this volume have discussed context in a variety of ways. At the broadest levels, context is discussed as culture or community. C. M. Moore calls for a reinvestment in the role of community as context. Folger and Bush elaborate on the implications of broad ideologies about conflict and social relationships. And Donohue and Bresnahan illuminate cultural implications for intergroup conflict and mediation. Working with a somewhat narrower conception of context, several contributors concentrate on institutional or organizational contexts, giving attention to the fit between third parties and their institutional settings. Karambayya and Brett's model of organizational intervention and Jones and Brinkman's analysis of peer mediation programs underscore the importance of considering organizational practice and culture in determining the design of dispute resolution systems. Jones points to an even narrower contextual influence in her discussion of dialectical tensions. She focuses on relationship contexts that shape interpretive and constructive implications of communicative behavior. The range of contexts considered throughout the volume attests to the embedded nature of contextual influences—there are layers of context that ultimately create disputants' and mediators' sense of what mediation is and what it can accomplish.

Implications for Practice

Program administrators and mediators can work toward developing more context-sensitive practice. The following suggestions may be useful in achieving this goal.

Define Contexts. Although defining contexts seems simplistic, all too often basic contextual influences on practice go unacknowledged. Definitions of context are assumed that prevent practitioners from appreciating important influences shaping practice. Or confusion results when different mediators or program administrators emphasize different contextual influences. Defining relevant contexts encourages mediators and administrators to step back and see the current dispute or overall mediation process in a larger frame that may alter their perception of its purpose and process.

Understand the Implications of Relevant Contexts. Mediators' understanding of context should involve attention to the external factors that shape their orientation to mediation and their specific views of the dispute at hand. Once mediators see themselves reflecting broader background influences, such as training, education, race, or gender, they can better appreciate their influence in reenacting or altering these influences. Program administrators' understanding of context should involve attention to ideological, cultural, and institutional influences that shape and sometimes dictate elements of practice and goals of the process.

Adjust Mediation Practice to Accommodate Contextual Concerns. The underlying logic of designing dispute systems is to match dispute resolution methods to the conflict situation. This logic is well illustrated in the chapters on contextual influences in this volume. On a more specific level, mediators and program administrators can match method and needs of particular parties, especially when cultural differences are key. Pairing mediators and disputants from similar cultures and backgrounds is a model already in use in several mediation programs. A more radical approach might involve allowing the participants to "negotiate" the nature of the mediation process with the mediator. Altering stages of the process, speaking orders, ground rules, preferred outcomes, criteria for success, and so forth, might be difficult but could yield the kind of responsiveness initially intended by some proponents of alternative dispute resolution.

Recognizing That Mediation Is a Mutual Influence Process

For quite some time, two myths permeated the folklore of mediation. Both center on the role of influence in practice. The first myth is that mediators are "neutral" parties in the process. The second is that mediators exert influence but are not influenced by the unfolding process—the belief in the "Teflon mediator." Both of these views have recently been discredited, and the communication perspective helps to explain their flaws.

The communication perspective asks us to acknowledge that as mediators attempt to manage disputants' conflicts, they also enter them. Mediators become parties involved with the conflict, albeit with their own outlooks and from their own unique stance as convener, interpreter, and overseer of the process. In short, mediators inevitably play an influential role in the way conflicts unfold during intervention. Mediator influence is inevitable because of what we know about the fundamental nature of any human interaction: We cannot be part of an interaction without continuously shaping, moving, and directing it.

Both intentionally and unintentionally, mediators influence interaction in a variety of ways. The work in this volume suggests that mediators' orientations—their explicit or implicit views of conflict, justice, and morality (Littlejohn, Shailor, & Pearce), their underlying ideological bent and their beliefs about the nature and use of problem solving (Folger & Bush), their views of which narratives are credible (Cobb), their selection of language to influence perceptions of mediator credibility and orientation (Tracy & Spradlin)—all contribute to the way a conflict, within mediation, ultimately unfolds.

Implications for Practice

   Recognizing the inevitability of influence has several important practice implications. We will briefly mention a few.

Specify Acceptable Forms of Mediator Influence. When we—as policy makers and practicing mediators—begin to see that some forms of influence are *inevitable*, we are forced to decide which forms of influence are *acceptable*. How we view these forms of influence says a great deal about what we think mediation is and what we expect it to accomplish. Some forms of mediator influence are viewed as totally unproblematic because they are seen as consistent with the goals of the process—they are expected as part of the mediator's role. Other forms of mediator influence are viewed as problematic or unacceptable because they are seen as inconsistent with the expectations for a mediator's role. Articulating why some forms of influence are acceptable and others are not is key to understanding what we want mediation to be the various arenas in which it is practiced. It may well provide a way to clarify the different conceptions of mediation we implicitly hold.

Decide What Forms of Influence Need to Be Made Explicit. Taking the principle of mutual influence to heart means considering whether some forms of mediator influence need to be acknowledged in ways that have not previously been considered. Although we have no definitive answers, practitioners need to address questions such as: Should mediators be asked or required to clarify the implicit orientations they carry with them as they practice? Should they be more reflective about, for instance, their views of conflict, morality, and justice as well as more content-related assumptions about the arena in which in they practice? Should *disputants* know any of this information about a mediator's outlook, assumptions, points of view before a session begins? Would giving parties such information change our views about what forms of mediator influence are acceptable? Does this "buyer beware" approach make sense, given the inevitability of mediator influence? These are the types of issues program administrators and mediators might wrestle with in considering the policy and design implications of taking the fact of mutual influence seriously.

Identify How Mediators' and Disputants' Discourse Defines and Shapes Interaction During the Process. The work in this volume suggests that mediators and disputants jointly participate in and create certain forms of talk as a mediation unfolds. Studies in this volume suggest that narrative structures, responses to dialectical tensions, sequences in which empowerment or recognition are achieved, and contexts in which mediators extend or drop disputants' prior comments are important discursive forms that shape the process. Seeing these forms of talk is important because they enable us to begin thinking of mediation as something more than a series of global stages that mediators initiate and lead disputants through (i.e., introduction, fact-finding, creation of options, etc.). Although these global stages provide useful frameworks for describing the basic direction mediation takes, they are at best introductory tools—they offer a series of snapshots that fail to capture the dynamic and interpretive properties of the process. Any experienced mediator knows that what happens as participants talk within and across these stages is what counts in understanding how a conflict unfolds during a session. Less often, mediators realize how *their* moves are part of these emerging patterns. And most mediators find it difficult to identify, discuss, or change these micro patterns of interaction.

Training programs can draw upon these forms of discourse, making them part and parcel of how mediators think about, discuss, and evaluate what occurs in any session. Trainers can ask mediators to identify these patterns in tapes, transcripts, or role plays and to discuss how these forms influence developments in the session. Through this kind of training, mediators can come to understand, for instance, how some disputants' narratives gain hold during a session. They can see how they might inadvertently seal off or ignore vulnerable places in some narratives, making it difficult for other disputants to challenge basic premises or interpretations. Or, mediators can come to see when they are likely to extend or drop a point raised in a disputant's prior comment and understand the impact these choices have on the direction of the session. This type of training could provide mediators with an accessible language for discussing the development of conflicts and understanding the role third parties play in them during sessions.

References

Abel, R. (1982). *The politics of informal justice.* New York: Academic Press.

Aboud, F. (1981). Egocentricism, conformity, and agreeing to disagree. *Developmental Psychology, 17*(6), 791-799.

Academy of Family Mediators. (1989a). *Initial mediation* [A training videotape]. Academy of Family Mediators. P.O. Box 10501. Eugene, OR 97440.

Academy of Family Mediators. (1989b). *Yours, mine, and ours: Property division mediation* [A training videotape]. Academy of Family Mediators. P.O. Box 10501. Eugene, OR 97440.

Acock, A. C. (1984). Parents and their children: The study of intergenerational influence. *Sociology and Social Research, 68,* 151-171.

Adalbjarnardottir, S., & Selman, R. (1989). How children propose to deal with the criticism of their teachers and classmates: Developmental and stylistic variations. *Child Development, 60*(3), 539-550.

Adams, J. S. (1965). Inequity in social exchange. In L. Berkowitz (Ed.), *Advances in experimental social psychology* (Vol. 2). New York: Academic Press.

Agar, M., & Hobbs, J. (1982). Interpreting discourse: Coherence and the analysis of ethnographic interviews. *Discourse Processes, 5,* 1-32.

Alberts, J. K., & Driscoll, G. (1992). Containment versus escalation: The trajectory of couple's conversational complaints. *Western Journal of Communication, 56,* 394-412.

Allport, G. (1954). *The nature of prejudice.* Reading, MA: Addison-Wesley.

Altman, I., Vinsel, A., & Brown, B. (1981). Dialectic conceptions in social psychology. *Advances in Experimental Social Psychology, 14,* 107-160.

Araki, C. T. (1990). Dispute management in the schools. *Mediation Quarterly, 8*(1), 51-62.

Askham, J. (1976). Identity and stability within the marriage relationship. *Journal of Marriage and the Family, 38,* 535-547.

Aubert, V. (1963). Competition and dissensus: Two types of conflict and conflict resolution. *Journal of Conflict Resolution, 7*(1), 26-42.

Auerbach, J. (1983). *Justice without law.* New York: Oxford University Press.

Backman, C. W. (1988). The self: A dialectical approach. *Advances in Experimental Social Psychology, 21,* 229-260.

Bamburg, J., & Isaacson, N. (1991). *A conceptual model of the instructionally effective school.* (ERIC Document Reproduction Service No. ED 333 533)

Bartunek, J. M., Benton, A. A., & Keys, C. B. (1975). Third party intervention and the bargaining behavior of group representatives. *Journal of Conflict Resolution, 19,* 532-557.

Basseches, M. A. (1981). *Beyond closed-system problem-solving: A study of meta-systemic aspects of mature thought.* Unpublished doctoral dissertation, Harvard University.

Bavelas, J., Black, A., Chovil, N., & Mullett, J. (1990). *Equivocal communication.* Newbury Park, CA: Sage.

Baxter, L. A. (1988). A dialectical perspective on communication strategies in relationship development. In S. W. Duck (Ed.), *Handbook of personal relationships* (pp. 257-273). New York: John Wiley.

Baxter, L. A. (1989, May). *On structure and its deconstruction in relational "texts": Toward a dialectical approach to the study of personal relationships.* Paper presented at the International Communication Association convention, San Francisco.

Baxter, L. A. (1990). Dialectical contradictions in relationship development. *Journal of Social and Personal Relationships, 7,* 69-88.

Belenky, M., Clinchy, B., Goldberger, N., & Tarule, J. (1986). *Women's ways of knowing.* New York: Basic Books.

Bellah, R. N., Madsen, R., Sullivan, W. M., Swidler, A., & Tipton, S. M. (1985). *Habits of the heart: Individualism and commitment in American life.* Berkeley: University of California Press.

Bellah, R. N., Madsen, R., Sullivan, W. M., Swidler, A., & Tipton, S. M. (1991). *The good society.* New York: Knopf.

Benenson, W. A. (1988). *Assessing the effectiveness of a peer based conflict management program in elementary schools.* Unpublished doctoral dissertation, University of Idaho, Boise.

Bennett, L., & Feldman, M. (1981). *Restructuring reality in the courtroom.* London: Tavistock.

Bercovitch, J. (1991). International mediation. *Journal of Peace Research, 28,* 3-6.

Berg-Cross, L., & Zoppetti, L. (1991). Person-in-culture interview: Understanding culturally different students. *Journal of College Student Psychotherapy, 5*(4), 5-21.

Berger, C. R., & Calabrese, R. J. (1975). Some explorations in initial interaction and beyond: Toward a developmental theory of interpersonal communication. *Human Communication Research, 1,* 99-112.

Berger, P., & Luckmann, T. (1966). *The social construction of reality.* Garden City, NY: Doubleday.

Bernard, S. E., Folger, J. P., Weingarten, H. R., & Zumeta, Z. R. (1984). The neutral mediator: Value dilemmas in divorce mediation. *Mediation Quarterly, 4,* 61-74.

Bernstein, R. (1983). *Beyond objectivism and relativism: Science, hermeneutics and praxis.* Philadelphia: University of Pennsylvania Press.

Billig, M., Condor, S., Edwards, D., Gane, M., Middleton, D., & Radley, A. (1988). *Ideological dilemmas: A social psychology of everyday thinking.* Newbury Park, CA: Sage.

Black, D. (1984). Social control as a dependent variable. In D. Black (Ed.), *Toward a general theory of social control* (pp. 1-36). New York: Academic Press.

Blades, J. (1984). Mediation: An old art revitalized. *Mediation Quarterly, 3,* 59-98.

Blake, R. R., & Mouton, J. S. (1964). *The managerial grid.* Houston: Gulf Publishing.

Blalock, H. M. (1982). *Race and ethnic relations.* Englewood Cliffs, NJ: Prentice Hall.

Bochner, A. P. (1984). The functions of human communicating in interpersonal bonding. In C. C. Arnold & J. W. Bowers (Eds.), *Handbook of rhetorical and communication theory* (pp. 544-621). Boston, MA: Allyn & Bacon.

Bochner, A. P., & Eisenberg, E. M. (1987). Family process: Systems perspectives. In C. R. Berger & S. H. Chaffee (Eds.), *Handbook of communication science* (pp. 540-563). Newbury Park, CA: Sage.

Bond, M., & Forgas, J. (1984). Linking person perception to behavior intention across cultures. *Journal of Cross-Culture Psychology, 15,* 337-353.

Bopp, M. J., & Weeks, G. R. (1984). Dialectical metatheory in family therapy. *Family Process, 23,* 49-61.

Borisoff, D., & Victor, D. A. (1989). *Conflict management: A communication skills approach.* Englewood Cliffs, NJ: Prentice Hall.

Boszormenyi-Nagy, I., & Spark, G. M. (1973). *Invisible loyalties: Reciprocity in intergenerational family therapy.* Hagerstown, MD: Harper & Row.

Boszormenyi-Nagy, I., & Ulrich, D. (1981). Contextual family therapy. In A. Gurman & D. Kniskern (Eds.), *Handbook of family therapy.* NY: Brunner/Mazel.

Brady, M. (1981). Narrative competence: A Navajo example of peer-group evaluation. *Bilingual Resources, 4*(22-23), 2-13.

Brenneis, D. (1988). Language and disputing. *American Review of Anthropology, 17,* 221-237.

Brenneis, D., & Lein, L. (1977). "You fruithead": A socio-linguistic approach to dispute settlement. In S. Ervin-Tripp & C. Mitchell-Kernan (Eds.), *Child discourse.* New York: Academic Press.

Bresnahan, M. I., & Kim, M. S. (1991, August). *American undergraduates' receptivity to international teaching assistants: An issue of English proficiency?* Paper presented at the Fourth International Conference on Language and Social Psychology, University of California, Santa Barbara.

Brett, J. M., & Rognes, J. (1986). Intergroup relations. In P. Goodman (Ed.), *Groups in organizations.* San Francisco: Jossey-Bass.

Bridge, K., & Baxter, L. A. (1992). Blended relationships: Friends as work associates. *Western Journal of Communication, 56,* 200-225.

Brinkman, H. (1991). *Conflict resolution training in the school environment.* Paper presented at the International Association for Conflict Management conference, Den Dolder, The Netherlands.

Brion-Meisels, S., Lowenheim, G., & Rendeiro, B. (1982). *The adolescent decisions program.* Boston, MA: Adolescent Issues Project.

Brion-Meisels, S., Rendeiro, B., & Lowenheim, G. (1984). Student decision-making: Improving school climate for all students. In S. Braaten, R. Rutherford, Jr., & C. Kardash (Eds.), *Programming for adolescents with behavioral disorders.* Reston, VA: Council for Exceptional Children.

Brion-Meisels, S., & Selman, R. (1984). Early adolescent development of new intervention. *School Psychology Review, 13*(3), 278-291.

Brophy, J. E. (1983). Classroom organization and management. *The Elementary School Journal, 83*(4), 265-285.

Burke, J., & Clark, R. (1982), An assessment of the methodological options for investigating the development of persuasive skills across childhood. *Central States Speech Journal, 33,* 437-445.

Burrell, N. A., Donahue, W. A., & Allen, M. (1990). The impact of disputants' expectations on mediation: Testing an interventionist model. *Human Communication Research, 17,* 104-139.

Burrell, N. A., & Vogl, S. M. (1990). Turf-side conflict mediation for students. *Mediation Quarterly, 7*(3), 237-252.

Bush, R. A. B. (1989). Efficiency and protection, or empowerment and recognition?: The mediator's role and ethical standards in mediation. *Florida Law Review, 41*(2), 253-286.

Buss, A. (1976). Development of dialectics and development of humanistic psychology. *Human Development, 19,* 248-260.

Cahn, E. S., & Cahn, J. C. (1970). Power to the people or the profession—The public interest in public interest law. *Yale Law Journal, 79,* 1005-1048.

Callias, M., Frosh, S., & Michie, S. (1987). Group social skills training for young children in a clinical setting. *Behavioural Psychotherapy, 15,* 367-380.

Camras, L. (1984). Children's verbal and nonverbal behaviors in a conflict situation. *Ethology and Sociobiology, 5,* 257-268.

Carnevale, P. J., Conlon, D. E., Hanisch, K. A., & Harris, K. L. (1989). Experimental research on the strategic-choice model of mediation. In K. Kressel & D. G. Pruitt (Eds.), *Mediation research: The process and effectiveness of third-party intervention* (pp. 344-367). San Francisco: Jossey-Bass.

Carnevale, P., Lim, R., & McLaughlin, M. (1989). Contingent mediator behavior and its effectiveness. In K. Kressel & D. G. Pruitt (Eds.), *Mediation research: The process and effectiveness of third-party intervention* (pp. 213-240). San Francisco: Jossey-Bass.

Carnevale, P. J., & Pegnetter, R. (1985). The selection of mediation tactics in public sector disputes: A contingency analysis. *Journal of Social Issues, 41*(5), 65-82.

Carter, L. (1988). *Understanding a society through its stories: The development and application of an approach for discovering norms through an analysis of narratives.* Paper presented to the Speech Communication Association, New Orleans.

Charny, I. W. (1986). An existential/dialectical model for analyzing marital functioning and interaction. *Family Process, 25,* 571-585.

Chatman, S. (1978). *Story and discourse.* Ithaca, NY: Cornell University Press.

Cissna, K. N., Cox, D. E., & Bochner, A. P. (1990). The dialectic of marital and parental relationships within the stepfamily. *Communication Monographs, 57,* 44-61.

Clark, R., O'Dell, L., & Willihnganz, S. (1986). The development of compromising as an alternative to persuasion. *Central States Speech Journal, 37*(4), 220-224.

232 NEW DIRECTIONS IN MEDIATION

Clark, R., Willihnganz, S., & O'Dell, L. (1985). Training fourth graders in compromising and persuasive strategies. *Communication Education, 34*, 331-342.

Cobb, S. (1991). Einsteinian practice and Newtonian discourse: Ethical crisis in mediation. *Negotiation Journal, 7*(1), 87-102.

Cobb, S. (1992a). *The pragmatics of empowerment in mediation: Towards a narrative perspective.* Report commissioned by National Institute for Dispute Resolution.

Cobb, S. (1992b). *"Theories of responsibility": The social construction of intentions in mediation.* Manuscript submitted for publication.

Cobb, S., & Rifkin, J. (1991a). Neutrality as a discursive practice: The construction and transformation of narratives in community mediation. In A. Sarat & S. Silbey (Eds.), *Studies in law, politics and society: Volume 11.* Greenwich, CT: JAI Press.

Cobb, S., & Rifkin, J. (1991b). Practice and paradox: Deconstructing neutrality in mediation. *Law and Social Inquiry, 161*, 35-62.

Cochrane, C. T., & Myers, D. V. (1980). *Children in crisis: A time for caring, a time for change.* Beverly Hills, CA: Sage.

Colby, A., & Kohlberg, L. (1981). *Invariant sequence and internal consistency in moral judgment stages.* (ERIC Document Reproduction Service No. ED 223 514)

Colby, A., Kohlberg, L., Gibb, J., & Leiberman, M. (1983). *A longitudinal study of moral judgment.* (ERIC Document Reproduction Service No. ED 223 512)

Commanday, P. M. (1985). "Peacemaking" confrontation management. *School Safety, 7,* 7-11.

Conforth, M. (1968). *Materialism and the dialectical method.* New York: International Publishers.

Conley, J., & O'Barr, W. (1990a). *Rules versus relationships.* Chicago: University of Chicago Press.

Conley, J., & O'Barr, W. (1990b). Rules versus relationships in small claims disputes. In A. D. Grimshaw (Ed.), *Conflict talk* (pp. 178-196). Cambridge: Cambridge University Press.

Coupland, N. (1988). Introduction: Towards a stylistics of discourse. In N. Coupland (Ed.), *Styles of discourse* (pp. 1-19). London: Croom Helm.

Coser, L. (1956). *The functions of social conflict.* New York: Free Press.

Craig, R. T. (1986). Goals in discourse. In D. Ellis & W. Donohue (Eds.), *Contemporary issues in language and discourse processes* (pp. 257-273). Hillsdale, NJ: Lawrence Erlbaum.

Craig, R. T., & Tracy, K. (Eds.). (1983). *Conversational coherence: Form, structure and strategy.* Beverly Hills, CA: Sage.

Cronen, V. E., Pearce, W. B., & Harris, L. M. (1982). The coordinated management of meaning: A theory of communication. In F. E. X. Dance (Ed.), *Human communication theory: Comparative essays* (pp. 61-89). New York: Harper & Row.

Cronen, V. E., Pearce, W. B., & Tomm, K. (1985). A dialectical view of personal change. In K. Gergen & R. Davis (Eds.), *The social construction of the person.* New York: Springer.

Cronen, V. E., Pearce, W. B., & Tomm, K. (1986). Radical change in the social construction of the person. In K. Davis & K. Gergen (Eds.), *The social construction of the person.* New York: Springer.

Cronin, M. (1980). *The relationship between story grammar and how grade 6 Cree students recall stories.* Paper presented to the University of Alberta.

Culler, J. (1975). *Structuralist poetics: Structuralism, linguistics and the study of literature.* Ithaca. NY: Cornell University Press.

Cummings, E. M., Iannotti, R. J., & Zahn-Waxler, C. (1985). Influence of conflict between adults on the emotions and aggressions of young children. *Developmental Psychology, 21,* 495-507.

Cupach, W. (1992). Dialectical processes in the disengagement of interpersonal relationships. In T. L. Orbuch (Ed.), *Close relationship loss: Theoretical approaches* (pp. 128-141). New York: Springer.

Davis, A. (1986). *From story to settlement.* Boston: District Court of Massachusetts.

Davis, A. M. (1986). Dispute resolution at an early age. *Negotiation Journal, 2,* 287-297.

Davis, A. M., & Porter, K. (1985). Dispute resolution: The fourth "R." *Missouri Journal of Dispute Resolution, 4,* 121-139.

Davis, A. M., & Salem, R. A. (1985). Resolving disputes, the choice is ours. *Update on Law-related Education, 9*(2), 20-24, 30.

Davis, G. (1988). The halls of justice and justice in the halls. In R. Dingwall & J. M. Eekelaar (Eds.), *Divorce mediation and the legal process: British practice and international experience* (pp. 95-115). Oxford: Oxford University Press.

Davis, G., & Bader, K. (1985). In-court mediation: The consumer view. *Family Law, 15,* 42-49, 82,86.

Delia, J., Kline, S., & Burleson, B. (1979). The development of persuasive communication strategies in kindergarteners through twelfth graders. *Communication Monographs, 46,* 24-56

Derrida, J. (1978). *Writing and difference.* Chicago: University of Chicago Press.

Derrida, J. (1980). The law of genre. In W. Mitchell (Ed.), *On narrative.* Chicago: University of Chicago Press.

Diez, M. (1984). Communicative competence: An interactive approach. In R. Bostrom (Ed.), *Communication yearbook 8* (pp. 56-79). Beverly Hills, CA: Sage.

Diez, M. (1986). Negotiation competence: A conceptualization of the rules of negotiation interaction. In D. Ellis & W. Donohue (Eds.), *Contemporary issues in language and discourse processes* (pp. 223-237). Hillsdale, NJ: Lawrence Erlbaum.

Dikaioi, P. (1980). *On justice.* Oxford: Clarendon Press.

Dingwall, R. (1988). Empowerment or enforcement? Some questions about power and control in divorce mediation. In R. Dingwall & J. M. Eekelaar (Eds.), *Divorce mediation and the legal process: British practice and international experience* (pp. 150-167). Oxford: Oxford University Press.

Dingwall, R. (1990). Divorce mediation: A study in the application of frame analysis. In J. Kurczewski & A. A. Czynczyk (Eds.), *Family, gender and body in law and society today* (pp. 141-168). University of Warsaw, Institute of Applied Social Sciences, Sociology of Custom and Law Department.

Dingwall, R., & Greatbatch, D. (1990). *Frame analysis and the study of social interaction.* Paper presented to the Society for Social Interaction Stone Symposium, San Francisco.

Dingwall, R., & Greatbatch, D. (1991). Behind closed doors: A preliminary report on mediator/client interaction in England. *Family and Conciliation Courts Review, 29,* 291-303.

Dingwall, R., & James, A. (1988). Family law and the psycho-social professions: Welfare officers in the English county courts. *Laws in Context, 6,* 61-73.

Dollerup, C. (1984). The ontological status, the formative elements, the filter, and the existences of folktales. *Fabula: Journal of Folktale Studies, 25*(3-4), 241-255.

Dolliver, R. (1972). The place of opposites in psychotherapy. *Journal of Contemporary Psychotherapy, 5,* 49-54.

Donohue, W. A. (1989). Communicative competence in mediators. In K. Kressel & D. Pruitt (Eds.), *Mediation research: The process and effectiveness of third-party intervention.* San Francisco: Jossey-Bass.

Donohue, W. A. (1991). *Communication, marital dispute and divorce mediation.* Hillsdale, NJ: Lawrence Erlbaum.

Donohue, W. A., Allen, M., & Burrell, N. (1988). Mediator communicative competence, *Communication Monographs, 55.*

Donohue, W. A., & Kolt, R. (1992). *Managing interpersonal conflict.* Newbury Park, CA: Sage.

Donohue, W. A., & Ramesh, C. (1992). Negotiation-opponent relationships. In L. Putnam & M. Roloff (Eds.), *Communication and negotiation* (pp. 209-234). Newbury Park, CA: Sage.

Doo, L. (1973). Dispute settlement in Chinese-American communities. *American Journal of Comparative Law, 21,* 627-657.

Douglas, A. (1957). The peaceful settlement of industrial and intergroup disputes. *Journal of Conflict Resolution, 1,* 69-81.

Douglas, A. (1962). *Industrial peacemaking.* New York: Columbia University Press.

Dworkin, R. (1977). *Taking rights seriously.* Cambridge, MA: Harvard University Press.

Eisenberg, A., & Garvey, C. (1981). Children's use of verbal strategies in resolving conflicts. *Discourse Processes, 4,* 149-170.

Epstein, D. (1984). *The political theory of the federalist.* Chicago: University of Chicago Press.

Etzioni, A. (1993). *The spirit of community.* New York: Crown.

Evans, S., & Boyte, H. C. (1986). *Free spaces: The sources of democratic change in America.* New York: Harper & Row.

Fairclough, N. (1989). *Language and power.* New York: Longman.

Feagin, J. R. (1989). *Racial and ethnic relations.* Englewood Cliffs, NJ: Prentice Hall.

Feagin, J. R. (1991). The continuing significance of race: Antiblack discrimination in public places. *American Sociological Review, 56*(February), 101-116.

Feldman, A. (1991). *Formations of violence: The narrative of the body and political terror in Northern Ireland.* Chicago: University of Chicago Press.

Felstiner, W. L. F. (1974). Influences of social organization on dispute processing. *Law and Society Review, 9,* 63-87.

Felstiner, W. L., Abel, R. L., & Sarat, A. (1980-1981). The emergence and transformation of disputes: Naming, blaming, claiming. *Law and Society Review, 15*(3-4), 631-654.

Ferguson, K. (1984). *The feminist case against bureaucracy.* Philadelphia, PA: Temple University Press.

Filley, A. C. (1975). *Interpersonal conflict resolution.* Glenview, IL: Scott, Foresman.

Fineman, M. (1988). Dominant discourse, professional language and legal change in child custody decisionmaking. *Harvard Law Review, 101*(4), 727-774.

Finley, G., & Humphreys, C. (1974). Naive psychology and the development of persuasive appeals in girls. *Canadian Journal of Behavioral Science, 6,* 75-80.

Fisher, R., & Ury, W. (1981). *Getting to yes: Negotiating agreement without giving in.* Boston: Houghton-Mifflin.

Fisher, W. (1987). *Human communication as narration.* Columbia: University of South Carolina Press.

Fisher, W. (1988). Clarifying the narrative paradigm. *Communication Monographs, 55,* 55-58.

Fleming, D. C. (1977). Teaching negotiation skills to preadolescents. (Doctoral dissertation, Syracuse University, 1976). *Dissertation Abstracts International, 38*(5-B), 2362.

Fleuridas, C., Nelson, T., & Rosenthal, C. (1986). The evolution of circular questions. *Journal of Marriage and Family Therapy, 12*(2), 113-127.

Folberg, J., & Taylor, A. (1984). *Mediation: A comprehensive guide to resolving conflicts without litigation.* San Francisco: Jossey-Bass.

Folger, J. P. (1991). Assessing community dispute resolution needs. In K. Grover Duffy, J. Grosch, & P. V. Olczak (Eds.), *Community mediation: A handbook for practitioners and researchers* (pp. 53-71). New York: Guilford.

Folger, J. P., & Bernard, S. (1985). Divorce mediation: When mediators challenge the divorcing parties. *Mediation Quarterly, 10,* 5-23.

Folger, J. P., & Bernard, S. (1986). *The mediator's role.* Paper delivered at the Speech Communication Association Conference, Chicago.

Folger, J. P., Poole, M. S., & Stutman, R. K. (1993). *Working through conflict: Strategies for relationships, groups and organizations.* New York: Harper-Collins.

Folger, R. (1984). Emerging issues in the social psychology of justice. In R. Folger (Ed.), *The sense of injustice: Social psychological perspectives* (pp. 4-24). New York: Plenum.

Forester, J. (1992). Envisioning the politics of public sector dispute resolution. In A. Sarat & S. Silbey (Eds.), *Studies in law, politics and society* (Vol. 12, pp. 247-286). Greenwich, CT: JAI Press.

Fraser, J. R., & Froelich, J. E. (1979). Crisis intervention in the court room: The case of the Night Prosecutor. *Community Mental Health Journal, 15,* 237-247.

Freeman, S., Littlejohn, S., & Pearce, B. (1992). Communication and moral conflict. *Western Journal of Communication, 56,* 311-329.

Frye, N. (1963). *Fables of identity.* New York: Harcourt Brace Jovanovich.

Friedrich, C. J. (1959). *Community.* New York: Liberal Arts Press.

Gadlin, H., & Oulette, P. (1987). Mediation Milanese: An application of systemic family therapy to family mediation. *Mediation Quarterly,* No. 14-15.

Garbarino, J., Scott, F. M., & Faculty of the Erickson Institute. (1989). *What children can tell us.* San Francisco: Jossey-Bass.

Garcia, A. (1991). Dispute resolution without disputes: How the interactional organization of mediation hearings minimizes argument. *American Sociological Review, 56,* 818-835.

Gardner, J. W. (1992). *Building community.* Washington DC: Independent Sector.

Garfinkel, H. (1967). *Studies in ethnomethodology.* Englewood Cliffs, NJ: Prentice Hall.

Genette, G. (1980). *Narrative discourse.* Ithaca, NY: Cornell University Press.

Gergen, K. (1980). Toward intellectual audacity in the social sciences. In R. Gilmour & S. Duck (Eds.), *The development of social psychology* (pp. 239-270). New York: Academic Press.

Gergen, K. J. (1985). The social constructionist movement in modern psychology. *American Psychologist, 40,* 266-275.

Gergen, K. (1986). Narratives and the self as relationship. In L. Borkowitz (Ed.), *Advances in experimental psychology.* New York: Academic Press.

Germane, C., Johnson, M., & Lemon, N. (1985). Mandatory custody mediation and joint custody orders in California: The dangers for victims of domestic violence. *Berkeley Women's Law Review, 1*(1).

Gilligan, C. (1982). *In a different voice: Psychological theory and women's development.* Cambridge, MA: Harvard University Press.

Gilligan, C. (1988). Adolescent development reconsidered. In C. Gilligan, J. V. Ward, & J. McLean Taylor (Eds.). *Mapping the moral domain* (pp. vi-xxxiv). Cambridge, MA: Harvard University Press.

Goffman, E. (1956). The nature of deference and demeanour. *American Anthropologist, 58,* 473-502

Goffman, E. (1959). *The presentation of self in everyday life.* Garden City, NY: Doubleday.

Goffman, E. (1975). *Frame analysis.* London: Penguin.

Gold, L. (1984). Interdisciplinary team mediation. *Mediation Quarterly, 6,* 27-46.

Goldsmith, D. (1990). A dialectic perspective on the expression of autonomy and connection in romantic relationships. *Western Journal of Speech Communication, 54,* 537-556.

Goodwin, M. (1990). Tactical uses of stories: Participation frameworks within girls' and boys' disputes. *Discourse Processes, 13*(1), 33-71.

Gramsci, A. (1971). *Selections from the prison notebooks.* London: Lawrence & Wishart.

Greatbatch, D., & Dingwall, R. (1989). Selective facilitation: Some preliminary observations on a strategy used by divorce mediators. *Law and Society Review, 23,* 613-641.

Grice, H. P. (1975). Logic and conversation. In P. Cole & J. L. Morgan (Eds.), *Syntax and semantics 3: Speech acts* (pp. 41-58). New York: Academic Press.

Grimshaw, A. D. (1990). Research on conflict talk: Antecedents, resources, findings, directions. In A. Grimshaw (Ed.), *Conflict talk* (pp. 280-324). Cambridge: Cambridge University Press.

Gudykunst, W. B., & Nishida, T. (1984). Individual and cultural influences on uncertainty reduction. *Communication Monographs, 51,* 23-36.

Guerra, N., & Slaby, R. (1989). Evaluative factors in social problem solving by aggressive boys. *Journal of Abnormal Child Psychology, 17*(3), 277-289.

Gulliver, P. H. (1979). *Disputes and negotiations.* New York: Academic Press.

Harms, R. A. (1987). *Conflict management; A secondary school curriculum.* Unpublished doctoral dissertation, Seattle University, Seattle, WA.

Harrington, C. (1985). *Shadow justice: The ideology and institutionalization of alternatives to court.* Westport, CT: Greenwood Press.

Harrington, C., & Rifkin, J. (1989). The gender organization of mediation: Implications for the feminization of legal practice. *Institute for Legal Studies, Working Papers, 4*(2).

Hartup, W., & Laursen, B. (1987). *Friendship and conflict: Synergies in child development.* (ERIC Document Reproduction Service No. ED 289 599)

Hartup, W., & Laursen, B. (1989). *Contextual constraints and children's friendship relations.* (ERIC Document Reproduction Service No. ED 310 848)

Hartup, W., Laursen, B., Stewart, M., & Eastenson, A. (1988). Conflict and friendship relations of young children. *Child Development, 59,* 1590-1600.

Haslett, B. (1983). Preschooler's communicative strategies in gaining compliance from peers: A developmental study. *Quarterly Journal of Speech, 69,* 84-99.

Hawaii State Department of Education (1985). *LRE ideas and lessons on citizenship/law-related education.* (ERIC Document Reproduction Service No. ED 266 994).

Haynes, J. (1983). The process of negotiations. *Mediation Quarterly, 1,* 75-92.

Haynes, J. M. (1982). A conceptual model of the process of family mediation: Implications for training. *American Journal of Family Therapy, 10,* 5-16.

Haynes, J. M., & Haynes, G. L. (1989). *Mediating divorce.* San Francisco: Jossey-Bass.

Hecht, M. L., Larkey, L. K., & Johnson, J. N. (1992). African American and European American perceptions of problematic issues in interethnic communication effectiveness. *Human Communication Research, 19*(2), 209-236.

Henderson, L. (1987). Legality and empathy. *Michigan Law Review, 85,* 1574-1653.

Heritage, J. (1988). *Garfinkel and ethnomethodology.* Cambridge: Polity.

Heritage, J. C., & Sefi, S. (1992). Dilemmas of advice: Aspects of the delivery and reception of advice in interactions between health visitors and first-time mothers. In P. Drew & J. Heritage (Eds.), *Talk at work: Interaction in institutional settings* (pp. 359-417). Cambridge: Cambridge University Press.

Hiltrop, J. M. (1985). Mediator behavior and the settlement of collective bargaining disputes in Britain. *Journal of Social Issues, 41,* 83-99.

Hiltrop, J. M. (1989). Factors associated with successful labor mediation. In K. Kressel & D. G. Pruitt (Eds.), *Mediation research: The process and effectiveness of third-party intervention* (pp. 241-262). San Francisco: Jossey-Bass.

Hocker, J. L., & Wilmot, W. W. (1992). *Interpersonal conflict* (3rd ed.). Dubuque, IA: William C. Brown.

Hofer, R. (1991). Stories in conversation. *Kansas Working Papers in Linguistics, 15.*

Hoffman, L. (1985). Beyond power and control: Toward a "second order" family systems therapy. *Family Systems Medicine, 3*(4), 381-396.

Hofstede, G. (1989). Measurement of individualism-collectivism. *Journal of Research in Personality, 22,* 17-36.

Holmes, M. A. (1992). Phase structures in negotiation. In L. Putnam & M. Roloff (Eds.), *Communication and negotiation* (pp. 83-105). Newbury Park, CA: Sage.

Hranitz, J. R., & Eddowes, E. A. (1990). Violence: A crisis in homes and schools. *Childhood Education, 67*(1), 4-7.

Hui, C. H., & Villareal, M. J. (1989). Individualism-collectivism and psychological needs: Their relationships in two cultures. *Journal of Cross-Cultural Psychology, 20,* 310-323.

Hutchins, L. M. (1990). *Mediation, not altercation: Student mediation in schools.* Unpublished manuscript, University of Denver, Denver.

Irving, H. H. (1981). *Divorce mediation: A rational alternative to the adversary system.* New York: Universe Books.

Jacobs, S. (1990). *Real-izing ideal argumentation through third party dispute mediation.* Paper delivered to the Speech Communication Association, Chicago.

Jacobs, S. (in press). Mediation as critical discussion. In F. H. van Emeren, R. Grootendorst, S. Jackson, & S. Jacobs (Eds.), *Reconstructing argumentative discourse.* Tuscaloosa: University of Alabama Press.

Jacobs, S., Jackson, S., Stearns, S., & Hall, B. (1991). Digressions in argumentative discourse: Multiple goals, standing concerns and implicatures. In K. Tracy (Ed.), *Understanding face-to-face interaction: Issues linking goals and discourse* (pp. 43-61). Hillsdale, NJ: Lawrence Erlbaum.

James, A. (1988). "Civil work" in the probation service. In R. Dingwall & J. M. Eekelaar (Eds.), *Divorce mediation and the legal process: British practice and international experience* (pp. 56-70). Oxford: Oxford University Press.

Jefferson, G. (1984). Transcript notation. In J. M. Atkinson, & J. C. Heritage (Eds.), *Structure of social action: Studies in conversation analysis* (pp. ix-xvi). Cambridge: Cambridge University Press.

Johnson, D. W. (1981). Student-student interaction: The neglected variable in education. *Educational Researcher, 10*(1), 5-10.

Johnson, J. M. (1993). *Dispute resolution directory*. Washington, DC: American Bar Association.

Johnson, K. K. (1988). *The impact of conflict management training on behavior and self-esteem of middle school students*. Unpublished doctoral dissertation, University of Houston, Houston, TX.

Jones, T. S. (1985). *"Breaking up is hard to do": An exploratory investigation of communication behaviors and phases in child-custody divorce mediation*. Unpublished doctoral dissertation, Ohio State University.

Jones, T. S. (1987, March). *An analysis of gender differences in mediator-disputant interaction for successful and unsuccessful divorce mediation*. Paper presented to the Temple University Discourse Conference, Philadelphia.

Jones, T. S. (1988). Phase structures in agreement and no-agreement mediation. *Communication Research, 15*, 470-495.

Jones, T. S. (1989a). Lag sequential analysis of mediator-spouse and husband-wife interaction in successful and unsuccessful divorce mediation. In M. A. Rahim (Ed.), *Managing conflict: An interdisciplinary approach* (pp. 93-107). New York: Praeger.

Jones, T. S. (1989b). A taxonomy of effective mediator strategies and tactics for nonlabor-management mediation. In M. A. Rahim (Ed.), *Managing conflict: An interdisciplinary approach* (pp. 221-229). New York: Praeger.

Jose, P., & Hennelly, S. (1987). *Measures of social cognitive development: Interpersonal conflict resolution and social rule understanding*. (ERIC Document Reproduction Service No. ED 283 609)

Karambayya, R., & Brett, J. M. (1989). Managers handling disputes: Third-party roles and perceptions of fairness. *Academy of Management Journal, 32*(4), 687-704.

Karambayya, R., Brett, J. M., & Lytle, A. (1992). The effects of formal authority and experience on third-party roles, outcomes and perceptions of fairness. *Academy of Management Journal, 35*(2), 426-438.

Katriel, T., & Shenhar, A. (1990). Tower and stockade: Dialogic narration in Israeli settlement ethos. *Quarterly Journal of Speech, 75*(4), 358-380.

Katz, D., & Kahn, R. L. (1966). *The social psychology of organizations*. New York: John Wiley.

Kaufmann, S. (1991, June). *Peer mediation in schools: Training models from a theoretical perspective*. Paper presented at the International Association for Conflict Management conference, Den Dolder, The Netherlands.

Kelly, J. B., & Gigy, L. L. (1989). Divorce mediation: Characteristics of clients and outcomes. In K. Kressel & D. G. Pruitt (Eds.), *Mediation research: The process and effectiveness of third-party intervention* (pp. 263-283). San Francisco: Jossey-Bass.

Kelvin, P. (1977). Predictability, power and vulnerability in interpersonal attraction. In S. Duck (Ed.), *Theory and practice in interpersonal attraction*. London: Academic Press.

Kemmis, D. (1990). *Community and the politics of place*. Norman: University of Oklahoma Press.

Kepner, C. H., & Tregoe, B. B. (1965). *The rational manager*. New York: McGraw-Hill.

Kilmann, R., & Thomas, K. (1975). Interpersonal conflict handling behavior as reflections of Jungian personality dimensions. *Psychological Reports, 37,* 971-980.

Koch, M. S., & Miller, S. (1987). Resolving student conflicts with student mediators. *Principal, 66,* 59-62.

Kochan, T. A., & Jick, T. (1978). The public sector mediation process: A theory and empirical examination. *Journal of Conflict Resolution, 22,* 209-240.

Kochman, T. (1981). *Black and white styles in conflict*. Chicago: University of Chicago Press.

Kolb, D. M. (1983). *The mediators*. Cambridge: MIT Press.

Kolb, D. M. (1985). To be a mediator: Expressive tactics in mediation. *Journal of Social Issues, 41*(2), 11-26.

Kolb, D. M. (1986). Who are organizational third parties and what do they do? In R. J. Lewicki, B. H. Sheppard, & M. H. Bazerman (Eds.), *Research on negotiations in organizations, 1* (pp. 207-278). Greenwich, CT: JAI Press.

Kolb, D. M. (1989). Labor mediators, managers, and ombudsmen: Roles mediators play in different contexts. In K. Kressel & D. G. Pruitt (Eds.), *Mediation research: The process and effectiveness of third-party intervention* (pp. 91-114). San Francisco: Jossey-Bass.

Kolb, D. M., & Glidden, P. (1986). Getting to know your conflict options. *Personnel Administrator, 31*(6), 77-90.

Kolb, D. M., & Putnam, L. (1991). Introduction: The dialectics of disputing. In D. M. Kolb & J. M. Bartunek (Eds.), *Hidden conflict in organizations* (pp. 1-31). Newbury Park CA: Sage.

Kolb, D. M., & Sheppard, B. H. (1985). Do managers mediate or even arbitrate? *Negotiation Journal, 1,* 379-388.

Krappmann, L., & Oswald, H. (1987). *Negotiation strategies in peer conflicts: A follow-up study in natural settings*. (ERIC Document Reproduction Service No. ED 282 641)

Kreidler, W. J. (1984). *Creative conflict resolution: More than 200 activities for keeping peace in the classroom*. Glenview, IL: Scott, Foresman.

Kressel, K. (1977). Labor mediation: An exploratory survey. In D. Lewin, P. Ffeuille, & T. Kochan (Eds.), *Public sector labor relations* (pp. 252-272). Glen Ridge, NJ: Horton.

Kressel, K., & Pruitt, D. G. (1989a). Conclusion: A research perspective on the mediation of social conflict. In K. Kressel & D. G. Pruitt (Eds.), *Mediation research: The process and effectiveness of third-party intervention* (pp. 394-435). San Francisco: Jossey-Bass.

Kressel, K., & Pruitt, D. G. (Eds.). (1989b). *Mediation research: The process and effectiveness of third-party intervention*. San Francisco: Jossey-Bass.

Kuczynski, L., & Kochanska, G. (1990). Development of children's noncompliance strategies from toddlerhood to age 5. *Developmental Psychology, 26*(3), 398-408.

Kuczynski, L., Kochanska, G., Radke-Yarrow, M., & Girnius-Brown, O. (1987). A developmental interpretation of young children's noncompliance. *Developmental Psychology, 23*(6), 799-806.

Labov, W., & Fanshel, D. (1977). *Therapeutic discourse: Psychotherapy as conversation.* New York: Academic Press.

Ladd, G., & Emerson, E. (1984). Shared knowledge in children's friendships. *Developmental Psychology, 20,* 932-940.

Lakoff, G., & Johnson, M. (1980). *Metaphors we live by.* Chicago: University of Chicago Press.

Lam, J. A. (1988, January). *The impact of conflict resolution training programs on schools: A review and synthesis of the evidence.* Amherst, MA: National Association for Mediation in Education.

Lam, J. A., Rifkin, J., & Townley, A. (1989). Reframing conflict: Implications for fairness in parent-adolescent mediation. *Mediation Quarterly, 7*(1), 15-31.

La Resche, D. (1992). Comparison of the American mediation process with a Korean-American harmony restoration process. *Mediation Quarterly, 9*(4), 323-339.

Lasch, C. (1991). *The true and only heaven: Progress and its critics.* New York: Norton.

Legge, N. J., & Rawlins, W. K. (1992). Managing disputes in young adult friendships: Modes of convenience, cooperation, and commitment. *Western Journal of Communication, 56,* 226-247.

Lein, L., & Brenneis, D. (1978). Children's disputes in three speech [sic] communities. *Language in Society, 7*(3), 299-303.

Leung, K., & Lind, E. A. (1986). Procedure and culture: Effects of culture, gender, and investigator status on procedural preferences. *Journal of Personality and Social Psychology, 50,* 1134-1140.

Levy, J. (1989). Conflict resolution in elementary and secondary education. *Mediation Quarterly, 7*(1), 73-87.

Lewicki, R. J., & Sheppard, B. H. (1985). Choosing how to intervene: Factors affecting the use of process and outcome control in third party dispute resolution. *Journal of Occupational Behavior, 6,* 49-64.

Leyva, F. A., & Furth, H. (1986). Compromise formation in social conflicts: The influence of age, issue, and interpersonal context. *Journal of Youth and Adolescence, 15*(6), 441-452.

Likert, R., & Likert, J. G. (1976). *New ways of managing conflict.* New York: McGraw-Hill.

Lissak, R. I., & Sheppard, B. H. (1983). Beyond fairness: The criterion problem in research on dispute intervention. *Journal of Applied Social Psychology, 13,* 45-65.

Littlejohn, S. W. (1992). *Theories of human communication.* Belmont, CA: Wadsworth.

Littlejohn, S. W., Higgins, M., & Williams, M. (1987). *Demanding dialogue: Moral conflict in an American protestant church.* Paper presented at the Speech Communication Association, Boston.

Littlejohn, S. W., Pearce, W. B., Hines, S., & Bean, W. (1986, February). *Coherence and coordination in mediation communication: Exploratory case studies.* Paper presented at the Western Speech Communication Association, Tucson, AZ.

Littlejohn, S. W., & Shailor, J. (1986). *The deep structure of conflict in mediation: A case study.* Paper presented at the Speech Communication Association, Chicago.

Littlejohn, S. W., & Stone, M. (1991, November). *Moral conflict in a small town.* Paper presented at the Speech Communication Association, Atlanta.

Lopez, D., & Espiritu, Y. (1990). Panethnicity in the United States: A theoretical framework. *Ethnic and Racial Studies, 13*(2), 198-224.

Lovins, A. B. (1977). *Soft energy paths: Toward a durable peace.* New York: Harper & Row.

Lubiano, W. (1992). Black ladies, welfare queens and state minstrels: Ideological war by narrative means. In T. Morrison (Ed.), *Race-ing justice, engendering power.* New York: Pantheon.

Maag, J. W. (1990). Social skills training in schools. *Special Services in the Schools, 6*(1-2), 1-19.

MacIntyre, A. (1981). *After virtue: A study in moral theory.* South Bend, IN: University of Notre Dame Press.

Mack, R. W., & Snyder, R. C. (1957). The analysis of social conflict: Toward an overview and synthesis. *Journal of Conflict Resolution, 1*(2), 212-248.

MacNeil, I. (1984). Bureaucracy, liberalism and community—American style. *Northwestern University Law Review, 79,* 900-948.

Maier, N. R. F. (1967). Assets and liabilities in group problem-solving: The need for an integrative function. *Psychological Review, 74,* 239-249.

Maier, N. R. F., & Solem, A. F., (1962). Improving solutions by turning choice situations into problems. *Personnel Psychology, 15*(2), 151-157.

Mandler, J. (1982). Some uses and abuses of story grammar. *Discourse Processes, 5*(3-4), 305-318.

Manning, M. L., & Allen, M. G. (1987). Social development in early adolescence: Implications for middle school educators. *Childhood Education, 63*(3), 172-176.

Mansbridge, J. (1983). *Beyond adversary democracy.* Chicago: University of Chicago Press.

Margolis, H. (1990). Helping to implement cooperative learning. *Journal of Reading, Writing, and Learning Disabilities International, 7*(2), 153-164.

Marlow, L. (1987). Styles of conducting mediation. *Mediation Quarterly, 18,* 85-90.

Marlow, L., & Sauber, R. (1990). *The handbook of divorce mediation.* New York: Plenum.

Martin, J., & Stent, G. (1990). I think therefore I thank: A philosophy of etiquette. *American Scholar, 59,* 237-254.

Masheter, C., & Harris, L. (1986). From divorce to friendship: A study of dialectical relationship development. *Journal of Social and Personal Relationships, 3,* 177-189.

Mather, L., & Yngvesson, B. (1980-1981). Language, audience and the transformation of disputes. *Law and Society Review, 15*(3-4), 775-821.

Maynard, D. (1985a). How children start arguments. *Language in Society, 14,* 1-30.

Maynard, D. (1985b). On the functions of social conflict among children. *American Sociological Review, 50,* 207-223.

Maynard, D. (1988). Narrative and narrative structure in plea bargaining. *Law & Society Review, 22*(3), 449.

Maynard, D. W., & Clayman, S. (1991). The diversity of ethnomethodology. *Annual Review of Sociology, 17,* 385-418.

Maxwell, J. P. (1989). Mediation in the schools: Self-regulation, self-esteem and self-discipline. *Mediation Quarterly, 7*(2), 149-156.

McEwen, C. A., & Maiman, R. J. (1981). Small claims mediation in Maine: An empirical assessment. *Maine Law Review, 37,* 237-268.

McEwen, C. A., & Maiman, R. J., (1986). The relative significance of disputing forum and dispute characteristics for outcome and compliance. *Law and Society Review, 20,* 439-447.

McGillicuddy, N. B., Welton, G. L., & Pruitt, D. G. (1987). Third-party intervention: A field experiment comparing three different models. *Journal of Personality and Social Psychology, 53,* 104-112.

McKersie, R. B. (1964). Avoiding written grievances by problem-solving: An outside view. *Personnel Psychology, 17,* 367-379.

Menkel-Meadow, C. (1984). Toward another view of legal negotiation: The structure of problem-solving. *UCLA Law Review, 31,* 754-842.

Merry, S. E. (1989). Mediation in nonindustrial societies. In K. Kressel & D. G. Pruitt (Eds.), *Mediation research: The process and effectiveness of third-party intervention* (pp. 68-90). San Francisco: Jossey-Bass.

Millar, F., & Rogers, E. (1987). Relational dimensions of interpersonal dynamics. In M. Roloff & G. Miller (Eds.), *Interpersonal processes: New directions in communication research* (pp. 117-139). Newbury Park, CA: Sage.

Miller, P., Danaher, D., & Forbes, D. (1986). Sex-related strategies for coping with interpersonal conflict in children aged five to seven. *Developmental Psychology, 22*(4), 543-548.

Minow, M. (1987). Forward: Justice engendered. *Harvard Law Review, 101,* 10-95.

Mintzberg, H. R. (1975). The manager's job: Folklore and fact. *Harvard Business Review, 53*(4): 49-61.

Mishler, E. (1986). *Research interviewing: Context and narrative.* Cambridge, MA: Harvard University Press.

Montgomery, B. M. (1992, October). *A dialectical approach to reconceptualizing familiar and marital relationship maintenance.* Paper presented to the Speech Communication Association convention, Chicago.

Moore, C. M. (1991). Community is where community happens. *National Civic Review, 80,* 352-357.

Moore, C. W. (1986). *The mediation process: Practical strategies for resolving conflict.* San Francisco: Jossey-Bass.

Moore, C. W. (1989). *Decision making and conflict management.* Boulder, CO: CDR Associates.

Morgan, G. (1986). *Images of organization.* Beverly Hills, CA: Sage.

Much, N., & Shweder, R. (1978). Speaking of rules: The analysis of culture in breach. In W. Damon (Ed.), *New directions for child development: Moral development* (pp. 19-39). San Francisco: Jossey-Bass.

Mumby, D. K. (1988). *Communication and power in organizations: Discourse, ideology and domination.* Norwood, NJ: Ablex.

Mumby, D. K., & Putnam, L. (1992). The politics of emotion: A feminist reading of "Bounded Rationality." *Academy of Management Review, 17,* 465-486.

Nadler, L., Nadler, M., & Broome, B. (1985). Culture and the management of conflict situations. In W. Gudykunst, L. Stewart, & S. Ting-Toomey (Eds.), *Communication, culture and organizational processes* (pp. 87-113). Beverly Hills, CA: Sage.

Neale, M. A., Pinkley, R. L., Brittain, J. W., & Northcraft, G. B. (1990). *Managerial third-party dispute resolution.* Final report to the Fund for Research in Dispute Resolution, Washington, DC.

Nelson, J., & Aboud, F. (1985). The resolution of social conflict between friends. *Child Development, 56*(4), 1009-1017.

Nicholas, P. (1982). African-American children's stories. Paper presented at the Third World Studies Symposium on Oral Sources and Third World Studies, Santa Clara, CA.

Nonet, P., & Selznick, P. (1978). *Law and society in transition: Toward responsive law.* New York: Harper & Row.

Northrup, T. A. (1989). The dynamic of identity in personal and social conflict. In L. Kriesburg, T. A. Northrup, & S. Therson (Eds.), *Intractable conflicts and their transformation* (pp. 55-82). Syracuse, NY: Syracuse University Press.

Northrup, T. A., & Segall, M. H. (1991). *Subjective vulnerability: The role of disempowerment in the utilization of mediation services by women.* Final report to the Fund for Research on Dispute Resolution, Washington, DC.

Nozick, R. (1974). *Anarchy, state and utopia.* New York: Basic Books.

O'Barr, W., & Conley, J. (1985). Litigant satisfaction versus legal adequacy in Small Claims's Court narratives. *Law & Society Review, 19*(14), 661-701.

O'Connor, R. A. (1981). Law as indigenous social theory: A Siamese Thai case. *American Technologist, 8,* 223-237.

O'Donnell, K. (1990). Difference and dominance: How labor and management talk conflict. In A. Grimshaw (Ed.), *Conflict talk* (pp. 210-240). Cambridge: Cambridge University Press.

Ohtsuka, K., & Brewer, W. (1988). *Discourse organization in the comprehension of narrative texts: Technical report #428.* Cambridge: Bolt, Beranek, & Newman.

Ohtsuka, K., & Brewer, W. (1992). Discourse organization in the comprehension of temporal order in narrative texts. *Discourse Processes, 15,* 317-336.

Omanson, R. (1982). An analysis of narrative: Identifying central, supportive and distracting content. *Discourse Processes, 5*(3-4), 195-224.

Pallai, P. (1991). *Center/margin relations and the politics of location.* Paper presented at the annual meetings of the Speech Communication Association, Atlanta.

Pearce, W. B. (1989). *Communication and the human condition.* Carbondale: Southern Illinois University Press.

Pearce, W. B., & Cronen, V. E. (1980). *Communication, action, and meaning: The creation of social reality.* New York: Praeger.

Pearce, W. B., Littlejohn, S. W., & Alexander, A. E. (1989). The quixotic quest for civility: Patterns of interaction between the new Christian right and secular humanism. In J. K. Hadden & A. Shupe (Eds.), *Secularization and fundamentalism reconsidered: Religion and the political order III* (pp. 152-177). New York: Paragon House.

Pearson, J. (1982). An evaluation of alternatives to court adjudication. *The Justice System Journal, 7,* 420-444.

Pearson, J., & Thoennes, N. (1989). Divorce mediation: Reflections on a decade of research. In K. Kressel & D. Pruitt (Eds.), *Mediation research: The process and effectiveness of third-party intervention* (pp. 9-30). San Francisco: Jossey-Bass.

Peirce, K., & Edwards, E. (1988). Children's construction of fantasy stories: Gender differences in conflict resolution strategies. *Sex Roles, 18*(7/8), 393-404.

Penman, R. (1987). Discourse in courts: Cooperation, coercion and coherence. *Discourse Processes, 10,* 201-218.

Perelman, C. (1963). *The idea of justice and the problem of argument.* New York: Routledge & Kegan Paul.

Philips, S. (1990). The judge as third party in American trial court conflict talk. In A. D. Grimshaw (Ed.), *Conflict talk* (pp. 197-209). Cambridge: Cambridge University Press.

Pipkin, R. (1993). *Project on integrating dispute resolution into the standard first year course: An evaluation.* Final report to the University of Missouri-Columbia School of Law.

Pipkin, R., & Rifkin, J. (1984). The social organization in alternative dispute resolution: Implications for the professionalization of mediation. *The Justice System Journal, 9*(2), 204-228.

Pocock, J. (1975). *The Machiavellian moment: Florentine political thought and the Atlantic republican tradition.* Princeton, NJ: Princeton University Press.

Polanyi, L. (1985). *Telling the American story: A structural and cultural analysis of storytelling.* Norwood, NJ: Ablex.

Polenski, J., & Launer, H. (Eds.). (1986). *Mediation: Contexts and challenges.* Springfield, IL: Charles C Thomas.

Polkinghorne, D. (1988). *Narrative knowing and the human sciences.* Albany: SUNY Press.

Pomerantz, A. (1984). Agreeing and disagreeing with assessments: Some features of preferred/dispreferred turn shapes. In J. M. Atkinson & J. Heritage (Eds.), *Structures of social action: Studies in conversation analysis* (pp. 57-101). Cambridge: Cambridge University Press.

Potter, J., & Witherell, M. (1987). *Discourse and social psychology.* Newbury Park, CA: Sage.

Prop, V. (1968). *Morphology of the folktale.* Austin: University of Texas Press.

Pruitt, D. G. (1981). *Negotiation behavior.* New York: Academic Press.

Pruitt, D. G. (1983). Achieving integrative agreements. In M. X. Bazerman & R. J. Lewicki (Eds.), *Negotiating in organizations* (pp. 35-50). Beverly Hills, CA: Sage.

Pruitt, D. G., Fry, W. R., Castrianno, L., Zubek, J., Welton, G., McGillicuddy, N. B., & Ippolito, C. (1989). The process of mediation: Caucusing, control, and problem-solving. In M. A. Rahim (Ed.), *Managing conflict: An interdisciplinary approach* (pp. 201-208). New York: Praeger.

Pruitt, D. G., & Kressel, K. (1989). Introduction: An overview of mediation research. In K. Kressel & D. Pruitt (Eds.), *Mediation research: The process and effectiveness of third-party intervention* (pp. 1-9). San Francisco: Jossey-Bass.

Pruitt, D. G., & Lewis, S. (1977). The psychology of integrative bargaining. In D. Druckman (Ed.), *Negotiations* (pp. 161-192). Beverly Hills, CA: Sage.

Pruitt, D. G., & Rubin, J. Z. (1986). *Social conflict: Escalation, stalemate, and settlement.* New York: Random House.

Putnam, L. (1992, May 12). *Storytelling and negotiation rituals.* Paper presented to Program on Negotiation, Harvard Law School.

Putnam, L. L., & Folger, J. P. (1988). Communication, conflict and dispute resolution: The study of interaction and the development of conflict theory. *Communication Research, 15*(4), 349-359.

References

References

References   245

References

Putnam, L. L., & Holmer, M. (1992). Framing, reframing and issue development. In L. L. Putnam & M. E. Roloff (Eds.), *Communication and negotiation* (pp. 128-155). Newbury Park, CA: Sage.

Putnam, L., & Poole, M. S. (1987). Conflict and negotiation. In F. Jablin, L. Putnam, K. Roberts, & L. Porter (Eds.), *Handbook of organizational communication* (pp. 549-599). Newbury Park, CA: Sage.

Putnam, L. L., & Roloff, M. (1992). Communication perspectives on negotiation. In L. Putnam & M. Roloff (Eds.), *Communication and negotiation* (pp. 1-17). Newbury Park, CA: Sage.

Rawls, J. (1971). *A theory of justice.* Cambridge, MA: Harvard University Press.

Rawlins, W. K. (1983a). Negotiating close friendships: The dialectic of conjunctive freedoms. *Human Communication Research, 9,* 255-266.

Rawlins, W. K. (1983b). Openness as problematic in ongoing friendships: Two controversial dilemmas. *Communication Monographs, 50,* 1-13.

Rawlins, W. K. (1989). A dialectal analysis of the tensions, functions, and strategic challenges of communication in young adult, friendships. In J. Anderson (Ed.), *Communication yearbook 12* (pp. 157-189). Newbury Park, CA: Sage.

Rawlins, W. K. (1992). *Friendship matter: Communication, dialects, and the life course.* Hawthorne, NY: Aldine de Gruyter.

Rifkin, J., Millen, J., & Cobb, S. (1991). Toward a new discourse for mediation: A critique of neutrality. *Mediation Quarterly, 9*(2), 151-164.

Riskin, L. (1984). Toward new standards for the neutral lawyer in mediation. *Arizona Law Review, 26,* 329-362.

Riskin, L. (1982). Mediation and lawyers. *Ohio State Law Journal, 43,* 29-60.

Roberts, M. (1992). Who is in charge? Reflections on recent research on the role of the mediator. *Journal of Social Welfare Law,* 372-387.

Roehl, J. A., & Cook, R. F. (1989). Mediation in interpersonal disputes: Effectiveness and limitations. In K. Kressel & D. G. Pruitt (Eds.), *Mediation research: The process and effectiveness of third-party intervention* (pp. 31-52). San Francisco: Jossey-Bass.

Rogers, N., & McEwen, C. (1989). *Mediation: Law, policy and practice.* San Francisco: Bancroft Whitney.

Roloff, M. (1987). Communication and conflict. In C. R. Berger & S. H. Chaffee (Eds.), *Handbook of communication science* (pp. 484-534). Newbury Park, CA: Sage.

Rouner, L. S. (1991). *On community.* South Bend, IN: University of Notre Dame Press.

Rowland, R. (1988). On limiting the narrative paradigm: Three case studies. *Communication Monographs, 55,* 39-54.

Ruble, T. L., & Thomas, K. W. (1976). Support for a two-dimensional model of conflict behavior. *Organizational Behavior and Human Performance, 16,* 143-155.

Rychlak, J. F. (1968). *A philosophy of science for personality theory.* Boston: Houghton Mifflin.

Sagan, E. (1985). *At the dawn of tyranny: The origins of individualism, political oppression and the state.* New York: Vintage.

Salfrank, L. (1991, May). *Student response teams: Deterring violence in our high schools.* Paper presented at the American Bar Association convention, Kansas City, MO.

Sancilio, M., Plumert, J., & Hartup, W. (1987). *Friendship and aggressiveness as determinants of conflict outcomes in middle childhood.* (ERIC Document Reproduction Service No. ED 282 638)

Sandel, M. (1982). *Liberalism and the limits of justice.* Cambridge: Cambridge University Press.

Sanders, J. A., & Wiseman, R. L. (1991). *Uncertainty reduction among ethnicities in the United States.* Paper presented at the meeting of the International Communication Association, Chicago.

Sarat, A. (1988). The "new formalism" in disputing and dispute processing. *Law and Society Review, 21*(3), 695-715.

Sarbin, T. (Ed.). (1986). *Narrative psychology: The storied nature of human conduct.* New York: Praeger.

Scherer, J. (1972). *Contemporary community: Sociological illusion or reality?* London: Tavistock.

Schmidt, W., & Tannenbaum, R. (1960). The management of differences. *Harvard Business Review, 38,* 107-115.

Selman, R. (1980). *The growth of interpersonal understanding.* New York: Academic Press.

Selman, R. (1981). The development of interpersonal competence: The role of understanding in conduct. *Developmental Review, 1,* 401-422.

Selman, R., Beardslee, W., Schultz, L., Krupa, M., & Podorefsky, D. (1986). Assessing adolescent interpersonal negotiation strategies: Toward the integration of structural and functional models. *Developmental Psychology, 22*(4), 450-459.

Selman, R., & Demorest, A. (1984). Observing troubled children's interpersonal negotiation strategies: Implications of and for a developmental model. *Child Development, 55,* 288-304.

Selman, R., & Glidden, M. (1987, Fall). Negotiation strategies for youth. *School Safety,* pp. 18-21.

Selvini-Palazzoli, M., Boscolo, L., Ceechin, G., & Prata, G. (1980). Hypothesizing-circularity-neutrality. *Family Process, 19,* 73-85.

Shailor, J. G. (in press). *Empowerment in dispute mediation: A critical analysis of communication.* New York: Praeger.

Shailor, J., & Pearce, W. B. (1986, October). *"The URP that ate mediation": A case study in the structure of human relationships.* Paper presented at the Communication and Culture Conference, Philadelphia.

Shantz, D. (1983). *Correlates of fighting in first and second grade children: A naturalistic study.* (ERIC Document Reproduction Service No. ED 229 127)

Shantz, C. (1984). *Conflicts and conundrums in child development.* (ERIC Document Reproduction Service No. ED 254 315)

Shantz, C. (1987a). Conflicts between children. *Child Development, 58*(2), 283-305.

Shantz, C. (1987b). *The promises and perils of social conflict.* (ERIC Document Reproduction Service No. ED 286 601)

Shantz, D., & Shantz, C. (1982, August). *Conflicts between children and social-cognitive development.* Paper presented at the American Psychological Association convention, Washington, DC.

Shapiro, D., Drieghe, R., & Brett, J. (1985). Mediator behavior and the outcome of mediation. *Journal of Social Issues, 41*(2), 101-114.

Sheppard, B. H. (1983). Managers as inquisitors: Some lessons from the law. In M. H. Brazerman & R.J. Lewicki (Eds.), *Negotiating in organizations* (pp. 193-213). Beverly Hills, CA: Sage.

Sheppard, B. H. (1984). Third party conflict resolution: A procedural framework. In B. M. Staw & L. L. Cummings (Eds.), *Research in organizational behavior* (Vol. 6, pp. 141-190). Greenwich, CT: JAI Press.

Sheppard, B. H., Blumenfeld-Jones, K., & Roth, J. (1989). Informal thirdpartyship: Studies of everyday conflict intervention. In K. Kressel & D. G. Pruitt (Eds.), *Mediation research: The process and effectiveness of third-party intervention* (pp. 166-189). San Francisco: Jossey-Bass.

Sheppard, B. H., Roth, J., Blumenfeld-Jones, K., & Minton, J. (1991). *Third party dispute interpretations: Simple stories and conflict interventions.* Paper presented at the national Academy of Management Meetings, Miami Beach, FL.

Sherry S. (1986). Civic virtue and the feminine voice in constitutional adjudication. *Virginia Law Review, 72,* 543-616.

Sherzer, J. (1980). *Telling, retelling, and telling within telling: The structure and organization of narrative in Kuna Indian discourse.* Paper presented at the Conference on Orality, Vibino, Italy.

Shotter, J. (1984). *Social accountability and selfhood.* Oxford: Basil Blackwell.

Shotter, J. (1987). The social construction of an "us": Problems of accountability and narratology. In R. Burnett, P. McGhee, & D. Clarke (Eds.), *Accounting for personal relationships: Social representations of interpersonal links.* New York: Methuen.

Shutz, A. (1962). *Collected papers I: The problem of social reality.* The Hague, The Netherlands: Martinus Nijhoff.

Simkin, W. E. (1971). *Mediation and the dynamics of collective bargaining.* Washington, DC: Bureau of National Affairs.

Silbey, S. S., & Merry, S. E. (1986). Mediator settlement strategies. *Law and Policy, 8,* 7-32.

Sillars, A., & Weisberg, J. (1987). Conflict as a social skill. In M. E. Roloff & G. R. Miller (Eds.), *Interpersonal processes: New directions in communication research* (pp. 140-171). Newbury Park CA: Sage.

Simmel, G. (1955). *Conflict.* New York: Free Press.

Simmel, G. (1964). *Conflict and the web of group affiliations* (K. H. Wolff & R. Bendix, Trans.). New York: Free Press. (Original work published 1908)

Slavin, R. E. (1991). Cooperative learning and group contingencies. *Journal of Behavioral Education, 1*(1), 105-115.

Sluzki, C. (1992). Transformations: A blueprint for narrative changes in therapy. *Family Process, 31,* 217-230.

Sluzki, C. (1993). *Better-formed stories.* Paper on file with the author [Sara Cobb, Department of Communication, University of Connecticut, West Hartford, CT]

Smith, D. A. (1987). Police responses to interpersonal violence: Defining the parameters of legal control. *Social Forces, 65*(3), 767-782.

Smith, D. A., Visher, C., & Davidson, L. (1984). Equity and discretionary justice: The influence of race on police arrest decisions. *Journal of Criminal Law and Criminology, 75,* 234-249.

Smith, P. (1989, Fall). The convenanted community. *Kettering Review,* 22-29.

Smith, R. C., & Eisenberg, E. M. (1987). Conflict at Disneyland: A root metaphor analysis. *Communication Monographs, 54,* 367-380.

Social Science Education Consortium, Inc. (1987). *Conflict resolution in the schools: Final evaluation report.* Boulder, CO: Author.

Solomon, V., & Rosenthal, D. (1984). *Meta-analysis on paradoxical interventions.* Copy on file with author [Sara Cobb, Department of Communication, University of Connecticut, West Hartford, CT].

Stalcup, C. (1981). An investigation of children's perceptions of peer conflicts. (Doctoral dissertations, University of Texas at Austin, 1980). *Dissertation Abstracts International, 41*(7-B), 2795-2796.

Stamp, G. H. (1992, October). *Toward generative family theory: Dialectal tensions within family life.* Paper presented to the Speech Communication Association convention, Chicago.

Stamp, G. H., & Banski, M. A. (1992). The communicative management of constrained autonomy during the transition to parenthood. *Western Journal of Communication, 56,* 281-300.

Stewart, E. C. (1987). American assumptions and values: Orientation to action. In L. F. Luce & E. C. Smith (Eds.), *Toward internationalism: Readings in cross cultural communication* (2nd ed.), (pp. 51-72). Cambridge, MA: Newbury House.

Stone, C. (1981). A structural developmental approach to the study of peer interaction. (Doctoral dissertation, Harvard University, 1981). *Dissertation Abstracts International, 42*(6-B), 2572-2573.

Stubbs, M. (1983). *Discourse analysis: The sociolinguistic analysis of natural language.* Chicago: University of Chicago Press.

Swadener, E. B. (1988). *Teaching toward peace and social responsibility in the early elementary years: A friends school case study.* (ERIC Document Reproduction Service No. 316 321)

Tabachnick, B. R. (1990). Studying peace in elementary schools: Laying a foundation for the "Peaceable kingdom." *Theory and Research in Social Education, 18*(2), 169-173.

Tajfel, H., & Turner, J. C. (1986). The social identity theory of intergroup behavior. In S. Worchel & W. Austin (Eds.), *Psychology of intergroup relations* (pp. 7-24). Chicago: Nelson-Hall.

Tan, N. T. (1988). Developing and testing a family mediation assessment instrument. *Mediation Quarterly, 19,* 53-67.

Tannen, D. (1986). *That's not what I meant: How controversial style makes or breaks your relations with others.* New York: Ballantine.

Taylor, T. (1986). *Enhancing interpersonal problem-solving skills in preschoolers.* (ERIC Document Reproduction Service No. ED 288 623)

Tedeschi, J. T., & Rosenfeld, P. (1980). Communication in bargaining and negotiation. In M. E. Roloff & G. R. Miller (Eds.), *Persuasion: New directions in theory and research* (pp. 225-248). Beverly Hills, CA: Sage.

Thibaut, J. W., & Walker, L. (1975). *Procedural justice: A psychological perspective.* Hillsdale, NJ: Lawrence Erlbaum.

Thomas, K. W. (1989). Norms as an integrative theme in conflict and negotiation: Correcting our "sociopathic" assumptions. In M. Rahim (Ed.), *Managing conflict: An interdisciplinary approach* (pp. 265-272). New York: Praeger.

Thompson, J. B. (1984). *Studies in the theory of ideology.* Cambridge: Polity.

Ting-Toomey, S. (1985). Toward a theory of conflict and culture. In W. Gudykunst, L. Stewart, & S. Ting-Toomey (Eds.), *Communication, culture and organizational processes* (pp. 71-86). Beverly Hills, CA: Sage.

Ting-Toomey, S. (1988). Intercultural conflict styles: A face-negotiation theory. In Y. Kim & W. Gudykunst (Eds.), *Theories in intercultural communication* (pp. 213-235). Newbury Park, CA: Sage.

Tomm, K. (1987). Interventive interviewing. Part II. *Family Process, 26,* 126-183.

Touval, S., & Zartman, I. W. (1989). Mediation in international conflicts. In K. Kressel & D. G. Pruitt (Eds.), *Mediation research: The process and effectiveness of third-party intervention* (pp. 115-137). San Francisco: Jossey-Bass.

Tracy, K. (1991). Introduction: Linking communicator goals with discourse. In K. Tracy (Ed.), *Understanding face-to-face interaction: Issues linking goals and discourse* (pp. 1-17). Hillside, NJ: Lawrence Erlbaum.

Triandis, H. C., Bontempo, R., Villareal, J., Asai, M., & Lucca, N. (1988). Individualism and collectivism: Cross-cultural perspectives on self-ingroup relationships. *Journal of Personality and Social Psychology, 54,* 323-338.

Triandis, H. C., Leung, K., Villareal, M. J., & Clark, F. L. (1985). Allocentric vs. idiocentric tendencies: Convergent and discriminant validation. *Journal of Research in Personality, 19,* 349-415.

Trubisky, P., Ting-Toomey, S., & Lin, S. (1991). The influence of individualism-collectivism and self-monitoring on conflict styles. *International Journal of Intercultural Relations, 15,* 65-83.

Ury, W. L., Brett, J. M., & Goldberg, S. B. (1988). *Getting disputes resolved: Designing systems to cut the costs of conflict.* San Francisco: Jossey-Bass.

Van Dijk, T. (1987). *Communicating racism: Ethnic prejudice in thought and talk.* Newbury Park, CA: Sage.

VanLear, C. A. (1991). Testing a cyclical model of communicative openness in relationship development: Two longitudinal studies. *Communication Monographs, 58,* 337-361.

Varela, F. (1979). *Principles of biological autonomy.* New York: Elsevier North-Holland.

Venkataramaiah, S., & Kumari, K. (1975). Socio-psychological analysis of children's quarrels: Theoretical concepts and implications. *Child Psychiatry Quarterly, 8,* 1-6.

Venkataramaiah, S., & Kumari, K. (1986). Socio-psychological analysis of children's quarrels, the empirical investigation: Results and discussion. *Child Psychiatry Quarterly, 10,* 1-7.

Volkema, R. J. (1988). The mediator as face manager. In J. A. Lemmon (Ed.), *Techniques and results in family mediation* (pp. 5-14). San Francisco: Jossey-Bass.

Wall, J. A., Jr. (1981). Mediation: An analysis, review and proposed research. *Journal of Conflict Resolution, 25,* 157-180.

Wall, J. A., & Blum, M. (1991). Communication mediation in the People's Republic of China. *Journal of Conflict Resolution, 35*(1), 3-20.

Wall, J. A., & Rude, D. E. (1989). Judicial mediation of settlement negotiations. In K. Kressel & D. G. Pruitt (Eds.). *Mediation research: The process and effectiveness of third-party intervention* (pp. 190-212). San Francisco: Jossey-Bass.

Walster, E., Berschied, E., & Walster, G. W. (1973). New directions in equity research. *Journal of Personality and Social Psychology, 25,* 151-176.

Watzlawick, P., Beavin, J., & Jackson, D. (1967). *Pragmatics of human communication.* New York: Norton.

Watzlawick, P., Weakland, J., & Fisch, R. (1974). *Change.* New York: Norton.

Weeks, G. R. (1977). Toward a dialectal approach to intervention. *Human Development, 20,* 277-292.

West, R. (1988). Jurisprudence and gender. *The University of Chicago Law Review, 55*(1), 1072.

White, M., & Epston, D. (1990). *Narrative means to therapeutic ends.* New York: Norton.

Wiseman, R. L., & Fiske, J. A. (1980). A lawyer-therapist team as mediator in martial crisis. *Social Work, 25,* 442-445.

Worchel, S. (1986). The role of cooperation in reducing intergroup conflict. In S. Worchel & W. Austin (Eds.), *Psychology of intergroup relations* (pp. 288-304), Chicago: Nelson-Hall.

Yeates, L., & Selman, R. (1989). Social competence in the schools: Toward an integrative developmental model for intervention. *Developmental Review, 9*(1), 64-100.

Yerby, J. (1992, October). *Family systems theory reconsidered: Integrating social construction theory and dialectal process into a systems perspective of family communication.* Paper presented to Speech Communication Association convention, Chicago.

Yu, E. Y. (1983). Korean communities in America: Past, present, and future. *Amerasia, 10*(2), 23-51.

Zartman, I. W. (1978). Negotiation as a joint decision-making process. In I. W. Zartman (Ed.), *The negotiation process: Theories and applications* (pp. 67-86). Beverly Hills, CA: Sage.

Zartman, I. W., & Touval, S. (1985). International mediation: Conflict resolution and power politics. *Journal of Social Issues, 41,* 27-45.

Index

About the Contributors

Mary I. Bresnahan (Ph.D., University of Michigan, 1985) is an Associate Professor in the Department of Communication at Michigan State University. She studies communication and gender, ethnic conflict, and discourse involving requests and refusals. Her work has been published in *Text, Discourse Processes, Journal of Asian Pacific Communication, The Howard Journal of Communication, Multilingua,* and *Philippine Studies.*

Jeanne M. Brett (Ph.D., University of Illinois, 1972) is a Professor of organizational behavior at Northwestern University's Kellogg School of Management. Her interests include the study of conflict resolution and third-party processes in organizational settings. She is coauthor (with W. Ury & S. Goldberg) of *Getting Disputes Resolved: Designing Systems to Cut the Costs of Conflict* and has published other work in this area in *The Journal of Organizational Behavior, Negotiation Journal, Journal of Management,* and *Journal of Applied Psychology.*

Heidi Brinkman (Ph.D., University of Denver, 1991) is an Instructor in the College of Business at the University of Denver. Her research interests include the impact of diversity-related change in organizational contexts, cultural influences in communication, and developmental influences in communication. She is a consultant specializing in diversity issues and has developed a diversity-sensitivity measure for organizational use.

Robert A. Baruch Bush (J.D., Stanford University, 1974) is the Harry H. Raines Distinguished Professor of Alternative Dispute Resolution Law at Hofstra University Law School. He teaches and researches in mediation and alternative dispute resolution and has published work in the *Journal of Contemporary Legal Issues, Florida Law Review, Denver Law Review,* and the *Wisconsin Law Review.* He is completing a book with Joseph Folger integrating theory and practice, titled *Mediation at the Crossroads.*

Sara Cobb (Ph.D., University of Massachusetts, 1988) is a Visiting Assistant Professor at the University of California, Santa Barbara, specializing in qualitative analyses of conflict resolution processes. Although much of her research has focused on the practice of neutrality in mediation, she has also examined the management of violence in dispute resolution processes. She has recently published in *Mediation Quarterly, The Negotiation Journal, Law and Social Inquiry, Discourse Processes,* and *Communication Theory.*

Robert Dingwall (Ph.D., University of Aberdeen, 1974) is Professor and Chair of the School of Social Studies, University of Nottingham, England. He studies the role of mediator influence in intervention from a discourse analytic perspective. He has coedited (with J. M. Eekelaar) *Divorce Mediation and the Legal Process: British Practice and International Experience* and has contributed to *Family and Conciliation Courts Review, Law in Context, Mediation Quarterly,* and *Law in Society Review.*

William A. Donohue (Ph.D., Ohio State University, 1976) is a Professor of Communication at Michigan State University. His interests include negotiation, mediation, and the study of interaction process. He has recently published *Communication, Marital Dispute and Divorce Mediation,* as well as articles in *Human Communica-*

tion Research, Communication Monographs, Mediation Quarterly, and *Communication Yearbook 7.*

Joseph P. Folger (Ph.D., University of Wisconsin-Madison,1978) is an Associate Professor at Temple University and is the Associate Dean for Research and Graduate Studies in the School of Communications and Theater. His recent research on mediation and conflict has been published in *Mediation Quarterly, Negotiation Journal,* and in the edited volume *Community Mediation: A Handbook for Practitioners and Researchers.* The second edition of his co-authored book (with M. S. Poole and R. K. Stutman) *Working Through Conflict: Strategies for Relationships, Groups and Organizations* has recently been published. He is currently completing a book on the ideological foundations of mediation, entitled *Mediation at the Crossroads*, with R. Baruch Bush.

David Greatbatch (Ph.D., University of Warwick, 1985) is a University Research Fellow at the School of Social Studies, University of Nottingham, England. He has written extensively on conversation analysis in relation to news interviews and professional/client interaction. He has published in *Family and Conciliation Courts Review* and *Law and Society Review.*

Tricia S. Jones (Ph.D., Ohio State University, 1985) is an Associate Professor and Chair of the Department of Rhetoric and Communication at Temple University. Her current research interests include children's conflict competence, mediation processes, nonverbal cues in conflict interaction, multiculturalism, and the dynamics of sexual harassment. Her recent publications include articles in *International Journal of Conflict Management, Sex Roles, Journal of Social Psychology,* and *Communication Research.* She is editing a special issue of *International Journal of Conflict Management* on multiculturalism and conflict in organizational settings and is preparing a book on peer mediation based on her research with the Philadelphia School District's peer mediation program.

Rekha Karambayya (Ph.D., Northwestern University, 1989) is an Assistant Professor in the Faculty of Administrative Studies at York University. Her current research interests include dispute resolution processes in organizations and organizational citizenship behavior. Her work has most recently been published in *The Academy of Management Journal.*

Stephen W. Littlejohn (Ph.D., University of Utah, 1970) is a Professor of Speech Communication at Humboldt State University. His research interests include the role of communication in conflict, mediation, and communication theory. He is the author of *Theories of Human Communication.*

Carl M. Moore (Ph.D., Wayne State University, 1972) recently retired from Kent State University where he served as a professor in Communication Studies. He is an active practitioner who facilitates a wide range of public policy disputes in government, nonprofit, and community contexts. His recent publications include *Group Techniques for Idea Building, A Colorful Quilt: The Community Leadership Story, The Facilitator's Manual,* and articles in *Nation's Cities Weekly, Journal of Intergroup Relations, Public Administration Review,* and the *National Civic Review.*

Christopher W. Moore (Ph.D., Rutgers University, 1983) is a partner in CDR Associates in Boulder, CO. He is an experienced mediator who works in a wide range of conflict arenas including family, interpersonal, and public policy disputes. He has published *The Mediation Process: Practical Strategies for Resolving Conflict* and articles in *Mediation Quarterly, Colorado Municipalities,* and the *NIDR Forum.*

W. Barnett Pearce (Ph.D., Ohio University, 1969) is a Professor and Chair of the Department of Communication at Loyola University of Chicago. His interests focus on social constructionism as a way of thinking about communication. His books include *Interpersonal Communication: Making Social Worlds, Reagan and American Public Discourse* (with Michael Weiler), *Cultures, Politics and Research Programs: An International Assessment of Practical Problems in Field Research* (with Uma Narula), *Communication, Action and Meaning: The Creation of Social Realities* (with Vernon Cronen), and *Communicating Personally* (with Charles Rossiter, Jr.).

Janet Rifkin (J.D., New York University, 1972) is a Professor of Legal Studies at the University of Massachusetts and is currently serving as the university ombudsperson. She is also the founder and director of the University of Massachusetts Mediation Project. Her writings focus on the role of the mediator and the way in which the concept of third-party neutrality is shaped by considerations of gender and the dispute resolution process. She has recently published in *Mediation Quarterly, Law and Social Inquiry,* and *Law, Politics and Society.*

Jonathan Shailor (Ph.D., University of Massachusetts, 1992) is an Assistant Professor of Speech Communication at Ithaca College. He is a practicing mediator who does research on communication and conflict and the role of empowerment in mediation. He is the author of *Empowerment in Dispute Mediation: A Critical Analysis of Communication.*

Anna Spradlin (Ph.D., University of Denver, 1990) is an Instructor in the Department of Communication at the University of Colorado. Her teaching and research interests include leadership and conflict in social movements, conflict processes, and mediation. She is an experienced mediator who practices in farmer-lender, landlord-tenant, family, and community mediation contexts.

Karen Tracy (Ph.D., University of Wisconsin, 1981) is an Associate Professor of Communication at the University of Colorado, Boulder. She is a discourse analyst who has studied the relationship between conversational practices and situation outcomes in a range of everyday communication situations. She has edited the volume *Understanding Face-to-Face Interaction: Issues Linking Goals and Discourse* and has contributed to *Human Communication Research, Communication Monographs, Journal of Language and Social Psychology, Research on Language and Social Interaction,* and *Discourse Processes.*